THE CHINESE ALMANAC
1991
THE YEAR OF THE RAM

COMPILED BY
KWOK MAN-HO

EDITED BY
JOANNE O'BRIEN AND
MARTIN PALMER

BANTAM BOOKS
TORONTO · NEW YORK · LONDON · SYDNEY · AUCKLAND

THE CHINESE ALMANAC 1991
A BANTAM BOOK   0 553 40057 6

First publication in Great Britain

PRINTING HISTORY
Bantam edition published 1990

Copyright © International Consultancy on Religion, Education
and Culture 1990

Conditions of sale
1. This book is sold subject to the condition that it shall not, by way
of trade *or otherwise*, be lent, re-sold, hired out or otherwise circulated
in any form of binding or cover other than that in which it is published
*and without a similar condition including this condition being imposed on the
subsequent purchaser.*
2. This book is sold subject to the Standard Conditions of Sale of Net
Books and may not be re-sold in the UK below the net price fixed by
the publishers for the book.

This book is set in 10/12 Garamond by
Photoprint, Torquay, Devon.

Bantam Books are published by Transworld Publishers Ltd.,
61–63 Uxbridge Road, Ealing, London W5 5SA, in Australia by
Transworld Publishers (Australia) Pty. Ltd., 15–23 Helles Avenue,
Moorebank, NSW 2170, and in New Zealand by Transworld
Publishers (N.Z.) Ltd., Cnr. Moselle and Waipareira Avenues,
Henderson, Auckland.

Made and printed in Great Britain by
Cox and Wyman Ltd., Reading, Berks.

CONTENTS

INTRODUCTION

THE BEGINNING OF HISTORY

When Stonehenge was still a dream in some prehistoric Briton's mind this book was already in annual production. For Chinese legend has it that this book, the yearly Almanac, was ordered by the great and mysterious Emperor Yao, one of the Five August Emperors who ruled China at the start of history. The story tells that in the year 2256 BC, over four thousand years ago, Yao ordered two brothers to calculate the arrival of the seasons of the year and the movements of the stars, sun and moon. The two brothers, Hsis and Ho, carried out their duties and thus we must assume that the first ever Almanac was produced for the year 2255 BC. It seems to have been an instant hit. The Emperor Yao ordered that such a useful book should be produced each and every year, for the orderly government of the country and the wellbeing of the people depended upon it.

Imagine then his anger when a few years later scandal hit the book. Something was going wrong. The predictions of the weather, the eclipses of the sun and moon, the days for planting certain crops and other such crucial daily details determined by the stars, had been miscalculated. The religious ceremonies of the court were wrong. The orderly organization of the country was in chaos. The emperor demanded to know what had gone wrong. Why were Hsis and Ho making such a mess of the crucial work of calculating the Almanac? Why were the stars not in the correct places at the times the astrological calculations had said they would be? What on earth, if not in Heaven, was going on?

The answer came back swift enough. The Shu Ching, an ancient book of Chinese History over three thousand years old, tells us that Hsis and Ho, presumably grown rich on their skills as astrologers, were sunk in wine, literally 'intoxicated' with their success. The Prince of Yin was immediately sent to punish the two brothers who had thrown the country into such chaos. Yin arrested the two and they were swiftly executed by imperial command. Then the emperor sent out his law on the Almanac and on astrology. It was a fearful law that said any astrologer miscalculating the Almanac or the movement of the stars would be 'put to death without mercy'.

So the Almanac is no ordinary book. In Chinese legend and history it has made and broken emperors and entire dynasties. It has been held to be so important that people have been killed for getting it wrong while others have risen to the highest offices because they got it right.

But what is this book that has had an effect on emperors and peasants and which is claimed to be the oldest annual book in the world? And why is it believed to be so powerful — not just for individual lives but for the health and wellbeing of entire nations?

ANCIENT ASTROLOGY

Let us start with its foundation — Chinese astrology. The Almanac is one of the many forms in which astrology influences the lives of the Chinese people to this day. Indeed, it is the earliest recorded use of astrology. In ancient China, and right up until the end of the Chinese

Empire in 1911, there was always a Board or an Office of Imperial Astrologers. Their job was to calculate the emperor's horoscope and those of his wives and children, and to work out the astrological forces at work for the coming year. The official in charge of the Office of Astrology was one of the most powerful of all the court officials and astrology is still ranked as one of the traditional five arts and sciences of Chinese culture. No ruler would dream of making a major decision or setting off on a journey until he had found out if the day was lucky or unlucky. To this day millions of Chinese around the world will look in the Almanac to see which is the best time to open a new business, move house, travel or hold a major function.

But this attitude is not only Chinese. In the past Christian and Muslim rulers have always had their official or semi-official astrologers. Marco Polo on his epic journey to China in the thirteenth century frequently tells us of courts governed by Muslim, Christian or Buddhist rulers where decisions were not made until the official astrologers had been consulted. In England Queen Elizabeth I relied heavily upon the Reverend Dr John Dee, the priest at Manchester parish church, as her astrologer. In our own day reports which have never been fully denied claim that ex-President Ronald Reagan and his wife Nancy depended upon the forecasts of a Californian astrologer to decide which days were good for major international meetings.

In China this was all part and parcel of the way the government worked. But what is really interesting is what lay behind this. For the belief in astrology was and is rooted in a very profound philosophy of the world and of life itself which lies behind most aspects of Chinese society even now. This is the belief in what is called the Triad. This is not the infamous Mafia-type gangs of the Chinese underworld, although they trace themselves back to this

3

ancient philosophy. It is a belief in three basic powers —
Heaven, Earth and Humanity.

THE THREE POWERS

The word 'Heaven' includes the skies, the heavens, the
supreme power, or everything that we think of as God.
But it is not a personal force. The word 'Earth' covers all
the material things of this world, the land, waters, trees,
mountains, valleys, creatures, humans and all our works
such as towns, roads, temples and so on. These are the two
great fundamental dimensions of reality. There is nothing
beyond or outside these two forces. They are also the main
expressions of what is called 'yin and yang'. This is probably the most important idea in Chinese belief. Yin and
yang are often shown as a symbol of a circle divided into
two parts which interlock but which are totally contrast-
ing — the one light, the other dark — and each of which
contain a small part of the other.

In traditional Chinese thought these two forces of yin
and yang are completely opposite to each other. They are
light and dark, hot and cold, fiery and wet, male and
female, summer and winter, and so on. They are
constantly struggling against each other, each one trying
to dominate and annihilate the other. And they are
present everywhere. So while the Earth is seen as yin, it

4

also contains yang within it. When volcanoes erupt or the earth quakes, this is the sign that the forces of yang have got the upper hand. When floods wash away towns and villages or the land sinks into marsh and quagmire, then that is a sign that the forces of yin are in the ascendancy. Through the struggle of these two dynamically opposite forces of yin and yang the whole of life is kept in motion, and the balance between the two forces is what keeps the world, the universe, the whole cosmos in harmony. But it is a harmony which exists precisely because the two forces can never completely conquer each other, although they are always trying to do so. It is a harmony of struggle and dynamism. If the balance were ever to be permanently tipped in favour of one of the two forces, chaos would break forth and the whole universe be destroyed.

This is where humanity comes in. We alone have the power to change our surroundings. We alone have the power to make moral choices and decisions which shape history and affect our environment and our relationships with all around us. We alone have the power to tip the balance in favour of either yin or yang. So, small as we are in comparison to the sun (yang) or the moon (yin), to the winds (yin) or the fires (yang), we stand like the tiny weight which can tip the scales. Or perhaps a better picture is to imagine an acrobat in a circus. There he stands in the middle of a tightrope balanced upon a large rolling ball. If he puts one foot too far to one side, down he will tumble and the balance will be lost. One foot too far the other way and the same will happen.

That is the precarious position of humanity in this Triad. Heaven and Earth are the two forces of yang and yin. They are in perfect balance, and even though one will try to overrule the other, it cannot do so. But if humans choose to act badly, we can tip the balance and cause irreparable damage. In traditional thought earthquakes, fires and floods were signs of the balance being tipped too far one way. Illness or disaster in your personal life was also a sign that in your own precarious balancing act between the forces of yin and yang both around you and within you, you were lopsided and could come to harm. Humanity's role therefore is to ensure that yin and yang stay in tense harmony and balance. We have to learn how to stay in balance with the forces of the Heavens, with the stars, sun, moon. We most know the seasons (themselves signs of yin and yang). We must know when to farm or travel, how and where to build, when it is right to start something new or to bury the dead. For all of these acts can tip the balance too far one way unless we perform them in accordance with, and work in harmony with the greater forces which surround us. If we do work, play, build, travel and plan in accordance with the flow of natural yin–yang forces, then we can expect success, for we are moving in harmony with the greatest forces in the cosmos. If we go against these forces, we will fail disastrously and might even threaten the future of the world itself.

THE MANDATE OF HEAVEN

We can see how important it is in this philosophy to know how the astrological forces are working and which force — yin or yang — is at its greatest power at any given time. But there is one other reason why the emperors of China were anxious to receive the correct calculations for each year, for if the Almanac was incorrect then they forfeited the right to rule China. If the emperor sanctioned an Almanac which proved to be inaccurate in major areas such as eclipses, the start of each season and so forth, then it was obvious that he had lost the ability to mediate between Heaven and Earth. He had lost what was called the 'Mandate of Heaven', the permission or approval by which he ruled. The emperor's role was that of the central point of the Triad of Heaven, Earth and Humanity. He stood, literally, as a symbol of all humanity and as this symbol he appeared before Heaven and Earth once a year to restore the balance. His most important job was to offer a sacrifice first at the Temple of Heaven and then at the Temple of Earth. The reason for these sacrifices was to restore the balance. It was assumed that the activities of the human race during the past year had disturbed the balance of Heaven and Earth and would lead to disaster and distress unless harmony was restored. The emperor, known as the Son of Heaven, acted on behalf of humanity and, through his sacrifice and apologies to Heaven and Earth, restored the balance.

Although the emperor was called the Son of Heaven, Heaven seems to have got rather fed up with its sons at times. So if a major natural disaster or foreign invasion took place, it was obvious to the Chinese that Heaven had not accepted the sacrifice of the emperor. If the Almanac got the dates wrong, then obviously Heaven and Earth were no longer sharing their secrets with the emperor. When this happened, rebellion and revolt was legitimate and the emperor and his dynasty could be overthrown.

THE PEOPLE'S BOOK

But it was not just the emperor who used and needed the Almanac. Over the centuries it has come to be the most popular book among ordinary Chinese families, so popular in fact, that as early as the eighth century AD the Chinese were producing it in mass printed editions. The Almanac is the world's oldest continuously published book, and as it has always come out in soft covers, presumably it is also the world's first paperback.

So many copies were being published during the eighth

7

century – the period known as the Dark Ages in Europe – that one Japanese monk travelling in China wrote home to his friends complaining that all you could buy in the markets were cheap, printed Almanacs. There is a copy of the book in the British Museum dated 877 AD – just about the time King Alfred the Great was alive.

One reason why the Almanac is so valued by the ordinary Chinese is because it is believed to have magical powers. The Chinese edition has a red string loop at the top of the spine. The Chinese buy their Almanac before the New Year. Then, just before midnight on New Year's Eve, while offerings are being made to Heaven, Earth and the ancestors, they take down the old Almanac and, using the red string loop, hang up the new one beside the main door into the house. There it will hang until the following New Year. But why? Quite simply because it is a magic charm and has the power to protect the family and all those who enter the house in friendship. Clearly, a book which links Heaven, Earth and Humanity in harmony must be filled with a supernatural power and this alone helps to protect the home. The Almanac is also used for healing. Pregnant women take the book into hospital with them and put it under the pillow to protect themselves and their baby. Many older people take the book with them if they go for any treatment in a hospital or clinic.

This, then, is no ordinary book. But let us look a little further into its extraordinary history, for the Almanac has many strange tales to tell and some of the world's most infamous and interesting people have been caught up in its creation.

THE VERY BEGINNING

The first of these characters takes the story of the Almanac back beyond the Emperor Yao! For the oldest legends say that the calendar was invented by no other than Fu Hsi. Fu Hsi is one of the great mythological figures of Chinese legend and history. He is supposed to have lived over five thousand years ago and to have attained a great age. He is counted as the father of everything Chinese and as such is revered as the inventor of just about everything distinctively Chinese, from the chopsticks to calligraphy, from sewing to sex, from agriculture to art. He was also a great observer of the stars and of the movements of the earth — in fact an early astrologer/astronomer. One of the most famous ancient accounts of this strange but creative figure describes him thus:

When in ancient times Fu Hsi ruled the world he looked up to observe the phenomena of the heavens and gazed down to observe the contours of the earth. He observed the markings of the birds and beasts and how they were adapted to their habitats. Some ideas he took from his own body and went beyond this to take other ideas from other things [From the Great Commentary of the *I Ching*].

Through observing the world and the stars so carefully, Fu Hsi created the first calendar to guide the people in their work and their rest. He also created the eight trigrams of the *I Ching*, the great divination book of the Chinese, which is almost as old as the Almanac itself. While it is doubtful that anyone called Fu Hsi ever lived, he symbolizes all the basic elements of being Chinese. High among these is the discovery of the calendar. However, it took the Emperor Yao to bring this general discovery to the point at which Chinese society deems the Almanac as such to have been invented.

For many hundreds of years after Yao the calendar simply existed and was used throughout the many small kingdoms which made up China. After centuries of skirmishes and wars these kingdoms were united into a single empire and our story continues from there.

9

THE EMPEROR OF THE TERRACOTTA SOLDIERS

One of the most famous of all the emperors of China must be the Yellow Emperor of the Ch'in. He was the emperor who ordered a complete army of terracotta soldiers to be made and buried to protect his tomb at modern-day Sian. His tomb with its buried army is now one of the wonders of the world and China's greatest tourist attraction after the Great Wall. He was a very brutal man and became the first ruler of what we now think of as China by conquering the two other kingdoms in the area. He kept a massive standing army which was excellently trained and renowned for its brutality and he suppressed any sign of dissent in his conquered lands by sheer terror and force. He was probably one of the world's most efficient and excellent military strategists and it is from his pioneering work that the real Empire of China can be dated. Indeed, the name 'China' comes from a corruption of 'Ch'in', the name of the emperor's own country which in 221 BC conquered its neighbours and became the Chinese Empire.

The picture we have given of the Yellow Emperor of the Ch'in shows a fierce warrior and ruthless ruler. Yet this same man was also deeply religious and in many ways superstitious. It is from his country of Ch'in that we have the earliest existing text of the Almanac, preserved almost by accident in one of the great classics of ancient China. The *Li Chi* – the *Book of Rites* – contains a copy of the Imperial Almanac of the Ch'in. It is not easy to date this Almanac but it is thought to have been compiled and authenticated by Lu Pu-wei, who was the Prime Minister of the Yellow Emperor in the days before he conquered the rest of China. This places it in about the year 250 BC.

The Five Classics of China, within which this text is embedded, were books that those wishing to become administrators had to learn by heart. They were like the Bible and the laws of China and shaped Chinese thought for over two thousand years. The Almanac which is preserved within it is called the *Yueh Ling* and is full of the astrological and practical details which are still the mainstay of the Almanac today.

In the first month of spring the sun is in Shih, the star culminating at dusk being Zhan, and that culminating at dawn, Wei. Its days are Chia and Yi [the first two Heavenly Stems; see p. 38 below]. Its divine ruler is Thai Hao, and the spirit is Kaumang. . . The east winds resolve the cold. Creatures that have been torpid during the winter begin to move. The fish rise up to the ice. Otters sacrifice fish. The wild geese make their appearance. . . In this month there takes place the inauguration of spring. Three days before this ceremony the Grand Recorder informs the Son of Heaven, saying, 'On such and such a day is the inauguration of the spring. The energies of the season are fully seen in wood.' . . . He also orders the Grand Recorder to guard the statutes and maintain the laws, and [especially] to observe the motions in the heavens of the sun and moon, and of the zodiacal stars in which the conjunction of these bodies takes place, so that there should be no error as to where they rest and what they pass over; that there should be no failure in the record of all these things, according to the regular practice of early times.

BRUTAL CENSORSHIP

The Yellow Emperor of Ch'in was not a democratic ruler, as the scholars of his day found out. Once he had conquered China one of the first things he tried to do was wipe out all the ancient scholarship except for those parts which he thought were politically harmless, such as medicine and divination. All the other classics, the histories and poems, were burnt and any scholar who tried to defend them was murdered, often brutally. The surviving texts which we have of the great classics were

11

made from memory by the scholars who survived this awful time and from the few copies of the ancient books which survived by being hidden away.

One of the books which the emperor did not ban was the Almanac. In fact he gave it added importance in order to show how his reign was introducing a whole new era to China; he had a new calendar drawn up which was supposed to show that he was not only master of China but had also received Heaven's blessing. The new Almanac was issued with full pomp and ceremony and strict rules were laid down prohibiting the use of anything but the Imperial Calendar. It is thought that it is from this time that the practice of sending a copy of the Almanac to every governor of a city and province in China arose.

However, Heaven obviously did not think that it had given its Mandate to the Ch'in Dynasty. Having been established in 221 BC, the dynasty collapsed in 207 BC, three years after the death of its founder! The new dynasty, the Han, dropped the Ch'in calendar and created a new one. However, Heaven seems to have found this calendar more acceptable, and the dynasty ruled for many centuries.

One of the most extraordinary things about the Ch'in Yellow Emperor was his love of magic and what today we would call superstition.

THE SEARCH FOR IMMORTALITY

During his reign, the Ch'in Yellow Emperor sent fleets of magicians and young people to search for the Isles of the Immortals. These were legendary islands which floated somewhere out in the ocean, and anyone who could find them, land there and harvest the fruit from them would gain immortality. The Ch'in Yellow Emperor believed profoundly in the possibility of immortality, in living for ever, either here on earth or in Heaven. But this could only be done by preserving not just what we call the soul but also the body. The Chinese believed that existence ended with physical death. So it was essential to preserve the metaphysical and the physical. The Ch'in Yellow Emperor spent a vast fortune on trying to find the isles and on hiring wise men who claimed they could make the Pill of Immortality. He became so absorbed in the pursuit of immortality that he would do anything to find it. When he was told that he would live for ever if he never went out of doors, he ordered over 70 miles of corridors to be built linking his palaces so he could travel between them without going into the open air.

It is probably to the Ch'in Yellow Emperor that we owe the first additions that were made to the Almanac and which have increased over the centuries. For it was during his reign that the calendar began to contain more than just the forecast for the crops and the seasons; it started to offer advice and warnings of a more 'spiritual' kind. And this brings us to another interesting character in the long and at times violent history of the Almanac.

CAMPAIGN AGAINST SUPERSTITION

While the Ch'in Yellow Emperor was trying to destroy the classics and find immortality, one of China's greatest philosophers was fighting a valiant battle against what he saw as creeping superstition and magic in the Almanac. Hsun Tzu was a great Confucian scholar and statesman. Confucianism is a vast area of study, but we must briefly look at what it taught because, without some understandings of Confucius, his teachings and significance in Chinese thought and life, it is very difficult to understand the world from which the Almanac comes.

In Chinese Confucianism is called K'ung Chiao, meaning the 'teachings of K'ung'. K'ung is K'ung Futzu, the great ethical teacher of the fifth century BC. He is better known in the West by his latinized name Confucius which was given him by admiring Jesuit priests. K'ung was born in 551 BC and died, to all appearances a failure, in 479 BC. During his lifetime his advice on how to run a state was largely ignored, even when he was employed in an official capacity. He taught a return to the old values, and central to this was his belief in a strict but benevolent hierarchy. This went from respect and obedience of the son for the father (filial piety) up to the loyalty of the subject to the Emperor. If everyone lived according to the demands and expectations of their station and were strict but kind to those below them and deferential and obedient to those above them, then society would run smoothy.

After K'ung's death his disciples wrote down his teachings in *The Analects*. Within about fifty years these had become accepted throughout China. Rulers liked his emphasis on respect and obedience, and his sense of history gave people a feeling of continuity which has always been typically Chinese.

Over the centuries people's atitudes to K'ung have undergone many changes. On the one hand, on questions of right and wrong, on how to run a state and on the duties of the young towards the old he is respected as a thinker and a teacher. On the other hand, he has come to be regarded as a god, on the same level as Buddha and Lao Tzu. And this is in spite of the fact that during his lifetime K'ung refused to answer questions concerning the gods or life after death. He was very down to earth and would only deal with what he could measure or analyse.

It was this side of K'ung that Hsun Tzu admired. He was one of the old school of Confucians who distrusted anything which was not useful and 'sensible'. He protested loudly that the usefulness of the Almanac was being compromised by the introduction of such things as lucky days, auspicious and inauspicious times, divination systems and omens. But his protests went in vain because since that time the Almanac has gathered within it and around it a vast array of divination systems, charms, magic, good- and bad-luck systems and so on. Later we look at some of these systems and how they affect the book which you now hold.

HEAVENLY MASTER CHANG

The next character to appear on the scene of the Almanac is a very weird one. To begin with, legend says that this person lived for over 120 years and never died but ascended to Heaven in a cloud by becoming an immortal. Secondly, his sword, which descended from the heavens into his hand, was considered the most powerful occult object in all China. Thirdly, the whole of the demonic world shudders with fear just at the sound of his name – Chang Tao-ling. He is the only person whom we shall meet in our history of the Almanac whose portrait actually appears in the book. There he is called Chang T'ien Shih – Heavenly Master Chang.

Chang Tao-ling is reputed to have been born in 35 AD and to have ascended to Heaven in 157 AD. By the time he was six he was a master of the great Taoist classic the *Tao Te Ching* and had grasped all the essential teachings of astrology and geomancy. He is usually described as the founder of religious Taoism, as distinct from philosophical Taoism. Philosophical Taoism is contained in the great writings of people such as Lao Tzu (who is supposed to have written the *Tao Te Ching*), Chuang Tzu and some of the wonderful poets of the T'ang dynasty (618–906 AD). Philosophical Taoism has always had a small following because it calls for tremendous concentration of mind and body. Often the Taoists of this school would live high in the mountains or deep in the forests where they would pass months and years without seeing another human being. Unlike the Confucians, they rejected civil jobs or indeed anything to do with government, but sought the Way or Tao of Nature. The essential teachings of philosophical Taoism are captured in the short but deeply profound book the *Tao Te Ching* – the *Book of the Way*. This is reputed to have been written by Lao Tzu in the sixth century BC. Its basic teaching is that there is a fundamental Way to the world and to all existence. This Way is the Way of Nature and is a balancing of opposites (like the yin–yang ideas we looked at earlier) which achieves a harmony. Those who follow the Way know how to live with these opposites in such a way as to be carried through life by their force. Those, like the Confucians, who wish to impose their own order on the Way will be broken by it. Those who flow or bend with the Way will find themselves borne along by it. The wisdom of the Taoist sages lies in finding the true Way. Once you are in full harmony with the Way, you can live in total peace, and you can also live for ever once you have conquered physical decay through special practices to achieve immortality.

Now for most people, and especially for the average Chinese reader of the Almanac, this was all far too complex and difficult. This is where Chang Tao-ling comes in. In the first century AD he made Taoism a popular religion by offering help to anyone wanting to be in contact with the Way through magic, charms and especially through healing. So popular did Chang Tao-ling become that before long he was ruling a semi-independent kingdom of devout followers who numbered many hundreds of thousands.

FIGHTING EVIL SPIRITS

It is said that Chang Tao-ling's power came from his

sword, his book of mystic charms and his magic seal. These were all given to him or revealed to him by Lao Tzu and the other gods. Chang founded a dynasty of Taoist masters which has lasted from the second century AD to this very day. For in Taiwan there lives the last of the line of Taoist masters. Until the late 1930s the Chang masters lived on Dragon Tiger Mountain in Kiangsi. When the Communist forces threw the family out, they destroyed the seal, books and great sword and overturned thousands of sealed jars containing evil spirits which the charms and magic of Chang Tao-ling had captured.

It is no accident that Chang Tao-ling's portrait appears in the Almanac. It is from his foundation of religious, popular, magical Taoism that much of the Almanac's teaching about auspicious days, evil forces and good and bad stars comes to have such influence on the ordinary Chinese of today. But, as we have seen, the Almanac is also a charm in its own right, and in part this comes from Chang Tao-ling. One of the most important sections in the full Almanac is the charms signed by Chang Tao-ling or issued in his name. With these charms the ordinary Chinese person feels safe from the dread forces of evil.

With the rise of religious Taoism the Almanac began to move away from being an official, imperial book and began to take the shape it has today – a book of fortune as well as a means of charting of the influence of the stars and seasons.

We have seen how the basic forces which gave life to the Almanac came into play. In the beginning are the legendary figures, followed by the early kings and statesmen; then the rise of Confucianism and the coming of the emperors. The emperors were interested in both the practical philosophy of Confucius and the pursuit of occult wisdom. Then comes religious Taoism and the consolidation of the Almanac as a book of both practical and spiritual advice.

17

THE GREAT KHAN

Now we need to leap forward a thousand years to the next remarkable phase in the Almanac's long history.

In the year 1227 Genghis Khan died. His soldiers and warriors had by this time begun their vast expansion which was to take them from Korea to Russia, from North India to the gates of Vienna. From a wandering, disorganized grouping of northern tribes, Genghis Khan had forged a formidable fighting force which settled down to rule after the initial bloodbaths were over. It is doubtful whether there has ever been quite such a violent and bloody eruption of one people against so many other peoples in the whole of history as was witnessed when the Mongol hordes burst out of Mongolia under Genghis.

Of Genghis Khan's descendants, probably the most famous was his grandson, Khublai Khan – known as the Great Khan. He ruled China and set the model for a civilized ruler which has affected both European and Chinese ideas ever since. His grandfather, Genghis, is reputed to have said, 'Man's highest joy is in victory; to conquer one's enemies, to pursue them, to deprive them of their possessions, to make their beloved weep, to ride on their horses, and to embrace their wives and daughters.' But Khublai Khan took pleasure in ordered but imaginative government, in religious debate, and in patronage of the arts and in ruling his people fairly.

Amongst the Great Khan's interests was the Almanac and, like all good rulers, he took great care to have the calendar updated and all relevant skills brought to bear upon it. It was during his time that two very significant developments took place. For the first time ever all the existing Almanacs were gathered together and edited by one person, the famous mathematician Kuo Shou-ching. Interestingly, his book, which became definitive as to what the Almanac should contain, is called the *Sou-shi-*

shuh, meaning 'A System of Divination'. Here he set out all the basic ingredients which any almanac should have, and these ingredients can still be found in the Almanac to this day.

The second significant development ordered by the Great Khan was the introduction of Islamic ideas of astronomy and astrology. The traditional Chinese calendar is based on both the sun and the moon, while the Islamic calendar uses only the moon. There was some debate for a while as to which system to use. Khublai Khan decided to stick with the old Chinese calendar but appointed Muslim astrologers to produce the Almanac. It was the instruments which the Muslim astrologers brought to China that made possible the modernization of the Almanac. Muslim astrologers continued to produce the Almanac for some hundred years, and throughout this time they kept the mixture of astrological and astronomical elements which were now so firmly established as the hallmark of this remarkable book.

MARCO POLO

It is into this scene that the first Westerner, the first European to encounter the Almanac and record his thoughts about it, appears.

Marco Polo still stirs the imagination of many in the West. His fascinating account of his tremendous journeys across the world leaves us astonished at the endurance and fortitude of this Venetian merchant. He not only travelled halfway round the world, but also became a close friend of the Great Khan and travelled extensively in China during the period 1275–93 AD. Here is his account, not just of the Almanac and its creators, but also of how it was used. What he describes as being the case seven hundred years ago is still the same today.

19

There are in the city of Kambalu, amongst Christians, Saracens and Cathaians, about five thousand astrologers and soothsayers. . . . They have their astrolabes upon which are described the planetary signs, the hours and their several aspects for the whole year. The astrologers of each distinct sect annually proceed to the examination of their respective tables, in order to ascertain the course of the heavenly bodies, and their relative positions. They discover therein what the state of the weather shall be, from the paths of the planets in the different signs, and from this foretell the peculiar phenomena of each month. For instance, they predict that there shall be thunder and storms in a certain month, earthquake in another, strokes of lightning and violent rains; in another, diseases, mortality, wars, discords, conspiracies.

As they find the matter in their astrolabes, so they declare it will come to pass; adding, however, that God, according to his good pleasure, may do more or less than they have set down. They write their predictions for the year upon certain small squares, which are called Tacuin, and these they sell, for a groat apiece, to all persons who are desirous of peeping into the future.

Those whose predictions are found to be the more generally correct are esteemed the most perfect masters of their art, and are consequently the most honoured.

When any person forms the design of executing some great work, of performing a distant journey in the ways of commerce, or of commencing any other undertaking, and is desirous of knowing what success may be likely to attend it, he has recourse to one of these astrologers, and, informing him that he is about to proceed on such an expedition, inquires in what disposition the heavens appear to be at the time. The latter thereupon tells him that, before he can answer, it is necessary he should be informed of the year, the month, and the hour in which he was born; and that, having learned these particulars, he will then proceed to ascertain in what resepct his horoscope corresponds with the aspect of the celestial bodies at the time of making the inquiry. Upon this comparison he grounds his prediction of the favourable or unfavourable termination of the adventure.

The importance of the Almanac in deciding major events and auspicious days accurately reflects its current use. By now not only was the Imperial Calendar in existence, but also other versions based upon the Imperial one, reflecting the specific interests of particular groups. For instance, the Almanac Polo encountered in Campichu was almost certainly a Buddhist one. In Kambalu he records Christians, Muslims (Saracens) and Taoists/Confucians (Cathaians) at work. Each group produced its own Almanac, and particular lords and powerful religious centres also produced their own.

CHRISTIANS AT COURT

The next group of people to appear in this strange history were not Chinese at all, nor followers of any Chinese philosophy. They did not believe in astrology but prided themselves on being experts in astronomy and counted the great Galileo as one of their friends. They were the Jesuits, fathers of the Roman Catholic intellectual Order of the Society of Jesus.

The extraordinary story of the Jesuits' control of the Almanac begins with an attempt by Matteo Ricci, the greatest of all the Jesuits who served in China, to suppress the 'superstitious' aspects of the Almanac. In 1602, after many decades in China during which he became an expert in Chinese, Ricci arrived at last in the capital city of Peking. Here he started translating Western astronomical books which he hoped would enable him to reform the calendar in order to make it more accurate (it had not been reformed since the days of the Great Khan) and to get rid of the occult material. His death in 1610 cut short this plan and it was left to his successors to see what they could achieve. Over the next few decades Western and Chinese Jesuits and Christians produced translations of the major

21

astronomical texts and proved time and time again that the old calendar was way out in its calculations. But still the great prize of heading the Bureau of Astronomy and the Department of Calendrical Studies eluded them.

TRIAL OF STRENGTH

Then in 1644 a strange duel took place. Father Adam Schall of the Jesuits challenged the officials of the Bureau and the Department to predict the exact time when an eclipse, due to take place on 1 September, would begin. The emperor gave his permission for the contest to take place. The Bureau and Department officials desperately turned to their old methods and tried to work out when the eclipse would start, reach its peak and finish. Schall meanwhile turned to his charts and his telescope and calculated the times. The official description of the contest spells out what happened.

On September 1st, 1644, the grand secretary Feng Ch'uan was ordered in company with Adam Schall to bring the telescopes and other instruments to the observatory and to command the officials and students of the Calendrical Department and Bureau of Astronomy to repair to the observatory to study the eclipse of the sun. Only the prediction calculated by the Western method coincided exactly with the primary eclipse, the total eclipse, the passing of the eclipse, the time, the percentage, the location and other details, whereas the predictions calculated by the [traditional Chinese] methods contained errors as to the time and percentage of the eclipse

From that day on Adam Schall was appointed to be the director of the Almanac. The oldest and most deeply religious of all the Chinese institutions had fallen into the hands of Christians from Europe. Although Schall was removed from his post in 1664 and died in 1666, he was

22

succeeded in the post in 1669 by another astonishing man, Father Ferdinand Verblist. From then on until the expulsion of the last Western Jesuit in 1773, the Almanac was produced under the direction of the Jesuits.

But the great dream of Ricci of reforming not just the calendrical basis of the Almanac but also the 'superstitious' elements never came to be. The calendar itself was reformed, but the good- and bad-luck days, the charms, the auspicious and inauspicious tasks for the day, all these survived and prospered under the Jesuits. Indeed, so much so that one Dominican priest wrote to Rome to complain about Adam Schall's role as director of the Almanac. 'Father Adam, being president of the College of Mathematics, had charge of, as well in Political as Religious respects, assigning lucky and unlucky days for everything they are to do (though some excused the said Father as to this particular).' His duties, according to the writer, were to choose 'days and hours for everything except eating, drinking and sinning'.

We now move to the mid-nineteenth century for yet another astonishing chapter in the history of the book. And for the first time we see an attempt to destroy the Almanac for ever.

REBELLION

In the early to mid-nineteenth century, the foreign dynasty of the Manchus had been in control for almost two hundred years. They had become corrupt and incompetent, and foreign powers, notably Britain, France and the USA, were making inroads into China. The time was ripe for rebellion against not just the Manchus but against much of old China. The attraction of the science, knowledge, industrial skills and religion of the West was very great to many young people of that time. One of these was a man who failed all the major exams for entry into the Chinese civil service and instead launched the world's most massive and destructive civil war ever. Hung Hsiuch'uan was a disgruntled failed scholar who by accident came across an early, simple evangelical Christian tract. In 1850 Hung launched armed resistance to the Manchu, proclaiming himself to be the younger brother of Jesus Christ sent to bring freedom to all humanity.

The revolt spread like wildfire. By 1853 Hung's troops had captured the southern capital Nanking and were heading for Peking. They never reached Peking, but for the next ten years they ruled over more than half of China. Hung established himself as the ruler of the Heavenly Kingdom of Great Peace and this gave the revolt its name. Great Peace is *t'ai ping* in Chinese and the revolt is known as the T'ai-ping Rebellion. During Hung's reign he banned the Almanac and insisted that a Western calendar be introduced. These new almanacs were devoid of any auspicious days or hours, contained no charms or magic, but simply told the dates and the movements of the sun and moon. Strict edicts were carved on stone and set up throughout the T'ai-ping areas forbidding the use of old, superstitious and magical Almanacs.

The T'ai-ping Rebellion eventually collapsed more from internal conflict than from the effectiveness of the imperial troops. In the end the first major threat to the survival of the Almanac was defeated by none other than General Gordon, the pious evangelistic Englishman who was to perish at the siege of Khartoum. He it was who formed a crack troop of Chinese soldiers who were able to turn the tide of military success and finally to defeat the T'ai-ping in the mid-1860s.

The Almanac was soon available in former T'ai-ping areas and all seemed well again for this most ancient of books. But within eighty years of the end of the T'ai-ping Rebellion, the Almanac was once more under attack.

'THE GODS HAVE HAD THEIR DAY'

This brings us to the last great figure in this long history of the Almanac. His name is known worldwide: Mao Tse-tung. In 1927 Mao Tse-tung produced his *Report on an Investigation of the Peasant Movement in Hunan* in which he laid the foundations of the Communist revolution which twenty-two years later would end with Mao declaring the Communist state of China from the great gate of the Imperial Palace, the very gate from which the Almanac was announced each year.

In his *Report* Mao included a whole section on religion and superstition which indicated what troubled times lay ahead for ancient traditions such as the Almanac. Mao entitled this chapter 'Overthrowing the Clan Authority of the Ancestral Temples and Clan Elders, the Religious Authority of Town and Village Gods, and the Masculine Authority of Husbands.' In it he proposed that the gods had had their day and the party should now form the focus of devotion for the peasants.

From 1949 onwards the Almanac has been suppressed in mainland China. In 1977 even the ancient agricultural calendar was suppressed and only the Western calendar dates given in newspapers. For years nothing was heard of the Almanac in China and it looked as if the book had run its course in its homeland. In the 1960s Mao's Red Guards seemed to provide the final nail in the Almanac's coffin.

OR HAVE THEY?

The liberalization of China in the late 1970s and 1980s has shown that this book cannot easily be killed. In 1985 the newspapers started printing both Western dates and traditional Chinese dates again. An official astrologer was licensed in China to produce the calculations and details necessary for the Almanac, and an overseas edition, complete with all the traditional charms, magic and so forth, began to be published for sale outside China.

It is difficult to say quite what role the Almanac now has in China. Certainly copies of it can be found in homes. People still turn to it to decide when to travel and when to get married and so on.

But if you want to find the Almanac still flourishing as it has done for hundreds, indeed for thousands of years in China, then go to the Chinese communities around the world. Go to Hong Kong, where the Almanac holds sway just as it did in ancient days, or Taiwan, where, despite the modernist attitudes of the Kuomingtang, the Almanac is still a formidable part of everyday life; visit Singapore, San Francisco, Boston, Amsterdam, London, Manchester, Glasgow. Here, as well as in any other cities with sizable Chinese communities, you will find the Almanac hanging by its red thread and influencing life.

There are now very few people who can prepare the Almanac according to the ancient wisdom. One lives in mainland China, one in Hong Kong, there are at least two in Taiwan, and the last one, whose skills have been used to work out this Almanac that you now hold, lives in Manchester in the United Kingdom. The Chinese Almanac sells tens of millions of copies each year. You are holding the first English edition of the Almanac that focuses on lucky and unlucky times and actions and offers daily advice.

THE FULL ALMANAC

The daily forecasts that fill this book are the most popular and essential parts of the Almanac. Millions of Chinese people throughout the world consult the traditional Almanac to discover the information that makes up the main body of this book. The daily forecasts reveal the fortune associated with each hour, then go on to give advice and guidance for the day ahead. The Almanac does not claim to know the future, but it does show you what is likely to happen. However, the final outcome is up to you.

The traditional Chinese Almanac contains many more sections than those included here. These are consulted under special circumstances, for example, if you need a charm to protect yourself from harm, or if you want to find out the meaning of the lines on your face and hands, or if you want to know in what direction a new house should face to bring good luck.

The book itself is a magical charm, to be hung in the doorway to protect the home against evil influences, or taken into hospital to help in childbirth or during an operation. Indeed, the Chinese title of the book and its nickname give a very clear picture of how this book is seen and valued in the Chinese world. The Chinese name is T'ung Shu – the Book of Everything. Its nickname is the T'ung Sing – Good Fortune in Everything. For in popular thought the Almanac contains within it all that is

27

necessary to live in full harmony with the world and to make your way.

We will now describe the contents of a typical Almanac so that you can get some flavour of the book. The typical Almanac produced in Hong Kong or China opens with a strange picture of a young boy leading a cow. This picture refers to a very ancient festival, one of only three solar festivals in the Chinese calendar. This celebrates the start of spring, Li Ch'un. This festival stretches back into the mists of antiquity, as does the strange ritual to which this picture refers. Over 3500 years ago it was the custom in China to sacrifice a cow at the start of spring to encourage fertility. In some parts of China this practice continued right up to to the end of the last century, but in most places the real cow had been replaced by a paper model. The Almanac gives instructions on how big the model for the New Year should be and, very importantly, what colours should be used. The colours are there to ward off the evil that lurks at the New Year, such as sickness in the early months or fire in the autumn. The picture is surrounded by details about the fortune of the coming year and advice. The original function of the Almanac was to help the farmers know when the seasons were coming and what to plant. Indeed, in some parts of the Chinese world the Almanac is known as the Farmer's Almanac.

The next section gives details of the *feng shui* directions for the year. One of the great arts of Chinese culture is that of *feng shui*. The words literally mean 'wind–water' and refer to the art of studying the land. The art of *feng shui* helps humans build, plant and bury in accordance with the forces of yin and yang* (represented here by wind and water) so that we live and are buried in harmony with the Way. This skill of knowing in which direction a house should be oriented, how high it should be, what colour it

* see pp. 4–6.

should be painted, what should be planted around it, and so on, is still practised very widely by the Chinese today. It has begun to attract interest from environmentalists, who see that there is much wisdom in trying to build in harmony with the scale, shape and meaning of the land, rather than just plonking buildings down in an environment with no regard for their surroundings. So this section ends with a list of the best and worst directions for building and for burials this year.

The first divination system which appears in the Almanac is not very accurate or highly regarded. It uses a complex system which uses your eight characters to tell you which 'house' of the Twelve Earthly Branches (see p. 39) you are in this year.

Recognizing that Chinese readers now have also to know something about the Western world, the Almanac has a number of sections which are designed to help. So next comes a list of the 200 years from 1801 to 2000 with the Chinese name (reign title and year) and the Western equivalent. Later comes a section which can only be described as being a mixed blessing. It claims to be an English dictionary with a Chinese pronunciation guide. Here you will find a list of English words with the Chinese meaning beside them. This has limited scope but it does have some interesting examples. However, it is the pronunciation guide which is most curious. For instance, for the English word 'foot' the Chinese character given as a pronunciation guide is pronounced 'fuk' in Cantonese (the Chinese spoken by people from South China around Hong Kong) and as 'fu' in Mandarin (the main dialect of Chinese spoken across the country). It is doubtful that a Chinese person who relied upon the Almanac's guide to English would be understood in the West.

Next in order comes one of the oldest sections. This lists the so-called Twenty-Four Joints and Breadths of the Solar Year. These are fascinating terms which describe the changes in the weather and land during the year. If you live in China you will find that they are still remarkably accurate. For instance, there is Yu Shui – 'constant rain which heralds the early part of spring'. This is followed two weeks later by Ching Chih – 'the awakening of the insects'. Anyone who has been in the Far East at this time of year (around 5 March) will know how accurate a description that can be. These terms are still used and published regularly in all Chinese newspapers, even in mainland China, because they have been found, century after century, to be a useful guide to what to expect at certain times of the year.

One of the most interesting sections is the text of Liu Po Wen, who might be described as China's Nostradamus. Nostradamus was a Western sage who is supposed to have produced cryptic statements about the future in the late sixteenth century which many claim to have been uncannily accurate. His Chinese equivalent was Liu Po Wen and he lived in the fourteenth century. He is reputed to have written his predictions in about 1370 AD. They are mostly given in code and it requires detailed knowledge of Chinese characters and history to be able to work them out. However, if the prediction was actually written in the fourteenth century, then it is remarkably accurate up to 1911, but then it becomes very vague. This great and much admired series of prophecies goes by a rather odd title. It is known as 'The Biscuit Poem of Liu Po Wen'. The reason for this strange title is explained within the first few lines of the poem. The first emperor of the Ming dynasty was eating a biscuit one day when a servant came to announce that Liu Po Wen was seeking an audience. The emperor knew of his powers of predictions, magic and such like, so he hid his half-eaten biscuit under a bowl before Liu Po Wen was admitted. The emperor asked Liu to tell him what was under the bowl. Liu replied, 'It looks like the sun or like the moon, and one piece has been bitten out by a golden dragon [terms used to describe the emperor].' The emperor was duly impressed. The poem goes on to tell of the predictions which Liu then gave to the emperor.

Following this comes 'The Yellow Emperor's Poem of the Four Seasons'. This is not the Ch'in Yellow Emperor but the original Yellow Emperor, who is supposed to have ruled at the beginning of history. This is a very simple divination system for which you need to know the Chinese 'hour' in which you were born, each Chinese 'hour' is two Western hours long and has a character attached to it (see p.39). You then look for your character on a picture of the emperor, and this will give you a basic forecast for the year.

This is followed by the major section on charms, headed by Chang Tao-ling, the Master of Charms. Various sets of charms appear throughout the Almanac — charms for purifying water, for 'everything', for protecting pregnant women, for sickness, for protecting the home, and so on.

The Twenty-Eight Constellations are hardly known in the West, yet they form an important part of Chinese astrology. One section in the Almanac gives a reading for the fortune of each constellation in the coming year. Each constellation is named after an animal — but not the ones we normally associate with the Chinese. The list is as follows:

Pig	Serpent
Porcupine	Earthworm
Wolf	Crocodile
Dog	Dragon
Pheasant	Badger
Cock	Hare
Crow	Fox
Monkey	Tiger
Gibbon	Leopard

31

Tapir	Griffon
Sheep	Ox
Deer	Bat
Horse	Rat
Stag	Swallow

One of the most popular divination systems in the Almanac is known as 'Fortune-Telling by Physical Sensations'. We all sometimes get a burning sensation in one ear; or a shudder runs through us and we say someone has just walked over our grave. Well, the Chinese have a whole system of meaning which is given to such events. To work this system you must note exactly which Chinese 'hour' in which the sensation starts. Perhaps you get a burning sensation in your ear at 6.30 a.m. This means that someone is coming from afar and has some good news for you. However, if the sensation comes at, say, 10.15 a.m., then you are about to lose money and any new venture will end in failure.

Another very popular section is 'Old Mr Chou's Book of Auspicious and Inauspicious Dreams'. Old Mr Chou was in fact the king of Chou, the founder of the Chou dynasty, who lived around 1000 BC. We do not know how old this system of interpreting dreams is but it is certainly old enough to have passed into folklore. So a child falling asleep in a lesson is likely to be teased by a teacher, who will ask if he has just been to visit Old Mr Chou. The interpretation of the dreams is mostly based on Chinese puns and on giving certain things such as kowtowing or receiving gifts a special significance. So if you dream about the sun or moon rising, then you will be prosperous and happy. If you dream about one of them setting, you will be cheated. If you dream about a statue of the Buddha, you will have very good fortune; if you dream your wife is pregnant, then she is having an affair. To dream of killing yourself with an axe is a sign of great fortune to come, while to dream of killing a lamb is very bad luck.

Shortly after Old Mr Chou comes yet another of the popular divination systems, one which you can see being practised every day in Chinese temples around the world. It is called 'Cup Divination'. The cups are in fact two pieces of wood, each a comfortable shape and size for the hand. They are flat on one side and curved on the other. To receive a message from the gods by the cup-divination system, you hold both pieces together and pray, asking the question you wish to have answered. Then you throw them on the ground. If one lands facing up and one down, this is called 'sheng' and means 'uncertain'. If both land facing up, then this means yang and is usually a positive reply. If both face down, this is yin and usually means 'no'. You throw the cups three times and then look for the explanation of the combination you have got. For example, sheng, sheng, yang means 'The time is not right for anything. You must avoid doing anything.'

A very strange, complex and, it is believed, powerful divination system in the Almanac is called 'The Secret Book of Chu-ko's Spirit of Calculation'. The section opens with a preface which makes it clear that this system is not to be played with lightly.

This book has been copied down through the ages from the old times. In the old times, only a few fragments of it were preserved and very few people knew of it or how to use it. According to legend, during the Han period it was written down by a man called Chu-ko Wu Hou and consists of a total of 384 predictions. Some of these prediction poems are short, some long but they all contain powerful explorations of both good and bad fortune. It is also very accurate and if you compare it with the fortune-telling of Chin Ch'ien or Ma Ch'ien you will find this method is more accurate. A friend of mine has a large library of books on many similar subjects but he says that this book is the most valuable and accurate of them all. The book of Chu-ko is able to tell everyone whether they will have good or bad fortune. It can also lead people to avoid evil things and guide them to fortune and safety. Those wishing to use it should be honest in order to ensure the utmost accuracy. Do not play with this book or else you will destroy its value.

Written on 7th month of the 7th year of the Republic of Wu Hsien by Chang Yin Hsiang (1918).

The system is very complicated but consists of writing down three characters which in some way encapsulate the question or concern that you want answered. Then, through a very detailed numbering system, you arrive at a magic number. You then look up that number which refers you to a poem. Let us say you find you have the magic number 302. You look up the poem for that number and then, using a highly involved system, you discover a whole series of messages in answer to your question.

You may never have wondered how to send a telegram or telex in Chinese, but for the Chinese this is a real problem. Telegrams and telexes can only work using alphabetic script: they cannot be used to transmit Chinese characters. So the Almanac has a solution. It provides nearly 8000 popular Chinese words and gives them each a number. This means that you send a string of numbers in your telegram or telex and then the person at the other end looks up each number in his or her Almanac and decodes the message. This is a very useful section.

Finally there are a number of sections containing good advice on how to run your business, your home, your relationships with friends, etc. They are full of proverb-type wisdom and are deeply marked by the Confucian values of respect and honour to those above you and care for those below you. They paint idealized pictures of the perfect Chinese family and business; these are intriguing because of the detail they give about everyday life in former times. They are imbued with the sense of filial piety, honour, ancestor worship, wives obeying husbands, the people obeying the rulers, and so on. They also contain hints on how to judge the moral worth of someone by his/her habits and behaviour — some of this is very perceptive if only because it is good common sense.

But it is the main section of the Almanac, the daily account of auspicious and inauspicious days — what it is good to do on a given day, what to avoid, and other such details, that is most famous; it is for this that most Chinese families buy the Almanac year after year, making it, after the works of Mao, the most popular Chinese book in the world. And this is the section that you will find translated and adapted in following pages.

THE ASTROLOGY AND DIVINATION
OF THE ALMANAC

The method by which the dates, lucky days and activities for each day of the Almanac are chosen is one of the best-guarded secrets in the Chinese world. In a moment we will look at Chinese horoscopes and astrology. We will look at some of the divination systems which the Almanac contains. We will tell stories of the Twelve Animals of the Chinese calendar and look at the fascinating systems which give the sixty-year cycle. What we cannot tell you, however, is how this Almanac is calculated for each day of any given year, for this secret is known to fewer than ten people and takes years of study to master. Amongst the Chinese, the Almanac Master Choi Pak-lai of Hong Kong is probably the most famous. His Almanacs are to be found all over the world, reaching much further than the Taiwanese versions, and only rivalled by the mainland Chinese edition.

It was from Choi Pak-lai that Kwok Man Ho, the astrologer responsible for this Almanac, learned the final details which he needed in order to master the ancient science of the Almanac. Now Kwok Man Ho joins the ranks of the few who can calculate their own Almanac for publication. He is also the first such astrologer to write in English as his main language for the Almanac.

Surrounded by books yellowed by age and stretching back into antiquity, and using the intricate geomancer's compass and other antique tools of astrology, Kwok Man Ho has scanned the heavens, listened to the Earth and drawn upon the wisdom of the centuries to prepare this Almanac. Through his calculations he has discovered which days Heaven had decreed will be auspicious and for what events. He has worked out exactly when each Chinese month will begin and end and when an extra month will need to be added. He has calculated (this time with a computer programme) how these Chinese dates correlate with the Western calendar. He has divined what forces are at work at certain times of the day and whether these are good or bad.

Many people think that there are just twelve years in the Chinese calendar cycle, but this is not so. Certainly there are the Twelve Animals and they form the basis of the Chinese calendar, but only that. For the Chinese calendar works on a sixty-year cycle and therefore someone who was born in the year of the Tiger in 1938 will not encounter the same kind of Tiger year again until 1998. For 1938 was the year of the Tiger passing through the mountain; sixty years on and 1998 will be the same kind of Tiger. Meanwhile 1950 was the year of the Tiger going down the mountain; 1962 was the Tiger passing through the forest; 1974 was the Tiger standing still; and 1986 was the Tiger in the forest. Each of these Tiger years makes a difference to the horoscope and it is never enough to simply say 'I am a Tiger' or 'I am a Snake' or whatever. You need to know if you are a Tiger in the forest or a Snake on the grass and so on. You will find a full list of the special names for each year of the sixty-year cycle on pp. 49–51.

THE TEN HEAVENLY STEMS AND THE TWELVE EARTHLY BRANCHES

The cycle of sixty is created by combining two different

sets of names, one of which has ten names in it, the other twelve. These are known as the Ten Heavenly Stems and the Twelve Earthly Branches. This reminds us of the Triad of traditional Chinese wisdom: Heaven, Earth and Humanity. Each of these systems is linked to certain key ideas in Chinese astrology and philosophy. Thus the Ten Heavenly Stems are linked to the Five Elements and to the five main directions (north, south, east, west and centre — Chinese count the centre as a direction). This gives the following chart:

HEAVENLY STEM	CHARACTER	ELEMENT	DIRECTION
Chia	甲	Wood	East
Yi	乙	Wood	East
Ping	丙	Fire	South
Ting	丁	Fire	South
Wu	戊	Earth	Centre
Chi	己	Earth	Centre
Keng	庚	Metal	West
Hsin	辛	Metal	West
Jen	壬	Water	North
Kuei	癸	Water	North

The Twelve Earthly Branches are linked to the hours of the day (remember, Chinese 'hours' are two Western hours long) and the Twelve Animals. This gives the following chart:

38

EARTHLY	CHARACTER	ANIMAL	'HOUR'
Tzu	子	Rat	23–1
Ch'ou	丑	Ox	1–3
Yin	寅	Tiger	3–5
Mao	卯	Hare	5–7
Ch'en	辰	Dragon	7–9
Szu	巳	Snake	9–11
Wu	午	Horse	11–13
Wei	未	Ram	13–15
Shen	申	Monkey	15–17
Yu	酉	Cock	17–19
Hsu	戌	Dog	19–21
Hai	亥	Pig	21–23

The cycle of sixty always starts with the first character of the Heavenly Stems and the first of the Earthly Branches – Chia and Tzu. The Heavenly Stems then have to be repeated six times and the Earthly Branches five times in order that Chia and Tzu can come together again. This is what produces the cycle of sixty.

Throughout the Almanac you will notice references to 'broken' days within the month or within the year. These are considered unlucky since the earthly branch for that day clashes with the earthly branch of the month or year in question.

THE TWELVE ANIMALS

There are many stories of how the Twelve Animals came to be associated with the Twelve Earthly Branches and why the Rat is always the first (Tzu). The story of the selection of the twelve goes like this:

The Jade King was extremely bored since he had little to do: he was waited on by his aides and servants and because he lived in Heaven he had no idea what happened on earth. In an effort to amuse himself he summoned his chief adviser.

'I have ruled for many years,' said the King, 'but I have never seen the animals on earth. What do they look like?'

The adviser told him that there were many animals on earth. Did the Jade King wish to see them all?

'Oh no!' replied the King. 'I shall waste too much time if I do that. Instead I want you to select the twelve most interesting animals and I will grade them according to their peculiarity.

The adviser thought long and hard as to which animals would please the King. First of all he decided to send an invitation to the rat; he also asked the rat to pass on an invitation to his friend the cat. Further invitations were also sent to the ox, the tiger, the rabbit, the dragon, the snake, the horse, the ram, the monkey, the cock and the dog, telling them to be at the palace at six o'clock the next morning.

The rat was extremely proud to be summoned before the Jade King and set off to tell the cat their good news. The cat was delighted to hear the news, but was afraid that he might oversleep. He therefore made the rat promise to wake him early the next morning. That night the rat pondered on how handsome the cat was and how ugly he would appear in comparison. The only way to prevent the cat taking the limelight was to let him oversleep the next morning.

Early the next day eleven animals were lined up before the Jade King. When the King reached the end of the line he turned to his adviser. 'They are all very interesting, but why are there only eleven?'

The adviser had no answer and, for fear that the King would think he had not performed his task properly, he sent a servant down to earth and ordered him to catch the first animal he found and to bring it up to Heaven. The servant arrived on a road and saw a man carrying a pig, so he took it to the parade.

Meanwhile the rat was afraid that the King might not see him because he was so small. The only thing to do was to sit on the ox's back and play a flute. That way the King would be sure to notice him.

The King did indeed notice him, and was so delighted with this unusual animal that he gave him first place. The Jade King gave the ox second place, since he had been so kind as to let the rat sit on his back. Because the tiger looked so courageous he was given third place, and the rabbit, because of his fine white fur, was given fourth place. The King thought the dragon looked like a strong snake on its legs, so he gave him fifth place. The snake was given sixth place, the horse seventh, the ram, eighth, the monkey ninth, the cock tenth (he was the only bird that the adviser knew his servant could catch), and the dog was given eleventh place. The pig was ugly, but the King gave him twelfth place.

After the ceremony had been performed the cat came dashing into the palace and begged the King to give him a chance.

'I'm sorry,' said the King. 'You are too late. I have arranged the Twelve Earthly Branches and cannot go back on my choice.'

When the cat spotted the rat, he chased him with the intention of killing him. That is why, even today, a cat cannot be friends with a rat.

41

Another story about why the rat is first goes thus:

One day the twelve animals of the calendar were arguing as to who should be first in the calendar. The gods, fed up with this bickering, stepped in to settle the argument. They suggested a contest. The first animal to reach the far bank of the river would be the first animal sign. All the creatures assembled on the river bank. The rat looked up and down the line. He could see that he stood the least chance of swimming swiftly across the river, so he decided to hitch a lift. Looking at his friends, he thought that the ox, with his great strength and tenacity, was most likely to reach the far bank first.

So as the animals plunged into the river, the rat jumped nimbly onto the ox's broad back. Just before the ox climbed out onto the river bank ahead of all the others, the rat leaped from his back and landed first. Although the other animals protested strongly that the rat had cheated, the gods declared him the winner because he had used his head rather than just his strength to win the race. This is why the cycle of twelve yearly animals signs starts with the rat and is followed by the ox.

CHINESE DATES

The Western calendar is a solar calendar. It works on the time it takes for the earth to travel a full circle around the sun. This takes 365¼ days per year, give or take a few minutes. This is why we have three years of 365 days and every fourth year a leap year. The days are divided into months which are 30 or 31 days long, with the exception of February. Although we use a solar calendar, some events are still based on the older, lunar, calendar which was used in the Middle East. So, for instance, Easter is a lunar date and this is why it can come anywhere between late March and mid-April.

The Chinese use a lunar calendar. They measure the months according to the waxing and waning of the moon and this gives them months which are either 29 or 30 days long. This means that, on average, the Chinese lunar year loses between ten and twelve days a year when set against the solar year. So every three or four years the Chinese calendar inserts an extra month.

There is a nice story told about the extra month. When the British seized Hong Kong from the Chinese in the First Opium War of 1839–42, they happened to take over the island in a year which had an extra month (1841). The local Chinese who were employed by the newly arrived British explained that there was an extra month according to their calendar and the British agreed to pay them thirteen months' salary instead of twelve. An enterprising Chinese worker then sold the British the idea that every Chinese year had thirteen months in it and the practice arose of paying thirteen months' salary every year.

NUMBERING THE YEARS

Chinese months, unlike Western months, do not have names. There does not seem to have been a tradition of naming months, though in certain documents they were known by their Heavenly Stem and Earthly Branch. Nor do the Chinese have a dating system for their years like we do. We take the assumed birthdate of Jesus Christ as the starting point of our numbering system. Thus 1991 is deemed to be the 1,991st year after the birth of Jesus. This is spelt out by the term 'Anno Domini' (AD) meaning 'the year of Our Lord'. In the Muslim calendar the starting point is the journey made by the Prophet Mohammed from Mecca to Medina in the year 622 AD. This is seen as being the first year of the Muslim calendar. Like the Chinese, Muslims follow a lunar calendar, except that they do not add an extra month. So the Muslim calendar loses ten to eleven days a year and moves backwards against the Western calendar. Thus for Muslims 1991 sees the start, on 13 July, of the year 1412 AH (After Hijrah — Hijrah is the name given to Mohammed's journey).

The Chinese do not use a fixed point in history. They have usually taken the name of the emperor and then counted how many years he has reigned. So 1837 AD, the year Queen Victoria came to the throne of England, is known as the 17th year of the reign of the Emperor Tao-kuang, the year of Ting Yu, the Lonely Cock. Thus, according to Chinese custom, if we were to follow a similar pattern in Britain, this year, 1991, would be the 38th year of the reign of Queen Elizabeth II.

But since 1911 there have been no emperors and this creates a problem once one sixty-year cycle has been completed. From 1912 until 1948 the Chinese name the years as years of the Republic. Thus 1948 is the 37th year of the Republic. From 1949 onwards they do not number the years, but use the full Heavenly Stem and Earthly Branch name instead. The present cycle of sixty will not be completed until the year 2009, but, being pragmatists, the Chinese are not speculating who or what will be ruling China then.

FORTUNE AND FATE IN THE ALMANAC

Before we turn to look at the Almanac day by day, it is important to spell out a few things about what the Chinese believe about fortune and fate. The Chinese believe that while there are certain ground rules laid down by Heaven, there is also a lot of space for personal action and choice. In the Chinese art of physiognomy, for instance, there are many tales of how people have changed their fate and therefore their physical features by acts of kindness or acts of cruelty. There is the charming tale told of P'eng Cho.

P'eng Cho spent his days ploughing the paddy fields with his oxen. It was a job he had done since his father died, and P'eng Cho's mother relied on her only son to support her. One day a wise fortune-teller was passing by and commented how hard the young boy was working. The wise man paused for a moment, then continued, 'I have looked at the five features of your face and read your physiognomy. I have to warn you that you will die on your twentieth birthday.' That evening P'eng Cho told his mother what the fortune-teller had foretold. She was heartbroken to hear this news. But what could she do — the wise man must have given an accurate prediction.

Several years later the Eight Immortals were walking by P'eng Cho's paddy fields and decided to cut across the narrow causeway which divided the watery expanses. For fear of splashing these strangers P'eng Cho pulled his oxen to a halt until they had crossed safely. The Immortals were impressed by P'eng Cho's kindness and commented on how thoughtful and hard-working he was. On returning home that evening the young boy told his mother how eight unusually dressed people had stopped to speak to him. From his description P'eng Cho's mother immediately realized that they must be the Eight Immortals and told her son to ask them for help if they ever walked by his fields again.

Two days later, the final day of P'eng Cho's life, the Eight Immortals did indeed walk by his paddy fields again. As he looked up from his plough, the boy's heart jumped, and he and his oxen knelt down in front of the holy people. The Eight Immortals wanted to find out what was troubling the young boy, and P'eng Cho revealed the fortune-teller's prediction. Finally P'eng Cho lifted his eyes to the Eight Immortals and pleaded, 'If it is within your power to grant me life, please do so.' The holy men and women were impressed with the young boy and promised him long life so he could serve his mother well. Each Immortal gave a gift of 100 years of life to P'eng Cho, and then they disappeared. P'eng Cho dropped his hoe in excitement, not realizing that as it fell it killed a poisonous snake. This was the very snake which would have killed P'eng Cho, just as the fortune-teller had predicted.

THIS LIFE AND THE NEXT

The Chinese believe that Heaven has laid out certain basic rules for each person's life. These give a certain fundamental shape to your life but not its direction, which is in your power to create. Those who seek to use their own gifts, the guidelines of Heaven, and who try to live in harmony with Heaven and Earth, can shape a very happy life. Those who abuse their gifts, kick against the constraints set by Heaven and ignore the signs of the Way that Heaven and Earth wish life to be lived, will find life hard and ultimately unrewarding. It is also important to realize that, behind many of the ideas in Chinese fortune-telling is the belief in reincarnation or rebirth. What you are now is a result of what you were and did in your previous life. You therefore start life weighed down with baggage made up of actions and their effects. This baggage is better known as karma. This will determine whether you are born into a wealthy family or a poor one; whether you are cared for or badly treated. However, by your actions in this life you can shape it to a better end and thus influence your next rebirth and incarnation. So Chinese people turning to the Almanac do not do so as slaves to a tyrannical master who tells them what they can and cannot do. The Chinese turn to the Almanac as a friend, drawing upon the wisdom of the heavens and of Earth to help guide them in the choices that they must make, in the way they should live and in the hopes that they might entertain for the future.

Let us take an example. You have decided to move house or to make a long journey. This is your decision. It has not been dictated to you. You have, for all sorts of reasons, made up your own mind to do such a thing. However, you want to ensure that this move or journey will fit in with the wider pattern, the yin and yang balance, of the world. You therefore turn to the Almanac and it will advise you. It cannot make every decision for you but it can suggest which day and time would be good or bad for such actions. It is then up to you. If you wish to go against the wider pattern – the Tao – of life, and move on a bad day for moving or travel on a bad day for travel,

47

that is your choice — but don't say Heaven didn't warn you!

You must make the basic decisions, but the Almanac will help you to make the most of what you decide to do. It might even fire the odd warning shot across your bows. But, inevitably, the final decision is yours.

THE TWELVE ANIMALS OF THE CHINESE CALENDAR

YOUR GUIDE TO THE ANIMAL FOR YOUR YEAR OF BIRTH

RAT

1924, 1984	Rat on the roof
1936, 1996	Rat in the field
1948, 2008	Rat in the warehouse
1900, 1960	Rat on the beam
1912, 1972	Rat on the mountain

OX

1925, 1985	Ox in the sea
1937, 1997	Ox in the lake
1949, 2009	Ox inside the gate
1901, 1961	Ox on the way
1913, 1973	Ox outside the gate

TIGER

1926, 1986	Tiger in the forest
1938, 1998	Tiger passing through the mountain
1950, 2010	Tiger going down the mountain
1902, 1962	Tiger passing through the forest
1914, 1974	Tiger standing still

RABBIT

1927, 1987	Rabbit looking at the moon
1939, 1999	Rabbit running out of the forest
1951, 2011	Rabbit in the burrow
1903, 1963	Rabbit running in the forest
1915, 1975	Buddha Rabbit

DRAGON

1928, 1988	Yielding Dragon
1940, 2000	Angry Dragon
1952, 2012	Dragon in the rain
1904, 1964	Cheerful Dragon
1916, 1976	Dragon flying to Heaven

SNAKE

1929, 1989	Prosperous Snake
1941, 2001	Snake sleeping in the winter
1953, 2013	Snake on the grass
1905, 1965	Snake coming out of the hole
1917, 1977	Snake in the fish pond

HORSE

1930, 1990	Horse in the hall
1942, 2002	Horse in the army
1954, 2014	Horse in the clouds
1906, 1966	Horse on the way
1918, 1978	Horse within the gate

RAM

1931, 1991	Prosperous Ram
1943, 2003	Ram in a flock of sheep
1955, 2015	Ram respected by others
1907, 1967	Lonely Ram
1919, 1979	Ram running on the mountain

MONKEY

1932, 1992	Elegant Monkey
1944, 2004	Monkey climbing a tree
1956, 2016	Monkey climbing up the mountain
1908, 1968	Lonely Monkey
1920, 1980	Monkey in a fruit tree

COCK

1933, 1993	Cock in the hen roost
1945, 2005	Singing Cock
1957, 2017	Lonely Cock
1909, 1969	Cock announcing the dawn
1921, 1981	Cock in the cage

DOG

1934, 1994	Dog on guard
1946, 2006	Sleepy Dog
1958, 2018	Dog going into the mountain
1910, 1970	Temple Dog
1922, 1982	Family Dog

PIG

1935, 1995	Pig passing by
1947, 2007	Pig passing the mountain
1959, 2019	Monastery Pig
1911, 1971	Pig in the garden
1923, 1983	Pig in the forest

YOUR HOROSCOPE FOR 1991

THE
YEAR OF
THE
RAM

FIRST MONTH

As the lion dances through the streets at New Year, firecrackers explode and frighten away evil spirits, which might otherwise carry misfortune into the year ahead.

1ST DAY OF THE 1ST MONTH –
FRIDAY, 15 FEBRUARY

THE HOURS OF FORTUNE

(G = good fortune; M = medium fortune; B = bad fortune)

23–01	M	07–09	B	15–17	B
01–03	B	09–11	G	17–19	G
03–05	M	11–13	M	19–21	B
05–07	M	13–15	M	21–23	G

ADVICE FOR THE DAY

Sit back and enjoy yourself today because this is the first day of the Chinese year of the Ram. Good fortune is in the air so take this opportunity to meet or make friends, to resolve arguments, to avoid disagreements and unnecessary risks. If you lose your temper today, or act without thinking first, the unhappiness that you cause could result in misfortune throughout the year.

New Year's Day is traditionally a day to celebrate with the family and to offer thanks to the gods but, whatever you do, remember that certain directions are more fortunate than others because lucky stars or helpful gods are resting there. The Almanac advises you to face south-west to receive the blessings of a happy god and west to receive the fortune associated with a god of nobility and a god of wealth. Avoid the east at all costs, because an unlucky star is shining there and it's also the direction of what the Almanac ominously refers to as 'Dead Door'.

WHAT TO AVOID TODAY

Spend as little time in the kitchen as possible today, and don't attempt cleaning or repair work unless it is absolutely necessary. Since this is a New Year's Day it's an unlucky time to attend or to arrange a burial.

56

This may not be such a lucky day for anyone born in the following years of the Dog: 1922, 1934, 1946, 1958, 1970.

2ND DAY OF THE 1ST MONTH – SATURDAY, 16 FEBRUARY

This is the day to worship and make offerings to Ch'e Kung who is usually depicted in Chinese mythology as a mad Buddhist monk.

THE HOURS OF FORTUNE

23–01	M		07–09	M		15–17	B
01–03	B		09–11	G		17–19	G
03–05	M		11–13	G		19–21	G
05–07	B		13–15	G		21–23	B

ADVICE FOR THE DAY

Now that the celebrations of the New Year are over it's a good time to settle down to work. As well as being a good time to pray or to reflect on the year ahead you're advised to set to work on painting or decorating around the house. However, if you're a motorist the gods of fortune have deserted you today because it's a perfect day for roadworks to begin.

WHAT TO AVOID TODAY

Be prepared for a day of delays and mishaps if you're planning to travel at home or abroad and, on a more personal note, don't risk having your hair cut or treating yourself to any other beauty routine.

This is an unlucky day for anyone born in the following years of the Pig: 1923, 1935, 1947, 1959, 1971.

3RD DAY OF THE 1ST MONTH –
SUNDAY, 17 FEBRUARY

THE HOURS OF FORTUNE

23–01	B	07–09	M	15–17	B
01–03	B	09–11	G	17–19	G
03–05	B	11–13	M	19–21	M
05–07	G	13–15	G	21–23	M

ADVICE FOR THE DAY

The good fortune associated with worship and prayer continues over from yesterday, but this is also a day to travel or set to work on DIY projects around your home. Lucky stars are also shining on gardeners, builders, tailors and farmers.

Don't turn down invitations to parties or other social gatherings today because you could be in for a welcome surprise.

WHAT TO AVOID TODAY

Stay well away from estate agents now because you might be forced to make an hasty decision which you will regret later. Although the general forecast for DIY is good, avoid cleaning or repair work in your bathroom.

Be prepared for a day of problems if you were born in the following years of the Rat: 1924, 1936, 1948, 1960, 1972.

4TH DAY OF THE 1ST MONTH – MONDAY, 18 FEBRUARY

THE HOURS OF FORTUNE

23–01	M	07–09	M	15–17	B
01–03	B	09–11	G	17–19	M
03–05	G	11–13	G	19–21	M
05–07	G	13–15	G	21–23	B

ADVICE FOR THE DAY

Give yourself time to reflect if you have worries on your mind because they may be sorted out more easily than you imagine. This is also a perfect time to start a new school or evening course, and romance is in the air if you are meeting or making friends.

If the weather is good you should try to fit in some gardening, and if you've been troubled by mice, slugs or rats this is the time to lay down repellent or traps.

WHAT TO AVOID TODAY

If you are thinking of clearing out your kitchen or repairing faulty electrical goods, leave it until another day. Be prepared for a day of disappointments if you were born in the following years of the Pig: 1923, 1935, 1947, 1959, 1971.

5TH DAY OF THE 1ST MONTH – TUESDAY, 19 FEBRUARY

The Almanac contains a traditional reminder to farmers that the spring rains begin at 11.58 this morning.

THE HOURS OF FORTUNE

23–01	B	07–09	G	15–17	B
01–03	B	09–11	G	17–19	M
03–05	B	11–13	G	19–21	B
05–07	M	13–15	G	21–23	M

ADVICE FOR THE DAY

Since this is a broken day within the month don't make any special plans or important decisions. You're advised instead to clean your house thoroughly and put some time aside for worship or quiet reflection.

WHAT TO AVOID TODAY

This is marked as a bad day for fishermen to repair nets but, even if you're only planning to sew or weave today, be extra careful. There's also a wave of bad luck associated with bedrooms, so don't attempt to move or buy bedroom furniture.

This is an unlucky day for anyone born in the following years of the Tiger: 1926, 1938, 1950, 1962, 1974.

6TH DAY OF THE 1ST MONTH – WEDNESDAY, 20 FEBRUARY

THE HOURS OF FORTUNE

23–01	M	07–09	G	15–17	B
01–03	B	09–11	G	17–19	B
03–05	G	11–13	G	19–21	M
05–07	B	13–15	M	21–23	M

ADVICE FOR THE DAY

Shopkeepers and other traders can look forward to a prosperous day, but if you're working in any other profession don't make important decisions today. The gods of fortune are on your side if you're arranging or attending a funeral, and your prayers may be unexpectedly answered now. On a more practical note, this is a suitable day to buy, sell or change the position of your bed.

WHAT TO AVOID TODAY

This is an unlucky day for cooks and home-brew enthusiasts, so spend as little time in your kitchen as possible and avoid making sauces or sampling your home-brew.

Don't expect your plans to work out as you expected today if you were born during the following years of the Rabbit: 1927, 1939, 1951, 1963, 1975.

7TH DAY OF THE 1ST MONTH – THURSDAY, 21 FEBRUARY

THE HOURS OF FORTUNE

23–01	M	07–09	B	15–17	B
01–03	B	09–11	G	17–19	M
03–05	G	11–13	M	19–21	G
05–07	G	13–15	G	21–23	G

ADVICE FOR THE DAY

This is an excellent day to be active and decisive because the stars favour anyone planning to begin a new college or evening course, to open a business or to collect outstanding debts. If you're planning to meet friends you can look forward to an interesting evening, and this is your opportunity to meet a new partner or begin a romance.

This is also your lucky day if you are a gardener or a DIY enthusiast because the forecast for digging and construction work is excellent. There's an optimistic note for farmers or anyone working with animals and, finally, if you have time left to yourself you should sit down and reflect on your good fortune or on your problems.

WHAT TO AVOID TODAY

If you're occupying yourself with housework or DIY stay well away from gutters, drains and other repair work that involves water. There's a note of caution for anyone planning a hunting trip – you may inflict more damage on yourself than you will on your prey.

This is an unlucky day for anyone born in the following years of the Dragon. 1928, 1940, 1952, 1964, 1976.

8TH DAY OF THE 1ST MONTH – FRIDAY, 22 FEBRUARY

This is the day to celebrate the grain god's birthday. He is particularly popular with farmers since he brings fertility to the land.

THE HOURS OF FORTUNE

23–01	M	07–09	G	15–17	B
01–03	B	09–11	B	17–19	M
03–05	G	11–13	G	19–21	G
05–07	G	13–15	B	21–23	G

ADVICE FOR THE DAY

This is a day for quiet reflection, and your prayers may be unexpectedly answered. If you work in the financial sector it's also an ideal time to collect outstanding debts or to take a risk in stocks and shares. If you're a keen gardener you should take this opportunity to buy new seeds or plants, and if your plants were plagued by insects last year or your house infested by vermin invest in traps or repellent today.

WHAT TO AVOID TODAY

Stay well away from your lawyer today and don't agree to a verbal or written contract until you're sure that you've been given all the background details.

This is an unlucky day for anyone born in the following years of the Snake: 1917, 1929, 1941, 1953, 1965, 1977.

9TH DAY OF THE 1ST MONTH – SATURDAY, 23 FEBRUARY

THE HOURS OF FORTUNE

23–01	G	07–09	G	15–17	B
01–03	B	09–11	M	17–19	M
03–05	G	11–13	B	19–21	M
05–07	M	13–15	G	21–23	M

ADVICE FOR THE DAY

The good fortune associated with prayer or religious ceremony continues over from yesterday but, on a more material note, it's also a well-starred day to open a business or to agree to a business deal. You can set off on journeys at home or abroad with confidence, and there's no need to worry about the future if you're beginning a new evening or college course. Your social life should be more exciting than you expected, and this is a good time to make new friends or to solve romantic problems. If you have some spare time on your hands today it would be well spent on DIY or gardening.

WHAT TO AVOID TODAY

If you've been saving food or drink for a special occasion don't be tempted to sample it today. If you're thinking of asking friends for advice or waiting for some news, prepare yourself for a shock.

This is an unlucky day for anyone born in the following years of the Horse: 1918, 1930, 1942, 1954, 1966, 1978.

10TH DAY OF THE 1ST MONTH – SUNDAY, 24 FEBRUARY

THE HOURS OF FORTUNE

23–01	G	07–09	M	15–17	B
01–03	B	09–11	B	17–19	M
03–05	G	11–13	M	19–21	M
05–07	G	13–15	B	21–23	M

ADVICE FOR THE DAY

Since this is a broken day within the year don't make important decisions or travel more than necessary. In fact, the only people who are likely to have a successful day are demolition workers.

WHAT TO AVOID TODAY

The Almanac specifically warns gardeners or farmers not to plough land or plant seeds today.

Be prepared for delays and setbacks throughout the day if you were born during the following years of the Ram: 1919, 1931, 1943, 1955, 1967, 1979.

11TH DAY OF THE 1ST MONTH – MONDAY, 25 FEBRUARY

THE HOURS OF FORTUNE

23–01	G	07–09	B	15–17	B
01–03	B	09–11	M	17–19	G
03–05	M	11–13	G	19–21	M
05–07	G	13–15	M	21–23	M

ADVICE FOR THE DAY

Lucky stars are shining on social events, so don't hesitate to accept social engagements because this is a day to meet or make friends and a perfect opportunity to begin a romance. You can look forward to years of happiness if you're announcing an engagement and if you're expecting to receive a present you'll be pleasantly surprised.

The Almanac also brings good news to anyone working with their hands, so if you're doing anything from knitting a jumper to putting a roof on your house you can be sure of a successful day. Finally, the Almanac offers a good forecast for farmers planning to buy or sell cattle.

WHAT TO AVOID TODAY

With an exception of burials you're advised not to attend

religious ceremonies, and while the forecast is good for manual and creative workers you should be extra careful if you're working with stone or repairing a cooker.

Your plans may not work out as you expected if you were born during the following years of the Monkey: 1920, 1932, 1944, 1956, 1968, 1980.

12TH DAY OF THE 1ST MONTH – TUESDAY, 26 FEBRUARY

THE HOURS OF FORTUNE

23–01	M	07–09	M	15–17	B
01–03	B	09–11	M	17–19	B
03–05	G	11–13	G	19–21	M
05–07	B	13–15	G	21–23	G

ADVICE FOR THE DAY

This is a day of activity whether you're in the office or at home. If you've been thinking about booking a holiday or making a business trip this is an ideal time to finalize arrangements or to begin your journey, and if you're moving to a new house or to a new country the upheaval may not be as painful as you imagined. Your financial prospects are excellent if you're negotiating a project, signing a contract or opening a business, and there's a secure future in store if you're announcing a marriage.

If you're celebrating today you've chosen an ideal day to receive and open presents and the forecast is excellent for meeting friends, beginning a romance and sorting out romantic difficulties. If you have any energy left after all this it would be a good idea to begin structural repair work on your house or to put some time aside to clean your kitchen or to repair faulty electrical goods.

WHAT TO AVOID TODAY

If you've been thinking of having your hair cut postpone your plans until another day, and if you're spending a day out in the open air, hunting, fishing or gardening, don't take unnecessary risks.

This is an unlucky day for anyone born in the following years of the Cock: 1921, 1933, 1945, 1957, 1969.

13TH DAY OF THE 1ST MONTH – WEDNESDAY, 27 FEBRUARY

THE HOURS OF FORTUNE

23–01	M	07–09	M	15–17	B
01–03	B	09–11	G	17–19	G
03–05	B	11–13	M	19–21	B
05–07	G	13–15	G	21–23	M

ADVICE FOR THE DAY

Now is the time to have the haircut that you were advised to postpone yesterday and, if you are confident with a pair of scissors, it's a good time to cut someone else's hair. Lucky stars are also shining on you if you're planning to sew, knit or weave, and the Almanac gives a special mention to fishing enthusiasts who intend to repair nets or fishing tackle. This is also a good day for recovery if you've been feeling ill, and if you're thinking of visiting a doctor the news will not be as bad as you expected. Finally, this is a perfect opportunity to sort out legal problems and to sign contracts.

WHAT TO AVOID TODAY

Although there's a good forecast for lawyers and their

clients you're advised not to agree to the sale of a house until tomorrow. On a more sombre note, if a close friend or relative has recently died you should try to stay as close as possible to your normal routine and delay funeral arrangements until tomorrow.

This is a day of unexpected delays and difficulties for anyone born in the following years of the Dog: 1922, 1934, 1946, 1958, 1970.

14TH DAY OF THE 1ST MONTH – THURSDAY, 28 FEBRUARY

THE HOURS OF FORTUNE

23–01	G	07–09	M	15–17	B
01–03	B	09–11	M	17–19	M
03–05	G	11–13	G	19–21	M
05–07	M	13–15	G	21–23	B

ADVICE FOR THE DAY

Today's good fortune is associated with handiwork around your home, particularly with painting and decorating. There's also a word of encouragement for anyone planning to repair paths or roads.

WHAT TO AVOID TODAY

Journeys by road, rail or sea are likely to be plagued with difficulties today so be prepared for delays, and if you are hoping to finalize travel arrangements you may be in for a disappointment. This is also a suitable day to end a period of mourning and put the past behind you.

This is an unlucky day for anyone born in the following
years of the Pig: 1923, 1935, 1947, 1959, 1971.

15TH DAY OF THE 1ST MONTH –
FRIDAY, 1 MARCH

THE HOURS OF FORTUNE

23–01	B	07–09	M	15–17	B
01–03	B	09–11	M	17–19	G
03–05	G	11–13	G	19–21	B
05–07	M	13–15	G	21–23	M

ADVICE FOR THE DAY

This is a good day for religious ceremony, particularly
marriage, and your prayers could be unexpectedly
answered. Now is the time to accept social engagements,
meet old friends, make new ones or begin a romance, and
if you're hoping to receive presents today you're in for a
welcome surprise. You needn't worry about the future if
you're announcing an engagement because the gods of
fortune are on your side, and the months ahead will be
prosperous for anyone opening a business. If you're
planning to travel today the roads should be clear and
delays at a minimum and the future looks bright if you are
moving to a new house or to a new country. This is also a
promising day for anyone working with animals and for
DIY enthusiasts or builders.

WHAT TO AVOID TODAY

Stick to journeys by land or air because there are hazards
ahead for anyone travelling by sea, and if you are planning
to launch a boat or dinghy postpone this until another
day.

This is a day of setbacks and delays for anyone born in the following years of the Rat: 1924, 1936, 1948, 1960, 1972.

16TH DAY OF THE 1ST MONTH – SATURDAY, 2 MARCH

THE HOURS OF FORTUNE

23–01	M	07–09	M	15–17	B
01–03	B	09–11	G	17–19	B
03–05	G	11–13	G	19–21	M
05–07	G	13–15	M	21–23	M

ADVICE FOR THE DAY

This is a good day for reflection and prayer, and if you have worries on your mind now is the time to talk them through with friends. This is also a promising time to make new friends or to begin a romance so, if you have the opportunity to go to a party today, don't turn it down. You're likely to find a bargain if you're planning your holidays, but even if you're only making your daily journey to work it will be trouble free. The gods of fortune are on your side if you are getting married today, and if you're moving into a new house or emigrating you've picked an excellent day to make the move. On the home front, it's a lucky day to garden, re-tile roofs or repair ceilings.

WHAT TO AVOID TODAY

Spend the minimum of time in the kitchen today even if you're a keen cook and take extra care if you're cooking elaborate sauces or organizing your own home-brew.

This is an unlucky day for anyone born in the following years of the Ox: 1925, 1937, 1949, 1961, 1973.

17TH DAY OF THE 1ST MONTH – SUNDAY, 3 MARCH

THE HOURS OF FORTUNE

23–01	G	07–09	G	15–17	B
01–03	B	09–11	G	17–19	G
03–05	B	11–13	M	19–21	M
05–07	G	13–15	G	21–23	M

ADVICE FOR THE DAY

This is a broken day within the month so you're advised by the Almanac to channel your energies into spring-cleaning, or if you've been thinking of clearing away rubbish or knocking down old fences or walls this is the day to do it.

WHAT TO AVOID TODAY

Unless your house or garden is in danger of flooding, don't attempt to mend gutters or drains. You should also avoid moving, buying or selling a bed.

Be prepared for delays and disappointments throughout the day if you were born during the following years of the Tiger: 1926, 1938, 1950, 1962, 1974.

18TH DAY OF THE 1ST MONTH –
MONDAY, 4 MARCH

THE HOURS OF FORTUNE

23–01	G	07–09	G	15–17	B
01–03	B	09–11	G	17–19	M
03–05	G	11–13	M	19–21	M
05–07	B	13–15	B	21–23	M

ADVICE FOR THE DAY

If you're beginning a new school or educational course today you can look forward to successful results in the future. It's also a safe day to travel, and if you're spending the day at home today try to put some time aside for gardening or DIY. Finally, it's a suitable day to attend or arrange a funeral.

WHAT TO AVOID TODAY

There's bad luck associated with solicitors today so avoid filing lawsuits, signing agreements or appearing in court. You're also warned not to build up your expectations if you're going to a party, meeting friends or business associates: there could be a disappointment in store.

Think before you act today if you were born in the following years of the Rabbit: 1927, 1939, 1951, 1963, 1975.

19TH DAY OF THE 1ST MONTH –
TUESDAY, 5 MARCH

THE HOURS OF FORTUNE

23–01	M	07–09	B	15–17	B
01–03	B	09–11	M	17–19	M
03–05	M	11–13	B	19–21	M
05–07	M	13–15	M	21–23	M

ADVICE FOR THE DAY

This is the day when your prayers may be unexpectedly answered, and it's a positive time for prayer and quiet reflection. There's still good fortune in the air if you're travelling or working on DIY, but the fortune has changed for the better if you're meeting friends. In fact, this is a promising time to make new friends or to begin a romance. The Almanac offers a word of support for tailors, dressmakers and weavers, and if you're laying down insect repellent or trying to get rid of vermin, this is a lucky day for you.

WHAT TO AVOID TODAY

Don't buy or mend jewellery today and resist the temptation to break into food supplies that you may have been saving for a celebration. This is also a bad time to begin a period of mourning, so try to stick as close as possible to your normal routine even if you feel like cutting yourself off from the rest of the world.

This is an ill-fated day for anyone born in the following years of the Dragon: 1928, 1940, 1952, 1964, 1976.

20TH DAY OF THE 1ST MONTH – WEDNESDAY, 6 MARCH

The period of Ching Chih begins at 10.14 this morning. Ching Chih literally means 'excited insect' and this is the time of year when insects wake with a start from their winter sleep, having been disturbed by the violent storms associated with the season.

THE HOURS OF FORTUNE

23–01	M	07–09	M	15–17	M
01–03	B	09–11	B	17–19	B
03–05	G	11–13	M	19–21	M
05–07	G	13–15	G	21–23	M

ADVICE FOR THE DAY

Lucky stars are shining on you if you're beginning a new college or evening course, and if you're making travel arrangements or setting off on a long journey you can expect a trouble-free day. You should feel on the road to recovery if you've been ill recently, and don't be afraid of visiting your doctor if you are waiting for medical results. There's also a good forecast for tailors and anyone else interested in needlework and, if your hobby is hunting or fishing, you can expect a good catch.

WHAT TO AVOID TODAY

There's bad fortune associated with marriage today, so if you are getting wed be prepared for arguments in the months ahead. You should also approach your work carefully if you're gardening and avoid re-potting shrubs or sowing seeds.

This is an unlucky day for anyone born in the following years of the Snake: 1929, 1941, 1953, 1965, 1977.

21ST DAY OF THE 1ST MONTH – THURSDAY, 7 MARCH

THE HOURS OF FORTUNE

23–01	G	07–09	B	15–17	M
01–03	B	09–11	G	17–19	B
03–05	M	11–13	B	19–21	G
05–07	M	13–15	M	21–23	G

ADVICE FOR THE DAY

Go ahead with plans to sign a contract or agree to a business deal, and don't be afraid of taking a risk today because it's likely to pay off. You should also take action now and buy traps or poison if you've been troubled by ants, slugs, mice or other vermin.

WHAT TO AVOID TODAY

There's bad luck associated with the kitchen today so be extra careful if you're handling sharp implements or hot liquids, and if you're planning to buy a cooker think carefully before you part with your money.

Don't make any hasty decisions or remarks today if you were born in the following years of the Horse: 1918, 1930, 1942, 1954, 1966, 1978.

22ND DAY OF THE 1ST MONTH – FRIDAY, 8 MARCH

THE HOURS OF FORTUNE

23–01	G	07–09	M	15–17	M
01–03	B	09–11	G	17–19	B
03–05	M	11–13	G	19–21	M
05–07	B	13–15	B	21–23	G

ADVICE FOR THE DAY

Since this is a broken day within the year the Almanac advises that your time would be well spent cleaning your house, but don't take on too much work outside unless it's necessary. There is, however, good fortune associated with prayer and worship so if you've had worries on your mind give yourself time to reflect today.

WHAT TO AVOID TODAY

Wait until another day if you were thinking of filling in holes or plastering ceiling cracks. There could also be a disappointment in store if you're thinking of having your hair cut today and beware of an accident if you're cutting your nails.

This is an unlucky day for anyone born in the following years of the Ram: 1919, 1931, 1943, 1955, 1967, 1979.

23RD DAY OF THE 1ST MONTH –
SATURDAY, 9 MARCH

THE HOURS OF FORTUNE

23–01	M	07–09	G	15–17	B
01–03	B	09–11	G	17–19	B
03–05	B	11–13	G	19–21	M
05–07	G	13–15	G	21–23	M

ADVICE FOR THE DAY

This is the perfect day not only to assess the repair work that needs doing on your house but also to begin work. Whether you're building an extension or painting a door, you'll be surprised and satisfied with your efforts by the end of the day. If you're working outside, concentrate on sowing seeds, planting trees or mending gutters. This is also a promising day for shopkeepers and for anyone signing a contract or initiating a business deal. Finally, good luck is on your side if you're sewing, weaving or knitting.

WHAT TO AVOID TODAY

Things may not work out as you expected today and if you made a request for something it may not be granted. The gods of fortune have also deserted you if you are buying property or land so don't put your name to a purchase agreement.

This is an ill-fated day for anyone born in the following years of the Monkey: 1920, 1932, 1944, 1956, 1968, 1980.

24TH DAY OF THE 1ST MONTH – SUNDAY, 10 MARCH

THE HOURS OF FORTUNE

23–01	G	07–09	M	15–17	M
01–03	B	09–11	M	17–19	B
03–05	G	11–13	G	19–21	M
05–07	G	13–15	G	21–23	B

ADVICE FOR THE DAY

If you're an enthusiastic gardener have a break from work today, but if you have to work be extra careful when digging. There's also a word of warning for anyone using tractors, bulldozers or other earth-moving equipment.

WHAT TO AVOID TODAY

This is not a day for commitment or strenuous activity although you can look forward to a safe journey if you're travelling by land, sea or air. The forecast is excellent for social activities so don't turn down party or dinner invitations – there could be a romantic surprise in store.

This is an unlucky day for anyone born in the following years of the Cock: 1921, 1933, 1945, 1957, 1969.

25TH DAY OF THE 1ST MONTH – MONDAY, 11 MARCH

THE HOURS OF FORTUNE

23–01	B	07–09	G	15–17	M
01–03	B	09–11	G	17–19	B
03–05	G	11–13	G	19–21	B
05–07	M	13–15	G	21–23	G

ADVICE FOR THE DAY

The prospect for travel is good so you can set off on journeys in your own country or abroad with confidence. If you think you can face the challenge, this is also a suitable day to give your house a thorough spring-clean, but try to put some time aside for yourself and indulge in a long relaxing bath or a haircut.

WHAT TO AVOID TODAY

If you've been mourning the death of a relative or friend, give yourself a little longer to recover from your loss. You're also advised not to arrange or attend a funeral.

This is an unlucky day for anyone born in the following years of the Dog: 1922, 1934, 1946, 1958, 1970.

26TH DAY OF THE 1ST MONTH – TUESDAY, 12 MARCH

This is a minor festival in the Chinese calendar, the festival of Pi Yi, the god of money.

THE HOURS OF FORTUNE

23–01	M	07–09	M	15–17	M
01–03	B	09–11	G	17–19	B
03–05	G	11–13	G	19–21	G
05–07	M	13–15	G	21–23	B

ADVICE FOR THE DAY

You should try to put some time aside for quiet reflection to resolve worries that are on your mind or simply to think through the day ahead. Don't be afraid to ask for help or advice: others will be willing to support you. Make an effort to meet friends or to accept social invitations; there could be a nice surprise in store. Finally, this is an appropriate day to buy, make or mend clothes.

WHAT TO AVOID TODAY

Be prepared for delays or minor accidents if you're travelling and if you're planning an important journey you're advised to postpone it until the 28th day of this month.

Think carefully before you act today if you were born during the following years of the Pig: 1923, 1935, 1947, 1959, 1971.

27TH DAY OF THE 1ST MONTH – WEDNESDAY, 13 MARCH

THE HOURS OF FORTUNE

23–01	B	07–09	M	15–17	B
01–03	B	09–11	G	17–19	B
03–05	G	11–13	M	19–21	M
05–07	G	13–15	G	21–23	G

ADVICE FOR THE DAY

You should try to put some time aside for prayer or quiet reflection and you could find that your requests are answered. The rest of today's forecast favours manual work in the house or garden. This is also a good opportunity to use your creative talents, particularly if you're interested in art.

WHAT TO AVOID TODAY

Don't attempt to tackle plumbing problems, however small. You should also beware of an accident in the bathroom, so take extra care if you're showering or taking a bath.

Be prepared for delays and disappointments throughout the day if you were born in the following years of the Rat: 1924, 1936, 1948, 1960, 1972.

28TH DAY OF THE 1ST MONTH – THURSDAY, 14 MARCH

THE HOURS OF FORTUNE

23–01	G	07–09	M	15–17	M
01–03	B	09–11	G	17–19	B
03–05	G	11–13	G	19–21	G
05–07	G	13–15	B	21–23	M

ADVICE FOR THE DAY

For the second day running this is an appropriate day for prayer or meditation. Any worries that have been on your mind should be resolved now. There's a prosperous and secure forecast for anyone working in trade, opening a business or getting married and journeys at home and abroad are blessed by good fortune. If you make the most of social opportunities that come your way you should find that friends and romantic partners are helpful and supportive. If you've the time and energy you should turn your attention to gardening and maintenance work around the house. Finally, the Almanac advises you to arrange a burial now or to put some time aside for yourself to mourn if a friend or close relative has recently died.

WHAT TO AVOID TODAY

If you're thinking of having acupuncture or other health treatments, you should postpone your visit until tomorrow. Don't initiate legal action now or sign contracts — you may not have been given sufficient information to make a sound decision. Today is a good day for travel. If your hobby is windsurfing, canoeing or sailing, you should take extra safety precautions.

Be prepared for setbacks and delays throughout the day if you were born in the following years of the Ox: 1925, 1937, 1949, 1961, 1973.

29TH DAY OF THE 1ST MONTH – FRIDAY, 15 MARCH

THE HOURS OF FORTUNE

23–01	G	07–09	G	15–17	G
01–03	B	09–11	G	17–19	B
03–05	B	11–13	B	19–21	M
05–07	M	13–15	G	21–23	M

ADVICE FOR THE DAY

This is a promising day to begin educational projects and you can expect successful results in the future. The gods of fortune are on your side if you're getting married, and you can look forward to a secure and prosperous partnership. For the second day running you should put some time aside for gardening or DIY. If you're working near water or planning to go swimming or sailing, it should prove to be a safe and satisfying day. Finally, if a close friend or relative has recently died you should find the practical and emotional support you need.

WHAT TO AVOID TODAY

Don't squander your money on unnecessary luxuries, you may need extra reserves sooner than you think. On a practical note, you should beware of an accident if you're clearing out bedroom cupboards or moving furniture.

This is an ill-fated day for anyone born in the following years of the Tiger: 1926, 1938, 1950, 1962, 1974.

SECOND MONTH

Chinese families gather before the family tomb to pray to the spirits of their ancestors and lay offerings upon their graves.

1ST DAY OF THE 2ND MONTH – SATURDAY, 16 MARCH

THE HOURS OF FORTUNE

23–01	G	07–09	G	15–17	G
01–03	B	09–11	B	17–19	B
03–05	G	11–13	M	19–21	M
05–07	B	13–15	M	21–23	M

ADVICE FOR THE DAY

Since this is a broken day within the month you should not make hasty decisions or commitments. Good fortune, however, is on your side if you're thinking of clearing away rubbish or demolishing a garden shed or a stone wall.

WHAT TO AVOID TODAY

Take extra care if you're working in the garden and don't plant seeds or trees. You should also avoid attending or arranging a funeral since it may be more upsetting than you thought.

This is an unlucky day if you were born in the following years of the Rabbit: 1927, 1939, 1951, 1963, 1975.

2ND DAY OF THE 2ND MONTH – SUNDAY, 17 MARCH

In every Chinese village and house there is a small shrine, set at ground level, dedicated to the local Earth god who guards the family. Each year, on the day of his festival, families lay offerings of fruit, fish, chicken, meat, candles and jossticks before his shrine.

THE HOURS OF FORTUNE

23–01	M	07–09	B	15–17	G
01–03	B	09–11	M	17–19	B
03–05	M	11–13	G	19–21	M
05–07	G	13–15	G	21–23	M

ADVICE FOR THE DAY

This is an ideal day for prayer, worship or quiet reflection and your prayers may be unexpectedly answered. If a relative or friend has recently died this is a suitable day to attend a funeral and don't be afraid to accept the support of those close to you. You can look forward to happiness and stability in the months ahead if you're marrying or moving to a new house or emigrating.

If it's your birthday or anniversary you may be pleasantly surprised by an unexpected present. Don't hesitate to sign or agree to a contract today because luck is on your side and if you're starting a new job there should be good promotion opportunities ahead. Finally, if you're working at home try to concentrate on needlework or gardening.

WHAT TO AVOID TODAY

There's the possibility of an accident in your kitchen today so spend as little time there as possible.

Be prepared for delays and disappointments throughout the day if you were born during the following years of the Dragon: 1928, 1940, 1952, 1964, 1976.

3RD DAY OF THE 2ND MONTH – MONDAY, 18 MARCH

THE HOURS OF FORTUNE

23–01	M	07–09	M	15–17	M
01–03	B	09–11	B	17–19	B
03–05	G	11–13	G	19–21	G
05–07	B	13–15	G	21–23	G

ADVICE FOR THE DAY

The good fortune associated with burials and all things spiritual continues over from yesterday as does the luck associated with gardening, starting a new job and moving to a new house or country. This should also be a profitable day for shopkeepers, stockbrokers and debt-collectors. If you have spare time on your hands this is an ideal day to put up or repair doors.

WHAT TO AVOID TODAY

Cancel appointments at the hairdresser unless you're certain of the cut that you want. You're also advised not to get married now unless you're prepared for months of arguments and recriminations.

This is an ill-fated day if you were born during the following years of the Snake: 1929, 1941, 1953, 1965, 1977.

4TH DAY OF THE 2ND MONTH –
TUESDAY, 19 MARCH

THE HOURS OF FORTUNE

23–01	M	07–09	G	15–17	G
01–03	B	09–11	G	17–19	B
03–05	B	11–13	B	19–21	M
05–07	G	13–15	M	21–23	M

ADVICE FOR THE DAY

Fortune has swung in the opposite direction from
yesterday and there's now an excellent forecast if you're
getting married or having your hair cut. If your clothes
need mending or darning, this is the day to do it. Finally,
if you've been plagued by slugs, ants, mice or mosquitoes
take this opportunity to lay down traps or insect
repellents.

WHAT TO AVOID TODAY

You're in danger of making a wrong decision if you're
buying property today so think very carefully before you
agree to a sale. If you're tempted to ask others for advice
today or even consult a fortune teller be prepared for
disappointing or unpleasant replies.

Don't make hasty decisions today if you were born during
the following years of the Horse: 1918, 1930, 1942,
1954, 1966, 1978.

5TH DAY OF THE 2ND MONTH –
WEDNESDAY, 20 MARCH

THE HOURS OF FORTUNE

23–01	G		07–09	M		15–17	G
01–03	B		09–11	G		17–19	B
03–05	G		11–13	M		19–21	M
05–07	G		13–15	B		21–23	B

ADVICE FOR THE DAY

Since this is both a broken day within the year and the day before the spring equinox you're advised to keep your head down to avoid confrontation. This is, however, an excellent time to pray or to work through worries that may be on your mind. If you do have surplus energy use it up cleaning your house since this is the time to sweep away the misfortune of winter.

WHAT TO AVOID TODAY

This is an unlucky day to work with, cut or collect wood. Anyone working at home should take extra care plastering walls or ceilings, and if you're setting off on a hunting trip beware of accidents.

This is an unlucky day for anyone born in the following years of the Ram: 1931, 1943, 1955, 1967, 1979.

6TH DAY OF THE 2ND MONTH –
THURSDAY, 21 MARCH

Ch'un Fen, the spring equinox, begins at 11.11 this morning.

THE HOURS OF FORTUNE

23–01	B	07–09	G	15–17	B
01–03	B	09–11	M	17–19	B
03–05	G	11–13	G	19–21	B
05–07	G	13–15	M	21–23	M

ADVICE FOR THE DAY

This is a perfect day to announce an engagement or to make a financial agreement. The gods of fortune are on your side if you're a shopkeeper or if your business involves any other sort of trade. The rest of today's luck is associated with work at home, so if you're gardening, painting, decorating or building you can be sure of a successful day. Finally, if you have to attend a funeral, accept the support offered by friends and family.

WHAT TO AVOID TODAY

With the exception of funerals try to avoid religious ceremonies. This is also an unlucky day for mending or darning, and the Almanac has a special word of warning for fishing enthusiasts who plan to repair nets.

Your plans may not work out as you expected today if you were born during the following years of the Monkey: 1920, 1932, 1944, 1956, 1968, 1980.

7TH DAY OF THE 2ND MONTH –
FRIDAY, 22 MARCH

THE HOURS OF FORTUNE

23–01	M		07–09	M		15–17	M
01–03	B		09–11	G		17–19	B
03–05	G		11–13	G		19–21	G
05–07	G		13–15	M		21–23	M

ADVICE FOR THE DAY

The misfortune associated with religious ceremony, prayer or quiet reflection has now disappeared and it's a good day to celebrate or to sort your problems out. Take this opportunity to accept party or dinner invitations: you could be in for a romantic surprise. Go ahead and finalize travel arrangements today, and if you're planning a special trip you can look forward to a safe journey. Finally, shopkeepers can expect a profitable day.

WHAT TO AVOID TODAY

If you're an enthusiastic gardener you should put your feet up and have a rest from work. You're also advised not to repair gutters or drains today: call in an expert instead.

This is an ill-fated day if you were born in the following years of the Cock: 1921, 1933, 1945, 1957, 1969.

8TH DAY OF THE 2ND MONTH – SATURDAY, 23 MARCH

THE HOURS OF FORTUNE

23–01	M	07–09	M	15–17	B
01–03	B	09–11	G	17–19	B
03–05	G	11–13	M	19–21	B
05–07	G	13–15	M	21–23	G

ADVICE FOR THE DAY

The good fortune associated with worship continues over from yesterday and you should find peace of mind, particularly if you've been mourning the death of a relative or friend. If you've been feeling under the weather this is an ideal time to consult a doctor – the news may not be as bad as you expected – and if you've recently been ill this is a good day for recovery and return to your normal routine. On the home front, there's a word of support for painters and decorators and if you've been troubled by ants, mice or other vermin, this is a suitable time to spray repellents or lay traps.

WHAT TO AVOID TODAY

There's still bad luck associated with gutters and drains so unless your house or garden is in danger of flooding, wait until tomorrow before you begin repairs.

This is an unlucky day if you were born in the following years of the Dog: 1922, 1934, 1946, 1958, 1970.

9TH DAY OF THE 2ND MONTH – SUNDAY, 24 MARCH

THE HOURS OF FORTUNE

23–01	G	07–09	G	15–17	G
01–03	B	09–11	G	17–19	B
03–05	M	11–13	M	19–21	G
05–07	G	13–15	B	21–23	B

ADVICE FOR THE DAY

For the third day running there's a good forecast for prayer, worship and quiet reflection. It's a profitable day for business so you can confidently sign a contract, retrieve debts, buy stocks and shares or open a business. You may bump into friends unexpectedly, and it's a positive day to sort out romantic problems or to begin a romance. Finally, if you're working on your home, concentrate on the kitchen or bathroom and take this opportunity to repair furnishings or darn clothes.

WHAT TO AVOID TODAY

Don't travel more than you have to today unless you have the patience to sit through endless delays. Check the facts very carefully if you're thinking of initiating legal action: your case may not be as strong as you imagine. There's also a threatening forecast for gardeners so be extra careful today, particularly if you're preparing the ground for planting.

This is an ill-fated day if you were born in the following years of the Pig: 1923, 1935, 1947, 1959, 1971.

10TH DAY OF THE 2ND MONTH – MONDAY, 25 MARCH

THE HOURS OF FORTUNE

23–01	B	07–09	M	15–17	M
01–03	B	09–11	M	17–19	B
03–05	G	11–13	B	19–21	M
05–07	M	13–15	G	21–23	M

ADVICE FOR THE DAY

This is a well-starred day for manual work and you should concentrate on repairing paths, driveways or walls.

WHAT TO AVOID TODAY

There's misfortune associated with jewellery today so be cautious if you're buying or selling and check locks and fasteners before you wear any expensive items. If friends or business associates ask for a loan, check the details very carefully and make sure that they can pay you back in the agreed time.

Be prepared for delays and disappointments in the following years of the Rat: 1924, 1936, 1948, 1960, 1972.

11TH DAY OF THE 2ND MONTH – TUESDAY, 26 MARCH

THE HOURS OF FORTUNE

23–01	G	07–09	M	15–17	G
01–03	B	09–11	B	17–19	B
03–05	G	11–13	M	19–21	G
05–07	G	13–15	M	21–23	G

ADVICE FOR THE DAY

This is a day for quiet reflection and your prayers may be unexpectedly answered. This is a positive day to start a new college or evening course. The future also looks bright for anyone beginning a new job or announcing an engagement. If you're planning to travel by land, sea or air you can look forward to a safe and delay-free journey. Make the most of social opportunities that come your way and you could be in for an unexpected romantic surprise. Finally, there's good news if you are planning DIY today and you can build, demolish or repair with confidence.

WHAT TO AVOID TODAY

Handle gardening tools with care today because there's the possibility of an accident. If you're mourning the death of someone close to you this is a suitable time to break from your day-to-day routine and reflect on your loss.

This is an unlucky day for anyone born in the following years of the Ox: 1925, 1937, 1949, 1961, 1973.

12TH DAY OF THE 2ND MONTH – WEDNESDAY, 27 MARCH

THE HOURS OF FORTUNE

23–01	G	07–09	B	15–17	G
01–03	B	09–11	G	17–19	B
03–05	B	11–13	M	19–21	G
05–07	M	13–15	G	21–23	G

ADVICE FOR THE DAY

The Almanac offers similar advice to yesterday. It is still a good day for prayer and worship, and travel and DIY continue to be well starred. If you missed the opportunity to meet friends or sort out romantic difficulties yesterday, there's still a chance for you today. The forecast for gardening is excellent and if you're thinking of setting off on a hunting trip you can be sure of a good catch. On a more sombre note, this is a suitable day to arrange or to attend a funeral.

WHAT TO AVOID TODAY

Although the forecast for DIY is good, don't take unnecessary risks if you're working in your kitchen or your bedroom and be extra careful if you're handling needles.

This is an ill-fated day for anyone born in the following years of the Tiger: 1926, 1938, 1950, 1962, 1974.

13TH DAY OF THE 2ND MONTH – THURSDAY, 28 MARCH

THE HOURS OF FORTUNE

23–01	M	07–09	M	15–17	M
01–03	B	09–11	M	17–19	B
03–05	M	11–13	G	19–21	M
05–07	B	13–15	G	21–23	G

ADVICE FOR THE DAY

Since this is a broken day within the month the lucky stars have abandoned you unless you're thinking of turning out cupboards, clearing away rubbish or demolishing a garden wall or shed.

WHAT TO AVOID TODAY

If you are thinking of having your hair cut cancel your appointment until another day to avoid disappointment. And there's also a word of caution for anyone opening a business or negotiating a business deal.

This is an unlucky day for anyone born in the following years of the Rabbit: 1927, 1939, 1951, 1963, 1975.

14TH DAY OF THE 2ND MONTH – FRIDAY, 29 MARCH

THE HOURS OF FORTUNE

23–01	M	07–09	B	15–17	G
01–03	B	09–11	M	17–19	B
03–05	B	11–13	G	19–21	M
05–07	G	13–15	G	21–23	M

ADVICE FOR THE DAY

This is a perfect day to announce an engagement or to receive presents. The forecast for business is good and it should prove to be a profitable day for shopkeepers so don't be afraid to take risks. If you're working at home channel your energies into gardening, mending home furnishings, painting or decorating the house or carrying out repair work in your kitchen or bedroom.

WHAT TO AVOID TODAY

If you're thinking of buying property today make sure that you have sufficient background information before you agree to a sale.

Think carefully before you make any decisions or commitments today if you were born in the following years of the Dragon: 1928, 1940, 1952, 1964, 1976.

15TH DAY OF THE 2ND MONTH – SATURDAY, 30 MARCH

THE HOURS OF FORTUNE

23–01	G	07–09	M	15–17	G
01–03	B	09–11	B	17–19	B
03–05	G	11–13	G	19–21	M
05–07	G	13–15	G	21–23	B

ADVICE FOR THE DAY

This could be the day when your prayers are answered; if you have worries on your mind try to put some time aside for quiet reflection. But this is also a day of activity and you can set out on a journey, open a business or begin a new college course with confidence. It's an ideal time to meet friends or begin a romance so make the most of social opportunities. If you're expecting to receive presents today you could be in for a welcome surprise. On the domestic front there's good news for DIY enthusiasts and gardeners and, if you have energy left after all this, it's a good time to treat yourself to a haircut or new clothes.

WHAT TO AVOID TODAY

Try to postpone getting married until another day because the gods of fortune have deserted you. The same is true if you're planning to sign a legal agreement or pursue legal action. This is also an inappropriate time to begin a period of mourning, so try to face the world as best you can.

This is an unlucky day for anyone born in the following years of the Snake: 1929, 1941, 1953, 1965, 1977.

16TH DAY OF THE 2ND MONTH – SUNDAY, 31 MARCH

THE HOURS OF FORTUNE

23–01	B	07–09	M	15–17	G
01–03	B	09–11	M	17–19	B
03–05	M	11–13	B	19–21	B
05–07	M	13–15	G	21–23	M

ADVICE FOR THE DAY

There is still good fortune in the air if you run your own business, and shopkeepers can expect a brisk trade today. If you're marrying today you can look forward to a happy and prosperous future with your partner. This is also a particularly good day to spoil yourself, so take this opportunity to have your hair cut or treat yourself to a long relaxing bath.

WHAT TO AVOID TODAY

The Almanac offers a word of caution to anyone who is using needles, particularly if you're sewing, darning or weaving. If you have problems on your mind, wait until tomorrow before you ask others for advice.

This is an unlucky day for anyone born in the following years of the Horse: 1918, 1930, 1942, 1954, 1966, 1978.

17TH DAY OF THE 2ND MONTH – MONDAY, 1 APRIL

THE HOURS OF FORTUNE

23–01	M	07–09	M	15–17	G
01–03	B	09–11	G	17–19	B
03–05	G	11–13	G	19–21	M
05–07	G	13–15	B	21–23	G

ADVICE FOR THE DAY

Since this is a broken day within the year you're advised to concentrate on spring-cleaning your home, but remember to put some time aside for quiet reflection.

WHAT TO AVOID TODAY

There's misfortune associated with wine and food today and you should avoid making elaborate sauces and brewing your own beer or wine. This may be a particularly painful day for you if you're in a period of mourning and, if possible, you shouldn't attend or arrange a funeral now.

This is an unlucky day for anyone born in the following years of the Ram: 1919, 1931, 1943, 1955, 1967.

18TH DAY OF THE 2ND MONTH – TUESDAY, 2 APRIL

THE HOURS OF FORTUNE

23–01	M	07–09	M	15–17	B
01–03	B	09–11	M	17–19	B
03–05	G	11–13	M	19–21	G
05–07	G	13–15	G	21–23	M

ADVICE FOR THE DAY

This is a busy day for anyone working at home because there's good fortune associated with plastering and general repair work, particularly in the bathroom. You should also lay down traps or insect repellent if you've been having problems with mice or other vermin. If you're out and about today it's a promising day to negotiate a business deal or to sign a contract.

WHAT TO AVOID TODAY

Watch out for accidents associated with gutters and drains today and, if you are having problems with water supplies, call in a plumber. You should also postpone religious ceremonies until tomorrow and, if you've been having emotional problems, don't try to sort them out today.

This is a day of disappointments if you were born in the following years of the Monkey: 1920, 1932, 1944, 1956, 1968, 1980.

19TH DAY OF THE 2ND MONTH – WEDNESDAY, 3 APRIL

This is the birthday of Kuan Yin, the goddess of Mercy, one of the most popular and beloved of all Chinese deities. The goddess is particularly revered by women as a protector of the poor and needy.

THE HOURS OF FORTUNE

23–01	G	07–09	M	15–17	M
01–03	B	09–11	M	17–19	B
03–05	G	11–13	M	19–21	G
05–07	G	13–15	B	21–23	M

ADVICE FOR THE DAY

If you're setting off on a journey everything should go according to plan, so go ahead and finalize travel arrangements today. There's also the promise of a good catch if you're planning a hunting or fishing trip.

WHAT TO AVOID TODAY

Don't pursue a lawsuit today even if you're sure that you're in the right. You're also advised to take things easy if you're digging your garden or sowing seeds.

This is an unlucky day for anyone born in the following years of the Cock: 1921, 1933, 1945, 1957, 1969.

20TH DAY OF THE 2ND MONTH – THURSDAY, 4 APRIL

THE HOURS OF FORTUNE

23–01	G	07–09	G	15–17	M
01–03	B	09–11	M	17–19	B
03–05	M	11–13	B	19–21	B
05–07	M	13–15	G	21–23	G

ADVICE FOR THE DAY

Don't miss this opportunity to make or meet new friends and be prepared for an unexpected romantic surprise. If you've been ill recently this is a good day to begin a period of convalescence and to get some fresh air, but it's also a good day to consult a doctor if you've been feeling under the weather. You might find renewed strength today if you've been in a period of mourning and it's a good time to face the world again. On a less serious note, the time is

103

right to lay down traps, poison or repellent if you've been plagued by insects or vermin.

WHAT TO AVOID TODAY

Before you wear jewellery check that safety chains and locks are secure and avoid buying or selling expensive jewellery until tomorrow. If you've been saving food or drink for a special occasion don't be tempted to sample it now; you will only regret your actions. While the Almanac says it is a good day to end a period of mourning there's still misfortune associated with funerals so try to avoid attending or arranging one.

You should think carefully before you commit yourself to new projects if you were born in the following years of the Dog: 1922, 1934, 1946, 1958, 1970.

21ST DAY OF THE 2ND MONTH – FRIDAY, 5 APRIL

This is the festival of Ching Ming which heralds the change in the weather with the start of spring. Ching Ming is the major festival of the dead, when Chinese families everywhere honour their ancestors by clearing graves or tombs and offering food and prayers to the spirits of the dead.

THE HOURS OF FORTUNE

23–01	G	07–09	M	15–17	G
01–03	B	09–11	B	17–19	G
03–05	M	11–13	M	19–21	B
05–07	M	13–15	M	21–23	B

ADVICE FOR THE DAY

Since this is Ching Ming you should limit your activities to spring-cleaning the house. This is, however, a good time for reflection and prayer, so if you have problems on your mind this could be the day to sort them out.

WHAT TO AVOID TODAY

Steer clear of gardening and journeys beyond your normal routine if you want to avoid accidents or delays.

This is an unlucky day for anyone born in the following years of the Pig: 1923, 1935, 1947, 1959, 1971.

22ND DAY OF THE 2ND MONTH – SATURDAY, 6 APRIL

THE HOURS OF FORTUNE

23–01	B	07–09	B	15–17	G
01–03	B	09–11	G	17–19	G
03–05	M	11–13	G	19–21	B
05–07	M	13–15	M	21–23	G

ADVICE FOR THE DAY

The good fortune associated with worship and prayer continues over from yesterday and this is generally a suitable day for religious ceremony, particularly for marriage or funerals. If you are beginning a period of mourning you should find renewed strength today.

WHAT TO AVOID TODAY

Don't spend more time in your kitchen than absolutely

necessary and don't attempt to repair faulty kitchen goods.

Don't expect your plans to work out as you expected if you were born in the following years of the Rat: 1924, 1936, 1948, 1960, 1972.

23RD DAY OF THE 2ND MONTH – SUNDAY, 7 APRIL

THE HOURS OF FORTUNE

23–01	M	07–09	M	15–17	M
01–03	B	09–11	G	17–19	G
03–05	M	11–13	G	19–21	B
05–07	B	13–15	G	21–23	G

ADVICE FOR THE DAY

This is a good day for practical activities, and you can expect successful results if you're painting and decorating or cleaning and weeding paths around the house.

WHAT TO AVOID TODAY

This isn't a good day to pamper yourself; in fact, you're more likely to cause an accident, particularly if you're cutting your hair or nails.

This is an ill-fated day for anyone born in the following years of the Ox: 1925, 1937, 1949, 1961, 1973.

24TH DAY OF THE 2ND MONTH –
MONDAY, 8 APRIL

THE HOURS OF FORTUNE

23–01	M	07–09	G	15–17	G
01–03	B	09–11	G	17–19	M
03–05	B	11–13	M	19–21	B
05–07	M	13–15	G	21–23	M

ADVICE FOR THE DAY

This is a well-starred day for prayer and your requests may be unexpectedly answered. This is also an excellent opportunity for financial negotiation so if you're running a business, lending money or buying stock, you can expect a profitable day.

WHAT TO AVOID TODAY

If you're working at home beware of an accident in your bedroom today. This is also an unlucky day to buy property so try to delay the final sale until tomorrow.

This is an unlucky day for anyone born in the following years of the Tiger: 1926, 1938, 1950, 1962, 1974.

25TH DAY OF THE 2ND MONTH –
TUESDAY, 9 APRIL

THE HOURS OF FORTUNE

23–01	G	07–09	G	15–17	G
01–03	B	09–11	G	17–19	M
03–05	M	11–13	G	19–21	B
05–07	B	13–15	G	21–23	B

ADVICE FOR THE DAY

The future looks bright if you're announcing an engagement or getting married and it's a perfect day to give or receive presents. This is also an appropriate time for prayer and reflection, and it's a good time to be grateful for your good fortune or think through your problems. The rest of today's forecast focuses on the home so, whether you're cleaning the house, building an extension or brewing your own beer, this is the day for you. Spend some time on your appearance: it's an ideal day to have your hair cut as you're sure to be pleased with the results.

WHAT TO AVOID TODAY

If you have taken the Almanac's advice and are busy around the house, don't be tempted to dig your garden or plant seeds. If you're mourning the death of someone close to you you should try to stick as closely as possible to your normal routine — this is not a good time for tears or recriminations.

Be prepared for disappointments throughout the day if you were born in the following years of the Rabbit: 1927, 1939, 1951, 1963, 1975.

26TH DAY OF THE 2ND MONTH – WEDNESDAY, 10 APRIL

THE HOURS OF FORTUNE

23–01	B	07–09	B	15–17	G
01–03	B	09–11	M	17–19	M
03–05	M	11–13	G	19–21	B
05–07	M	13–15	G	21–23	M

ADVICE FOR THE DAY

Since this is a broken day within the month you should turn your attention to any walls, sheds or buildings that need demolishing.

WHAT TO AVOID TODAY

This is an unlucky day for money matters, therefore you are advised not to open a business or make any financial commitments today. There's a word of advice if you're working with needles today — handle them with care and put them away safely.

This is an unlucky day for anyone born in the following years of the Dragon: 1928, 1940, 1952, 1964, 1976.

27TH DAY OF THE 2ND MONTH – THURSDAY, 11 APRIL

THE HOURS OF FORTUNE

23–01	M	07–09	M	15–17	M
01–03	B	09–11	B	17–19	B
03–05	G	11–13	G	19–21	B
05–07	G	13–15	G	21–23	M

ADVICE FOR THE DAY

The lucky stars are shining brightly on you if you're meeting friends, and you're likely to hear good news. There's the chance of a romantic meeting so make the most of social invitations that come your way. The rest of today's fortune is directed towards domestic affairs, so if you're doing anything from arranging flowers to cleaning your house you can expect satisfying results. While it's a good day for buying pets or caring for animals, it's also a good time to organize pest control if you've been bothered by vermin.

WHAT TO AVOID TODAY

Take care in the kitchen particularly if you're preparing soups or sauces. There's also a threatening forecast if you're marrying today, and if you've been in a period of mourning give yourself more time to recover from your loss.

Expect delays and setbacks now if you were born in the following years of the Snake: 1929, 1941, 1953, 1965, 1977.

28TH DAY OF THE 2ND MONTH – FRIDAY, 12 APRIL

THE HOURS OF FORTUNE

23–01	G	07–09	G	15–17	B
01–03	B	09–11	G	17–19	M
03–05	G	11–13	B	19–21	B
05–07	G	13–15	G	21–23	M

ADVICE FOR THE DAY

Your prayers may be unexpectedly answered, but this is also a day for quiet reflection especially if you're in mourning. There's good news ahead if you're marrying, giving or receiving presents, beginning a new educational course or setting out on a journey. There's also a good financial forecast so you can open a business or negotiate a business deal with confidence. If you've been thinking of getting your hair cut you should do so today. Finally, it's a promising day for general DIY around the house, particularly in your kitchen.

WHAT TO AVOID TODAY

There's an unlucky forecast for sports enthusiasts and there's a special word of warning for anyone planning to swim or set out on a hunting or fishing trip. Unless it's absolutely necessary you should avoid repairing faulty gutters or drains.

This is an ill-fated day for anyone born in the following years of the Horse: 1930, 1942, 1954, 1966, 1978.

29TH DAY OF THE 2ND MONTH – SATURDAY, 13 APRIL

THE HOURS OF FORTUNE

23–01	G	07–09	G	15–17	G
01–03	B	09–11	G	17–19	G
03–05	M	11–13	M	19–21	B
05–07	M	13–15	B	21–23	M

ADVICE FOR THE DAY

Since this is a broken day within the year you should channel your energies into spring-cleaning your home, but you should also put some time aside for quiet reflection.

WHAT TO AVOID TODAY

Be careful if you're buying or selling jewellery and, since there's the possibility of accident or loss, make sure it's secure. If you're thinking of filing a lawsuit, give yourself more time to check the facts thoroughly. You should also exercise will-power today — don't be tempted to sample food or drink that you may have been saving for a special occasion.

Don't make any hasty decisions or commitments today if you were born in the following years of the Ram: 1919, 1931, 1943, 1955, 1967, 1979.

30TH DAY OF THE 2ND MONTH – SUNDAY, 14 APRIL

THE HOURS OF FORTUNE

23–01	M	07–09	G	15–17	B
01–03	B	09–11	M	17–19	G
03–05	G	11–13	B	19–21	B
05–07	M	13–15	G	21–23	M

ADVICE FOR THE DAY

There is good fortune in store on this last day of the month if you're moving to a new house, emigrating, beginning a new college or evening course. There's the prospect of a day free of delays and accidents if you're travelling by land, sea or air and, if you're planning to meet friends or sort out romantic problems, there's a pleasant surprise in store. You can feel confident that you're making the right decision if you're opening a business or signing a contract, but even if you're just staying at home it's a good day for DIY and gardening. You should have renewed strength if you've been ill recently, and if you have just received bad news give yourself time to think things through before you act.

WHAT TO AVOID TODAY

There's still bad luck associated with jewellery so be careful whether you're wearing or buying it, and once again you are advised not to break into food or drink supplies that you've been saving for a celebration. Finally, if you have invested a lot of time and emotion into a project, it may not work out as you expected so don't be too disappointed. You should also avoid mulling over problems now because you may not have the strength or resources to sort them out.

This is an unlucky day for anyone born in the following years of the Monkey: 1920, 1932, 1944, 1956, 1968, 1980.

THIRD MONTH

The birthday of Tin Hau, the Queen of Heaven is marked by festivities that last several days. She is the guardian of those in danger at sea.

1ST DAY OF THE 3RD MONTH –
MONDAY, 15 APRIL

THE HOURS OF FORTUNE

23–01	M	07–09	M	15–17	G
01–03	B	09–11	B	17–19	B
03–05	G	11–13	M	19–21	B
05–07	G	13–15	G	21–23	G

ADVICE FOR THE DAY

The month begins with an excellent forecast for travelling or opening a new business. The rest of today's advice is focused on work at home. You should concentrate on general maintenance in your bathroom or bedroom, and if you've been planning to repair broken furniture or plaster walls this is the day to do it. This is also a positive day to attend a funeral and you should find much needed support from friends or family.

WHAT TO AVOID TODAY

There's misfortune associated with water today so don't attempt to repair gutters or drains, and if you're thinking of going swimming be extra careful.

This is an unlucky day for anyone born in the following years of the Cock: 1921, 1933, 1945, 1957, 1969.

2ND DAY OF THE 3RD MONTH – TUESDAY, 16 APRIL

THE HOURS OF FORTUNE

23–01	M	07–09	B	15–17	G
01–03	B	09–11	G	17–19	G
03–05	M	11–13	M	19–21	B
05–07	M	13–15	M	21–23	G

ADVICE FOR THE DAY

You should try to rest today and don't take unnecessary risks. The only support the Almanac offers today is for painters and decorators, so if you're planning to strip walls or choose a new colour scheme for your house you're in for a successful day.

WHAT TO AVOID TODAY

There's a possibility of an accident in the kitchen today so try to avoid unnecessary work there. If you're mourning the loss of someone close to you you will feel particularly low so don't push yourself too far and you should avoid attending or arranging a funeral.

Don't take any unnecessary risks today if you were born in the following years of the Dog: 1922, 1934, 1946, 1958, 1970.

3RD DAY OF THE 3RD MONTH – WEDNESDAY, 17 APRIL

THE HOURS OF FORTUNE

23–01	M	07–09	M	15–17	M
01–03	B	09–11	G	17–19	G
03–05	M	11–13	G	19–21	B
05–07	B	13–15	G	21–23	B

ADVICE FOR THE DAY

There's luck in the air if you're waiting for news or making a request and your prayers may be unexpectedly answered. Make every effort to accept social invitations because you could be in for a pleasant surprise, and if you've been having romantic problems this is the day to sort them out. There's happiness and prosperity in store if you're announcing an engagement or getting married, and the forecast for giving or receiving presents is excellent.

If you're on the move to a new house or new country you can be sure that you've made the right decision, and if you're opening a new business or investing money there's many profitable months ahead of you. If you're keen on needlework or have money to spare this is an ideal time to make or buy new clothes. Meanwhile, anyone who is staying at home today is advised to concentrate on gardening, general DIY, stocking up on food or drink supplies, and if you've been brewing your own beer and wine this is an excellent opportunity to sample it. Finally, there's good news for anyone working with animals or thinking of buying a new pet.

WHAT TO AVOID TODAY

If you're planning to get your hair cut wait until another day to avoid disappointment. Be prepared for travel delays and if you're making travel arrangements you can expect setbacks. There's a final word of warning if you're working in the kitchen – look out for faulty electrical goods and be extra cautious if you're cutting or chopping food.

This is an unlucky day for anyone born in the following years of the Pig: 1923, 1935, 1947, 1959, 1971.

4TH DAY OF THE 3RD MONTH – THURSDAY, 18 APRIL

THE HOURS OF FORTUNE

23–01	B	07–09	M	15–17	G
01–03	B	09–11	G	17–19	G
03–05	B	11–13	M	19–21	B
05–07	G	13–15	G	21–23	M

ADVICE FOR THE DAY

Once again it's a good day to ask for favours and it's an appropriate time for religious ceremony. Good fortune is still on your side if you're travelling, meeting friends or beginning a romance. Be prepared to take a risk today, particularly if you're investing money or opening a new business. Now is the time to clear out cupboards or drawers in your bedroom and to buy or sell a bed. Take this opportunity to mend clothes or home furnishings. Finally, if you have money to spare it's a good day to treat yourself to something you've been thinking of buying for a long time.

WHAT TO AVOID TODAY

If you're thinking of buying property give yourself another

day to think your decision through and check that you have been given sufficient background information.

This is an ill-fated day for anyone born in the following years of the Rat: 1924, 1936, 1948, 1960, 1972.

5TH DAY OF THE 3RD MONTH – FRIDAY, 19 APRIL

THE HOURS OF FORTUNE

23–01	M	07–09	M	15–17	G
01–03	B	09–11	G	17–19	M
03–05	G	11–13	G	19–21	B
05–07	G	13–15	G	21–23	B

ADVICE FOR THE DAY

You can be sure of a safe day and a good catch if you're setting off on a hunting or fishing trip. If you've been thinking of having your hair cut this is the day to visit the hairdresser. If you have the energy the forecast is also good for painting and decorating and for clearing or repairing garden paths or driveways.

WHAT TO AVOID TODAY

There's the threat of financial problems in the months ahead if you're opening a new business or negotiating a business deal. You're also advised against buying or mending clothes. If you're mourning the death of a friend or relative don't cut yourself off from others and try to stick as close as possible to your normal routine.

This is an unlucky day for anyone born in the following years of the Ox: 1925, 1937, 1949, 1961, 1973.

6TH DAY OF THE 3RD MONTH –
SATURDAY, 20 APRIL

Ku Yu, which begins at 22.30, is a date that has been fixed in the agricultural calendar for thousands of years. It is a reminder that sufficient rains will fall around this time to nourish their crops. This is why it is known as Grain Rain.

THE HOURS OF FORTUNE

23–01	B	07–09	G	15–17	G
01–03	B	09–11	G	17–19	M
03–05	B	11–13	G	19–21	B
05–07	M	13–15	G	21–23	M

ADVICE FOR THE DAY

Now is the time to sort out your personal problems. It's a good day for prayer and quiet reflection but it's also an opportunity to ask others for advice and, if you've just been through an unhappy period in your life, it's time to put the past behind you. If, however, you're mourning the recent death of a friend or relative this is a suitable time to attend a funeral and to accept the support of friends. On a practical note, the forecast is excellent if you're thinking of giving your house a thorough spring-cleaning. You can also expect a successful day if you're working with animals and the Almanac specifically advises farmers to buy livestock now.

WHAT TO AVOID TODAY

Avoid gardening, and do not plant seeds or trees. If you're working at home take extra care if you're sewing or carrying out repair work in your bedroom.

Be prepared for delays and disappointments throughout the day if you were born in the following years of the Tiger: 1926, 1938, 1950, 1962, 1974.

7TH DAY OF THE 3RD MONTH – SUNDAY, 21 APRIL

THE HOURS OF FORTUNE

23–01	M	07–09	G	15–17	M
01–03	B	09–11	G	17–19	B
03–05	G	11–13	G	19–21	B
05–07	B	13–15	M	21–23	M

ADVICE FOR THE DAY

This is a busy and fruitful day for dressmakers and sewing enthusiasts, but it's also a good day to buy new clothes. You should feel well on the road to recovery now if you've been ill, and if you're worried about your health this is a promising day to consult a doctor. If you have energy to spare you should once again channel it into cleaning the house, and if you've been troubled by vermin you should lay down repellent or traps today. It's a positive day for sport, and hunting or fishing enthusiasts can look forward to a successful day. Finally, it's a suitable day to attend a burial, but if you've just been through a period of depression now is the time to make a new start.

WHAT TO AVOID TODAY

There are hazards lurking in the kitchen and garden so be wary if you're gardening, brewing your own beer and wine, or preparing food.

This is an unlucky day for anyone born in the following years of the Rabbit: 1927, 1939, 1951, 1963, 1975.

8TH DAY OF THE 3RD MONTH – MONDAY, 22 APRIL

THE HOURS OF FORTUNE

23–01	M	07–09	B	15–17	B
01–03	B	09–11	G	17–19	M
03–05	G	11–13	M	19–21	B
05–07	G	13–15	G	21–23	G

ADVICE FOR THE DAY

This is a broken day within the month so you're advised to turn your attention to clearing away rubble or demolishing an old garden shed or wall. There's still good news for anyone recovering from an illness or consulting a doctor.

WHAT TO AVOID TODAY

There's misfortune associated with water and the Almanac advises you not to repair drains or gutters: employ a professional instead.

Don't make any hasty decisions or commitments today if you were born in the following years of the Dragon: 1928, 1940, 1952, 1964, 1976.

9TH DAY OF THE 3RD MONTH – TUESDAY, 23 APRIL

THE HOURS OF FORTUNE

23–01	M	07–09	G	15–17	M
01–03	B	09–11	B	17–19	M
03–05	G	11–13	G	19–21	B
05–07	G	13–15	B	21–23	G

ADVICE FOR THE DAY

It's a good day for mending clothes or home furnishings, but it's also a day of rest and you should treat yourself to a relaxing bath or sauna.

WHAT TO AVOID TODAY

Unless you're ready for months of recriminations, don't get married today. You're also advised not to sign legal agreements or file lawsuits: you may not have been given enough information to make the right decision.

This is an unlucky day for anyone born in the following years of the Snake: 1917, 1929, 1941, 1953, 1965, 1977.

10TH DAY OF THE 3RD MONTH – WEDNESDAY, 24 APRIL

THE HOURS OF FORTUNE

23–01	G	07–09	G	15–17	G
01–03	B	09–11	M	17–19	M
03–05	G	11–13	B	19–21	B
05–07	M	13–15	G	21–23	M

ADVICE FOR THE DAY

There's good fortune associated with worship and your prayers may be unexpectedly answered. It's an ideal time to begin a college or evening course. Travel at home or abroad is well starred, and you can look forward to a profitable day if you're negotiating a business deal, collecting debts or opening a new business. Don't refuse social invitations because it's a good opportunity to renew friendships or begin a romance. There's a good forecast for general renovation work around the home, particularly if you're working in your kitchen or bedroom. There's good news for farmers, vets and anyone else buying, selling or working with animals. Finally, it's a suitable day to attend or arrange a funeral.

WHAT TO AVOID TODAY

Think carefully before you invest in jewellery; you may not be getting the bargain you imagined. If you've been stocking up on food and drink for a special occasion, don't be tempted to break into it. Be prepared for bad news if you're asking others for advice; they may be able to see the problems ahead more clearly than you. Finally, leave your gardening tools where they are today since there's the possibility of an accident.

This is an ill-fated day for anyone born in the following years of the Horse: 1918, 1930, 1942, 1954, 1966, 1978.

11TH DAY OF THE 3RD MONTH – THURSDAY, 25 APRIL

THE HOURS OF FORTUNE

23–01	G	07–09	M	15–17	G
01–03	B	09–11	B	17–19	M
03–05	G	11–13	M	19–21	B
05–07	G	13–15	B	21–23	M

ADVICE FOR THE DAY

Since this is a broken day within the year you should concentrate on minor demolition work in the garden or clearing away rubble.

WHAT TO AVOID TODAY

Once again it's an unlucky day in the garden and you're advised to avoid planting seeds or trees and cutting or arranging flowers.

This is a day of delays and setbacks for anyone born in the following years of the Ram: 1919, 1931, 1943, 1955, 1967, 1979.

12TH DAY OF THE 3RD MONTH – FRIDAY, 26 APRIL

THE HOURS OF FORTUNE

23–01	G	07–09	B	15–17	B
01–03	B	09–11	M	17–19	G
03–05	M	11–13	G	19–21	B
05–07	G	13–15	M	21–23	M

ADVICE FOR THE DAY

Lucky stars are shining on romance and friendship now so don't miss out on social opportunities. You should hear good news if you've taken exams recently, and you can look forward to a successful career if you're beginning a new college or evening course. The gods of fortune are on your side if you're announcing an engagement and it's a perfect time to give or receive presents. Don't worry about delays or setbacks if you're moving house or emigrating, and go ahead with plans to open a business or invest money. You're unlikely to have any regrets if you're buying property, and if you're looking for a new home you will be pleasantly surprised. Finally, if you have time on your hands it's a promising day for DIY and gardening.

WHAT TO AVOID TODAY

Steer clear of electrical repairs in your kitchen and handle crockery with care. It's a bad time to consult a doctor or acupuncturist. And, on a more spiritual note, try to postpone religious ceremonies until tomorrow.

This is an unlucky day for anyone born during the following years of the Monkey: 1920, 1932, 1944, 1956, 1968, 1980.

13TH DAY OF THE 3RD MONTH – SATURDAY, 27 APRIL

THE HOURS OF FORTUNE

23–01	M	07–09	M	15–17	M
01–03	B	09–11	M	17–19	B
03–05	G	11–13	G	19–21	B
05–07	B	13–15	G	21–23	G

ADVICE FOR THE DAY

The fortunes of yesterday have changed and it's now a good time for religious ceremony or quiet reflection. The gods of fortune are on your side if you're marrying now or setting off on a journey by land, sea or air. This is a profitable day for shopkeepers and a promising time to invest money. Once again, it's a safe day for general DIY and gardening. It's also an appropriate day to attend or arrange a funeral.

WHAT TO AVOID TODAY

If you're thinking of getting your hair cut, postpone it until tomorrow to avoid disappointment. You should also be extra careful if you're mending water pipes, gutters or drains.

This is an ill-fated day for anyone born in the following years of the Cock: 1921, 1933, 1945, 1957, 1969.

14TH DAY OF THE 3RD MONTH – SUNDAY, 28 APRIL

THE HOURS OF FORTUNE

23–01	M	07–09	M	15–17	G
01–03	B	09–11	G	17–19	G
03–05	B	11–13	M	19–21	B
05–07	G	13–15	G	21–23	M

ADVICE FOR THE DAY

Once again, it's a good day for worship and your prayers may be unexpectedly answered. Travel difficulties should be resolved today and you can set off on journeys with confidence. It's a suitable day for enthusiastic dressmakers but it's also an ideal opportunity to treat yourself to some new clothes. Finally, painters and decorators should be more than happy with the results of their work at the end of the day.

WHAT TO AVOID TODAY

There's misfortune associated with land and housing so don't work in the garden or agree to the sale of a property now.

This is an unlucky day for anyone born in the following years of the Dog: 1922, 1934, 1946, 1958, 1970.

15TH DAY OF THE 3RD MONTH –
MONDAY, 29 APRIL

THE HOURS OF FORTUNE

23–01	G	07–09	M	15–17	G
01–03	B	09–11	M	17–19	M
03–05	G	11–13	G	19–21	B
05–07	M	13–15	G	21–23	B

ADVICE FOR THE DAY

Now is the time to sort out romantic problems, renew friendships and make the most of social invitations: you could be in for a pleasant surprise. You can expect a prosperous outcome if you're opening a business, but if you're tied to the house today you should channel your efforts into spring-cleaning, and renovation work to your doors, ceilings or your kitchen. It's also a lucky day for gardening.

WHAT TO AVOID TODAY

If you're mourning the death of someone close to you, turn to your friends for support instead of cutting yourself off from the world.

Your plans or ideas will not be realized today if you were born in the following years of the Pig: 1923, 1935, 1947, 1959, 1971.

16TH DAY OF THE 3RD MONTH – TUESDAY, 30 APRIL

THE HOURS OF FORTUNE

23–01	B	07–09	M	15–17	G
01–03	B	09–11	M	17–19	G
03–05	G	11–13	G	19–21	B
05–07	M	13–15	G	21–23	M

ADVICE FOR THE DAY

If you have worries on your mind, put some time aside to reflect on them today. But this is also a day of activity and a perfect time to begin a journey, to meet old friends, or to make new ones. There's the prospect of happiness in the years ahead if you're announcing an engagement now. If you've been thinking of buying new clothes you're likely to find exactly what you want and if you're investing money there should be a profitable outcome. Finally, it's a good time to put the sadness or the regrets of the past behind you and if you're attending a funeral you should resolve past differences.

WHAT TO AVOID TODAY

If you're a DIY enthusiast you should steer clear of repair work on ceilings. There's also the threat of an accident if you're sewing or knitting so take extra care when you're handling needles.

This is an unlucky day for anyone born in the following years of the Rat: 1924, 1936, 1948, 1960, 1972.

17TH DAY OF THE 3RD MONTH – WEDNESDAY, 1 MAY

THE HOURS OF FORTUNE

23–01	M	07–09	M	15–17	G
01–03	B	09–11	G	17–19	B
03–05	G	11–13	G	19–21	B
05–07	G	13–15	M	21–23	M

ADVICE FOR THE DAY

This is a good day for quiet reflection and your prayers may be unexpectedly answered. The rest of the day's fortune is given over to renovation work around the house and garden.

WHAT TO AVOID TODAY

Beware of an accident in the kitchen if you're handling hot liquids, making sauces or soups, or organizing your own home-brew.

This is an ill-fated day for anyone born in the following years of the Ox: 1925, 1937, 1949, 1961, 1973.

18TH DAY OF THE 3RD MONTH – THURSDAY, 2 MAY

THE HOURS OF FORTUNE

23–01	G	07–09	G	15–17	B
01–03	B	09–11	G	17–19	G
03–05	B	11–13	M	19–21	B
05–07	G	13–15	G	21–23	M

ADVICE FOR THE DAY

There's still good news for anyone sorting out personal problems or resolving difficulties with others. Don't be afraid to ask others for support today, particularly if you're mourning the death of a friend or relative. On a more practical note, it's a promising day to start a new educational course, to open a business or invest money. If you've been thinking of painting, repairing or putting up new doors, this is the day to do it. It's also a good day to make or mend home furnishings.

WHAT TO AVOID TODAY

Avoid moving, buying or selling a bed today and postpone housework in your bedroom until another day.

Be prepared for disappointments and setbacks throughout the day if you were born in the following years of the Tiger: 1926, 1938, 1950, 1962, 1974.

19TH DAY OF THE 3RD MONTH – FRIDAY, 3 MAY

THE HOURS OF FORTUNE

23–01	G	07–09	G	15–17	G
01–03	B	09–11	G	17–19	M
03–05	G	11–13	M	19–21	B
05–07	B	13–15	B	21–23	M

ADVICE FOR THE DAY

It's still a good time for prayer or personal reflection. If you're marrying today you can look forward to a prosperous and happy future. Take some fresh air or exercise if you've recently been ill because it's a good day for recovery. There's also good news for anyone buying, selling or working with animals. The forecast for renovation work around the home is excellent, particularly if you're building an extension. And, finally, it's a suitable day to attend or arrange a burial.

WHAT TO AVOID TODAY

It's a good day to stock up on food supplies but an unlucky time to use them all at once. Be prepared for an unexpected visitor. Have a rest from gardening today, it's likely to be more trouble than it's worth. You're also warned not to sign contracts or initiate legal action.

Don't make any hasty decisions or commitments today if you were born in the following years of the Rabbit: 1927, 1939, 1951, 1963, 1975.

20TH DAY OF THE 3RD MONTH – SATURDAY, 4 MAY

THE HOURS OF FORTUNE

23–01	M	07–09	B	15–17	M
01–03	B	09–11	G	17–19	M
03–05	G	11–13	B	19–21	B
05–07	G	13–15	G	21–23	M

ADVICE FOR THE DAY

Since this is a broken day within the month you should concentrate on clearing away rubble or pulling down a garden wall or shed. This is also an important day for dealing with health matters. If you're feeling ill, make an appointment to see your doctor or try to put some time aside to rest.

WHAT TO AVOID TODAY

Handle jewellery carefully and if you're thinking of buying an expensive piece of jewellery get a second opinion on its value. You should also think twice before you lend money, even to friends.

This is an unlucky day for anyone born in the following years of the Dragon: 1916, 1928, 1940, 1952, 1964, 1976.

21ST DAY OF THE 3RD MONTH – SUNDAY, 5 MAY

THE HOURS OF FORTUNE

23–01	G	07–09	M	15–17	M
01–03	B	09–11	B	17–19	M
03–05	G	11–13	M	19–21	B
05–07	G	13–15	G	21–23	M

ADVICE FOR THE DAY

Since this is the day before Li Hsia, don't take unnecessary risks. The Almanac advises you to put some time aside for prayer or quiet reflection.

WHAT TO AVOID TODAY

Steer clear of gardening today and you're particularly warned not to plant seeds or trees.

This is an unlucky day for anyone born in the following years of the Snake: 1917, 1929, 1941, 1953, 1965, 1977.

22ND DAY OF THE 3RD MONTH – MONDAY, 6 MAY

Li Hsia, the day that marks the start of summer, begins at 8.51 this morning.

THE HOURS OF FORTUNE

23–01	G	07–09	B	15–17	M
01–03	B	09–11	G	17–19	G
03–05	M	11–13	B	19–21	G
05–07	M	13–15	M	21–23	B

ADVICE FOR THE DAY

This is a good day for anyone who is on the move or making decisions. You should make travel plans now and if you're setting off on a journey you can expect to arrive there safely and on time. It's an ideal time to meet friends or begin a romance, so don't hesitate to accept social invitations. It's also a promising day to get married and to receive presents. Don't worry about the future if you're opening a business, finalizing a business deal or investing money. Stay calm if you're having medical treatment today, it should prove to be effective. There's a good forecast for anyone on the move, whether it's to a new house or country. Finally, it's a fruitful day for gardeners or DIY enthusiasts.

WHAT TO AVOID TODAY

Although there's a good forecast for DIY stay well away from electrical repair work in your kitchen. If you're a keen sailor, take extra safety precautions today or, better still, postpone your activities until tomorrow. This is not a good time to end a period of mourning or loss so give yourself some more time before you face the world again.

This is an ill-fated day for anyone born in the following years of the Horse: 1918, 1930, 1942, 1954, 1966, 1978.

23RD DAY OF THE 3RD MONTH – TUESDAY, 7 MAY

The birthday of Tin Hau, the queen of Heaven, is celebrated today.

THE HOURS OF FORTUNE

23–01	G	07–09	M	15–17	M
01–03	B	09–11	G	17–19	G
03–05	M	11–13	G	19–21	M
05–07	B	13–15	B	21–23	B

ADVICE FOR THE DAY

Since this is a broken day within the month you should concentrate on clearing away rubble or pulling down old walls or sheds. On a more spiritual note, it's an appropriate time for prayer or quiet reflection.

WHAT TO AVOID TODAY

Don't be tempted to buy expensive jewellery, and if you're wearing valuable rings, bracelets or chains make sure they are securely fastened. Avoid breaking into food or drink you've been saving for a special occasion.

Be prepared for delays and setbacks if you were born in the following years of the Ram: 1919, 1931, 1943, 1955, 1967, 1979.

24TH DAY OF THE 3RD MONTH – WEDNESDAY, 8 MAY

THE HOURS OF FORTUNE

23–01	M	07–09	G	15–17	B
01–03	B	09–11	G	17–19	M
03–05	B	11–13	G	19–21	M
05–07	G	13–15	G	21–23	B

ADVICE FOR THE DAY

Fishing enthusiasts are in for an enjoyable day and can be sure of a good catch. There's also a word of support for builders and anyone planning to get rid of mice, ants, mosquitoes or any other insects should act today.

WHAT TO AVOID TODAY

Keep yourself busy with practical activities and postpone religious ceremonies until tomorrow. You should, however, have a rest from gardening; your efforts will hardly be rewarded.

This is an unlucky day for anyone born in the following years of the Monkey: 1920, 1932, 1944, 1956, 1968, 1980.

25TH DAY OF THE 3RD MONTH – THURSDAY, 9 MAY

THE HOURS OF FORTUNE

23–01	G	07–09	M	15–17	M
01–03	B	09–11	M	17–19	B
03–05	G	11–13	G	19–21	M
05–07	G	13–15	G	21–23	B

ADVICE FOR THE DAY

Fortunes have changed and it's now a good day for worship, prayer and quiet reflection. It's also an ideal time to offer your support to others who may need it. There's success in store for you if you're waiting for exam results or starting a new educational project. Travel will be blessed by good fortune today so journey as far as you like. The gods of fortune are shining on you so don't worry about the future if you're getting married. If you're thinking of buying or making clothes, set to work now. This is also an appropriate time to concentrate on general maintenance work around the house.

WHAT TO AVOID TODAY

There's misfortune associated with water today so don't go swimming, and be extra careful if you're mending water pipes, gutters or drains.

Your plans may not work out as you expected if you were born in the following years of the Cock: 1921, 1933, 1945, 1957, 1969.

26TH DAY OF THE 3RD MONTH – FRIDAY, 10 MAY

THE HOURS OF FORTUNE

23–01	B	07–09	G	15–17	M
01–03	B	09–11	G	17–19	M
03–05	G	11–13	G	19–21	B
05–07	M	13–15	G	21–23	B

ADVICE FOR THE DAY

Try to put some time aside for prayer or quiet reflection.

It's a lucky day for anyone on the move so if you're travelling, moving to a new house or emigrating you can look forward to a safe journey. This is also a profitable day for shopkeepers and anyone thinking of investing money. If you're spending the day at home, concentrate on work in your bedroom or garden. This is also a suitable day to attend a funeral, and don't be afraid of turning to friends or relatives for support.

WHAT TO AVOID TODAY

Postpone trips to the doctor or acupuncturist until tomorrow. If you're sewing, darning or knitting today, handle needles with care.

This is a day of disappointments if you were born in the following years of the Dog: 1922, 1934, 1946, 1958, 1960, 1972.

27TH DAY OF THE 3RD MONTH – SATURDAY, 11 MAY

THE HOURS OF FORTUNE

23–01	M	07–09	M	15–17	M
01–03	B	09–11	G	17–19	B
03–05	G	11–13	G	19–21	G
05–07	M	13–15	G	21–23	B

ADVICE FOR THE DAY

The good fortune associated with prayer and quiet reflection continues today and this could be the time when your prayers are unexpectedly answered. But this is also an opportune moment to offer your support to others who may need it. The gods of fortune are on your side if you're marrying now and it's a perfect time to give or receive presents. There may be an unexpected surprise if you're meeting friends or going to a party and there's the possibility of a new romance. There's a happy and secure future in store if you're moving to a new house or emigrating. If you've been feeling ill you should take this opportunity to consult a doctor and don't worry if you're going for an operation – everything should work out well. Finally, if you're planning to do maintenance work on your home, you'll be more than satisfied with your efforts at the end of the day.

WHAT TO AVOID TODAY

Be prepared for difficulties if you're making holiday arrangements today and postpone journeys beyond your normal routine. On the domestic front, avoid making soups or sauces and don't work or sample home-brewed beer or wine.

This is an unlucky day for anyone born in the following years of the Pig: 1923, 1935, 1947, 1959, 1971.

28TH DAY OF THE 3RD MONTH – SUNDAY, 12 MAY

THE HOURS OF FORTUNE

23–01	B	07–09	M	15–17	B
01–03	B	09–11	G	17–19	M
03–05	G	11–13	M	19–21	M
05–07	G	13–15	G	21–23	B

ADVICE FOR THE DAY

It's still a promising day for prayer and reflection and

there's still good fortune in the air for meeting friends or beginning a romance. It's now an ideal day to travel or to finalize travel arrangements. You can open a new business or begin a new job with confidence and there's good luck in store if you're making investments or retrieving debts. If you've been ill recently this is a good day to return to work but it's also a positive day to recuperate from an illness. The forecast for builders is hopeful although you should be careful if you're painting or mending ceilings.

WHAT TO AVOID TODAY

Don't attempt to unblock drains or mend gutters yourself. Don't expect too much of yourself if you're mourning the loss of a close friend or relative. Give yourself more time to recover before you take on the pressures of work or company.

This is an unlucky day for anyone born in the following years of the Rat: 1924, 1936, 1948, 1960, 1972.

29TH DAY OF THE 3RD MONTH – MONDAY, 13 MAY

THE HOURS OF FORTUNE

23–01	G	07–09	M	15–17	M
01–03	B	09–11	G	17–19	M
03–05	G	11–13	G	19–21	G
05–07	G	13–15	B	21–23	B

ADVICE FOR THE DAY

Everything is going in your favour if you're buying or selling property now. On the home front, you should concentrate on gardening, painting or plastering.

WHAT TO AVOID TODAY

Avoid legal complications today, don't sign contracts or file lawsuits, and, if possible, postpone an appearance in court. It's also an unlucky day to attend or arrange a funeral.

Don't make any hasty decisions or commitments today if you were born in the following years of the Ox: 1925, 1937, 1949, 1961, 1973.

FOURTH MONTH

The Plum month, when the abundant plum trees are harvested, is the most humid time of the year.

1ST DAY OF THE 4TH MONTH – TUESDAY, 14 MAY

THE HOURS OF FORTUNE

23–01	G	07–09	G	15–17	G
01–03	B	09–11	G	17–19	G
03–05	B	11–13	B	19–21	M
05–07	M	13–15	G	21–23	B

ADVICE FOR THE DAY

This is an appropriate time to resolve personal problems but before you say anything think the situation through carefully. This is also a suitable day for prayer, worship and quiet reflection. If you're getting married or finalizing marriage plans the gods of fortune are on your side and you can look forward to a stable future. Finally, if you're feeling energetic, turn your attention to spring-cleaning.

WHAT TO AVOID TODAY

There could be unexpected guests on the way so don't be tempted to break into supplies of food or drink that you've been saving for a special occasion. If you are spring-cleaning the house today beware of an accident in the bedroom. Finally, you should handle jewellery carefully.

Don't make any commitments or hasty decisions now if you were born in the following years of the Tiger: 1926, 1938, 1950, 1962, 1974.

2ND DAY OF THE 4TH MONTH –
WEDNESDAY, 15 MAY

THE HOURS OF FORTUNE

23–01	G	07–09	G	15–17	G
01–03	B	09–11	B	17–19	G
03–05	G	11–13	M	19–21	M
05–07	B	13–15	M	21–23	B

ADVICE FOR THE DAY

This is a good day for prayer, reflection or quiet meditation. There's a bright future in store for you if you're getting married today and you can expect to receive some unexpected but welcome presents. You can look forward to successful results if you're starting a new evening course or sitting an exam. The gods of fortune are on your side if you're on the move to a new house, setting off on your holidays, or emigrating. There's also a word of support for anyone considering DIY so why not begin work on the jobs around the house that you've been postponing? Finally, it's a positive time to put the worries of the past behind you and come to terms with decisions that have been made or events that are beyond your control.

WHAT TO AVOID TODAY

This is a bad time to start a creative project and it's a particularly dangerous time to handle plants or flowers. You should also beware of accidents if you're playing sports or setting off on a hunting trip.

This is an unlucky day for anyone born in the following years of the Rabbit: 1927, 1939, 1951, 1963, 1975.

3RD DAY OF THE 4TH MONTH –
THURSDAY, 16 MAY

THE HOURS OF FORTUNE

23–01	G	07–09	B	15–17	G
01–03	B	09–11	G	17–19	G
03–05	G	11–13	M	19–21	G
05–07	G	13–15	M	21–23	B

ADVICE FOR THE DAY

Once again it's a suitable day to sort out personal problems or to put some time aside for prayer or quiet reflection. The good fortune associated with marriage is carried over from yesterday, but there's also a word of encouragement for anyone beginning a romance or trying to sort out romantic problems. Don't hesitate to accept social invitations – you're likely to hear some good news from a friend. If you are at home today you should turn your attention to general cleaning and to mending clothes or home furnishings.

WHAT TO AVOID TODAY

Don't attempt electrical repair work and be especially careful if you're handling electrical goods in your kitchen. On a more personal note, you should try to resolve family feuds, particularly if someone in your family has recently died. You should also begin to make plans for your future.

This is a day of disappointments for anyone born in the following years of the Dragon: 1916, 1928, 1940, 1952, 1964, 1976.

4TH DAY OF THE 4TH MONTH –
FRIDAY, 17 MAY

THE HOURS OF FORTUNE

23–01	M		07–09	M		15–17	M
01–03	B		09–11	B		17–19	G
03–05	G		11–13	G		19–21	G
05–07	B		13–15	G		21–23	B

ADVICE FOR THE DAY

Since this is a broken day within the month it is an appropriate time to demolish old walls or dilapidated buildings and to clear away rubble.

WHAT TO AVOID TODAY

If you're planning to have your hair cut, cancel the appointment to avoid disappointment. On a more serious note, don't get married now unless you're prepared for arguments and unhappiness in the months ahead.

This is a day of delays and setbacks for anyone born in the following years of the Snake: 1929, 1941, 1953, 1965, 1977.

5TH DAY OF THE 4TH MONTH –
SATURDAY, 18 MAY

THE HOURS OF FORTUNE

23–01	M		07–09	G		15–17	G
01–03	B		09–11	G		17–19	G
03–05	B		11–13	B		19–21	M
05–07	G		13–15	M		21–23	B

147

ADVICE FOR THE DAY

Lucky stars are shining on you if you're getting married, going to parties or meeting friends, and you could be in for an unexpected surprise. Travel for business or pleasure is blessed by good fortune so you can set off on journeys with confidence. Gardeners can look forward to a satisfying day's work and it's a good day for DIY. If you have been through a period of loss this is an appropriate time to mourn or to arrange a funeral.

WHAT TO AVOID TODAY

Make sure that you've been given sufficient background information before you agree to the sale of a property.

This is an unlucky day for anyone born in the following years of the Horse: 1930, 1942, 1954, 1966, 1978.

6TH DAY OF THE 4TH MONTH – SUNDAY, 19 MAY

THE HOURS OF FORTUNE

23–01	G	07–09	M	15–17	G
01–03	B	09–11	G	17–19	G
03–05	G	11–13	M	19–21	M
05–07	G	13–15	B	21–23	B

ADVICE FOR THE DAY

Since this is a broken day within the year it's an opportune time to give your house a thorough clean. You should also try to find some time to concentrate on spiritual matters: by the end of the day you may find renewed peace of mind.

WHAT TO AVOID TODAY

Take sufficient legal advice before you sign a contract or take legal action, for there could be unexpected problems. Be prepared for delays or damage to your belongings if you're moving to a new house or travelling abroad. Sports enthusiasts who are using dangerous or heavy equipment should take extra safety precautions to avoid accident.

This is an unlucky day for anyone born in the following years of the Ram: 1931, 1943, 1955, 1967, 1979.

7TH DAY OF THE 4TH MONTH – MONDAY, 20 MAY

THE HOURS OF FORTUNE

23–01	B	07–09	G	15–17	B
01–03	B	09–11	M	17–19	M
03–05	G	11–13	G	19–21	B
05–07	G	13–15	M	21–23	B

ADVICE FOR THE DAY

This is an ideal day to begin a journey, to move house or to emigrate. The gods of fortune are on your side if you're getting married and if you have romantic problems this is also a lucky day to resolve them. Don't miss this opportunity to meet or make new friends. Anyone buying or selling goods can look forward to a profitable day and extra efforts made today by builders or DIY enthusiasts should prove rewarding. This is a positive time to reflect on personal matters or to begin a period of mourning. It's also an appropriate day to arrange or attend a funeral.

WHAT TO AVOID TODAY

Gardeners are advised to take a rest from their hobby at least until tomorrow to avoid accident. With the exception of marriages and funerals, try to avoid religious ceremony and you should, as far as possible, try to focus your attention on practical, not spiritual matters.

Don't take unnecessary risks now if you were born in the following years of the Monkey: 1920, 1932, 1944, 1956, 1968, 1980.

8TH DAY OF THE 4TH MONTH – TUESDAY, 21 MAY

THE HOURS OF FORTUNE

23–01	M	07–09	M	15–17	M
01–03	B	09–11	G	17–19	B
03–05	G	11–13	G	19–21	G
05–07	G	13–15	M	21–23	B

ADVICE FOR THE DAY

Once again there's an excellent forecast for anyone who is on the move, getting married or meeting friends. Financial matters are still well-starred, so, if you're thinking of opening a business, now is the time to do it. The time is right to buy land or property and to carry out structural repair work around the house.

WHAT TO AVOID TODAY

Be extra careful in the kitchen if you're handling hot liquids and don't be tempted to over-indulge in alcohol – you'll only regret your actions. You should also be careful if you're going swimming, sailing, or working with water.

Be prepared for a day of problems if you were born in the following years of the Cock: 1921, 1933, 1945, 1957, 1969.

9TH DAY OF THE 4TH MONTH – WEDNESDAY, 22 MAY

Shiao Mun, the period which marks the beginning of the growing season, begins officially at 9.52 this evening.

THE HOURS OF FORTUNE

23–01	M	07–09	M	15–17	B
01–03	B	09–11	G	17–19	G
03–05	G	11–13	M	19–21	B
05–07	G	13–15	M	21–23	B

ADVICE FOR THE DAY

This should prove to be a profitable day if you're buying or selling goods, so be prepared to take a risk. It's an appropriate time to turn your attention to gardening or general maintenance work in the house, and if you've been infested by insects or vermin now is the time to take the necessary measures to get rid of them. If you have spare time on your hands you should try to catch up on needlework that you've been postponing, but it's also a fine opportunity to put your creative talents to good use.

WHAT TO AVOID TODAY

Don't try to solve plumbing problems and be careful if you're working with or near water. If you've recently been through a period of unheaval, give yourself more time to recover before you return to the normal demands of daily life.

This is an unlucky day for anyone born in the following years of the Dog: 1922, 1934, 1946, 1958, 1970.

10TH DAY OF THE 4TH MONTH – THURSDAY, 23 MAY

THE HOURS OF FORTUNE

23–01	G	07–09	G	15–17	G
01–03	B	09–11	G	17–19	M
03–05	M	11–13	M	19–21	G
05–07	G	13–15	B	21–23	B

ADVICE FOR THE DAY

Lucky stars are shining on you if you're beginning a romance or meeting old friends so make the most of invitations that come your way. Career prospects are also excellent if you're starting a new job or beginning a new project.

WHAT TO AVOID TODAY

Check your facts carefully before you take legal action and don't commit yourself to a verbal agreement or written contract. There's likely to be serious delays in store if you're travelling, so try to make your journeys as simple and short as possible.

Don't tie yourself down to commitments today if you were born in the following years of the Pig: 1923, 1935, 1947, 1959, 1971.

11TH DAY OF THE 4TH MONTH –
FRIDAY, 24 MAY

THE HOURS OF FORTUNE

23–01	B	07–09	M	15–17	M
01–03	B	09–11	M	17–19	G
03–05	G	11–13	B	19–21	M
05–07	M	13–15	G	21–23	B

ADVICE FOR THE DAY

You could find your personal problems eased today for this is a positive day for prayer or quiet reflection. Social events and journeys at home and abroad are well-starred today. Anyone getting engaged or married now can look forward to good fortune in the years ahead, and the time is right to give or receive presents. If you're moving to a new house or emigrating you can be sure that you have made the right decision. This is also a good day to return to your normal routine or to begin a period of convalescence if you've been ill recently. If you've been considering spring-cleaning your house, attempting general repair work, or gardening, this is the day to do it. Finally, this is a suitable time to arrange or attend a funeral, but if you have been through a period of loss you should put the past behind you.

WHAT TO AVOID TODAY

Handle money wisely today and don't be tempted to over-spend or to lend it to others. If you are concentrating on DIY around the house, avoid repair work on ceilings or in the bathroom.

This is an unlucky day for anyone born in the following years of the Rat: 1924, 1936, 1948, 1960, 1972.

12TH DAY OF THE 4TH MONTH – SATURDAY, 25 MAY

THE HOURS OF FORTUNE

23–01	G	07–09	M	15–17	G
01–03	B	09–11	B	17–19	M
03–05	G	11–13	M	19–21	G
05–07	G	13–15	M	21–23	B

ADVICE FOR THE DAY

This is an excellent day for quiet reflection and prayer, and you could find that your requests are unexpectedly answered. Don't be afraid to ask others for advice for you could find help from unexpected sources. On a more practical note, it's an ideal day to give your house a thorough cleaning.

WHAT TO AVOID TODAY

Beware of an accident in the garden and avoid planting shrubs, trees, seeds or flowers.

This is a day of disappointments and setbacks for anyone born in the following years of the Ox: 1925, 1937, 1949, 1961, 1973.

13TH DAY OF THE 4TH MONTH – SUNDAY, 26 MAY

THE HOURS OF FORTUNE

23–01	G	07–09	B	15–17	G
01–03	B	09–11	G	17–19	G
03–05	B	11–13	M	19–21	G
05–07	M	13–15	G	21–23	B

ADVICE FOR THE DAY

Good luck is on your side if you're planning journeys, lending money, receiving gifts or buying clothes. You can look forward to a happy and prosperous future if you're announcing an engagement or getting married. Make an effort to renew contact with old friends and you could be in for a pleasant surprise or an unexpected romance. On a practical note, this is a positive day to stock up on supplies of food and drink, to turn your attention to maintenance work on paths or driveways and to spend time painting and decorating.

WHAT TO AVOID TODAY

The general reading for DIY is positive, but you should stay away from electrical and structural repair work in your kitchen. This is also an unlucky day to move or buy bedroom furniture. If you have recently been bereaved you are advised not to begin a period of mourning, try to focus your attention on practical and routine affairs.

This is an unlucky day for anyone born in the following years of the Tiger: 1926, 1938, 1950, 1962, 1974.

14TH DAY OF THE 4TH MONTH – MONDAY, 27 MAY

This is the birthday of Lu Tung Pin, one of the eight immortals of Taoist legend. He is said to have been a Taoist monk famed for his wisdom and healing powers, and is believed to help the sick and destitute. He is also revered by hairdressers and barbers because he can guarantee safety when one is using scissors or razors.

THE HOURS OF FORTUNE

23–01	M	07–09	M	15–17	M
01–03	B	09–11	M	17–19	G
03–05	M	11–13	G	19–21	M
05–07	B	13–15	G	21–23	B

ADVICE FOR THE DAY

For the second day running lucky stars are shining on you if you are travelling, getting married or setting up a business. There's also good luck in store if you're emigrating, beginning a new job, signing a contract or finalizing a business agreement. If you're owed money, the Almanac suggests that you retrieve your debts. Once again there's a positive reading for DIY and other practical domestic matters. If you have recently been bereaved you're advised to allow yourself time alone to mourn your loss. This is also an appropriate time to arrange or attend a funeral.

WHAT TO AVOID TODAY

Although this is a good day to dig or plough land you're advised against planting seeds, shrubs or trees. You should also avoid beauty treatments, particularly if you're intending to have a haircut, manicure or pedicure.

Be prepared for problems and arguments throughout the day if you were born in the following years of the Rabbit: 1927, 1939, 1951, 1963, 1975.

15TH DAY OF THE 4TH MONTH – TUESDAY, 28 MAY

THE HOURS OF FORTUNE

23–01	M	07–09	B	15–17	G
01–03	B	09–11	M	17–19	M
03–05	B	11–13	G	19–21	M
05–07	G	13–15	G	21–23	B

ADVICE FOR THE DAY

You should find peace of mind today through prayer or meditation. For the third consecutive day you're advised to meet friends and to make the most of business or romantic opportunities that come your way. The gods of fortune are still on your side if you're getting married, receiving presents or are on the move to a new house or country. The forecast is still positive for gardening and structural work around the house, and it's an opportune time to concentrate on work in your bedroom. If you've been feeling ill recently you should consult a doctor and if you've just started a course of health treatments, they should prove to be effective. If you've been in a period of mourning, try to put the past behind you and concentrate on the day to day demands of your life.

WHAT TO AVOID TODAY

Don't buy property or land now, you could be making an expensive mistake.

Don't take unnecessary risks today if you were born in the following years of the Dragon: 1928, 1940, 1952, 1964, 1976.

16TH DAY OF THE 4TH MONTH – WEDNESDAY, 29 MAY

THE HOURS OF FORTUNE

23–01	G	07–09	M	15–17	G
01–03	B	09–11	B	17–19	M
03–05	G	11–13	G	19–21	M
05–07	G	13–15	G	21–23	B

ADVICE FOR THE DAY

Since this is a broken day within the month it is a suitable time to clear away rubbish or to knock down walls or dilapidated buildings.

WHAT TO AVOID TODAY

If you've just been through a period of mourning or upheaval, don't take on too many demands. It may take longer than you thought to recover. You should also avoid getting married or finalizing wedding arrangements.

Be prepared for delays and setbacks throughout the day if you were born in the following years of the Snake: 1929, 1941, 1953, 1965, 1977.

17TH DAY OF THE 4TH MONTH – THURSDAY, 30 MAY

THE HOURS OF FORTUNE

23–01	B	07–09	M	15–17	G
01–03	B	09–11	M	17–19	G
03–05	M	11–13	B	19–21	B
05–07	M	13–15	G	21–23	B

ADVICE FOR THE DAY

This is an appropriate day for prayer or quiet reflection. It is also a lucky time to get married and if you make the most of social opportunities that come your way you could be in for an unexpected and welcome surprise. If you're planning to go shopping you'll be more than pleased with your purchases. Travel at home or abroad is well-starred and if you've been having difficulty finalizing travel arrangements, they should be resolved now. Finally, if you have time on your hands you should concentrate on DIY in the kitchen or bedroom and it's a safe time to repair electrical goods. Now is the time to buy or sell animals and if you're working with animals you can expect a satisfying day. Finally, this is an appropriate day to arrange or to attend a funeral.

WHAT TO AVOID TODAY

Beware of an accident if you're going fishing or sailing; you should, if possible, postpone your trip until tomorrow. This is not an appropriate time to ask others for help or advice on your future for you may hear some unwelcome and upsetting news.

This is an unlucky day for anyone born in the following years of the Horse: 1918, 1930, 1942, 1954, 1966, 1978.

18TH DAY OF THE 4TH MONTH –
FRIDAY, 31 MAY

THE HOURS OF FORTUNE

23–01	M	07–09	M	15–17	G
01–03	B	09–11	G	17–19	B
03–05	G	11–13	G	19–21	M
05–07	G	13–15	B	21–23	B

ADVICE FOR THE DAY

Since this is a broken day within the year it's a good time to give your house a thorough spring-cleaning. You should also put some time aside for quiet thought or to discuss personal matters.

WHAT TO AVOID TODAY

Don't pursue legal matters today and don't sign contracts. There are hazards in the kitchen so check electrical goods for safety, handle pans and crockery with care, and beware of an accident if you're making sauces or using alcohol.

Don't take unnecessary risks today if you were born in the following years of the Ram: 1931, 1943, 1955, 1967, 1979.

19TH DAY OF THE 4TH MONTH –
SATURDAY, 1 JUNE

THE HOURS OF FORTUNE

23–01	M	07–09	M	15–17	B
01–03	B	09–11	M	17–19	M
03–05	G	11–13	M	19–21	G
05–07	G	13–15	G	21–23	B

ADVICE FOR THE DAY

This is a suitable time to catch up on needlework that you've been postponing or to start work on a new creative product. On a more mundane note, you should lay down traps or insect repellent if you've been having problems with insects or vermin in or around the house.

WHAT TO AVOID TODAY

If you have plumbing problems, don't attempt to fix them yourself, call in an expert instead. This is not the right time to reflect on personal or spiritual concerns, so try to keep yourself busy with practical matters.

Think twice before you agree to important plans or make commitments if you were born in the following years of the Monkey: 1920, 1932, 1944, 1956, 1968, 1980.

20TH DAY OF THE 4TH MONTH – SUNDAY, 2 JUNE

THE HOURS OF FORTUNE

23–01	G	07–09	M	15–17	M
01–03	B	09–11	M	17–19	B
03–05	G	11–13	M	19–21	G
05–07	G	13–15	B	21–23	B

ADVICE FOR THE DAY

This is a promising time to start a new educational course, to open a business, or to invest money. This is also a good day to exercise your creative talents, particularly if you're making or designing clothes. Lucky stars are shining on anyone who is getting married, renewing contact with old friends, or beginning a romance. The rest of the day's advice focuses on general house maintenance and gardening.

WHAT TO AVOID TODAY

Stay well away from lawyers now and don't commit yourself to contracts or become involved in other legal matters. There's misfortune associated with water so you should be extra careful whether you're watering the garden or going swimming.

This is an unlucky day for anyone born in the following years of the Cock: 1921, 1933, 1945, 1957, 1969.

21ST DAY OF THE 4TH MONTH – MONDAY, 3 JUNE

THE HOURS OF FORTUNE

23–01	G	07–09	G	15–17	M
01–03	B	09–11	M	17–19	G
03–05	M	11–13	B	19–21	B
05–07	M	13–15	G	21–23	B

ADVICE FOR THE DAY

Try to put some time aside for prayer or quiet reflection and don't be afraid to ask for help – your requests could be granted. It's an ideal time to make a move to a new house or to emigrate and everything should work according to plan. Now is the time to turn your attention to plastering, painting and getting rid of insects or vermin that have infested your house or garden. This should be a fruitful day for putting creative talents to use and the forecast is excellent for anyone who is designing or making clothes.

Finally, it should prove to be a successful day for enthusiasts of competitive sports.

WHAT TO AVOID TODAY

If you're wearing jewellery make sure that it is securely fastened and if you're thinking of buying expensive jewellery, get a second opinion before you buy. If you're thinking of consulting an acupuncturist, wait until tomorrow when the forecast for healing is more favourable. If you've been saving food or drink for a special occasion, don't be tempted to break into it now.

This is a day of delays and disappointments for anyone born in the following years of the Dog: 1922, 1934, 1946, 1958, 1970.

22ND DAY OF THE 4TH MONTH – TUESDAY, 4 JUNE

THE HOURS OF FORTUNE

23–01	G	07–09	M	15–17	G
01–03	B	09–11	B	17–19	G
03–05	M	11–13	M	19–21	G
05–07	M	13–15	M	21–23	B

ADVICE FOR THE DAY

You should try to give yourself some time alone during the next two days to sort out personal problems – they may not seem as serious as you imagined. This is also a good day for physical recovery and you can expect medical treatments to be successful.

WHAT TO AVOID TODAY

Your journeys are likely to be plagued by delays so try to avoid travel by bus, train or plane unless absolutely necessary. Farmers and gardeners are advised to take extra care now if they are planting crops, flowers, shrubs or trees.

Don't make hasty remarks or decisions now if you were born in the following years of the Pig: 1923, 1935, 1947, 1959, 1971.

23RD DAY OF THE 4TH MONTH – WEDNESDAY, 5 JUNE

THE HOURS OF FORTUNE

23–01	B	07–09	B	15–17	G
01–03	B	09–11	G	17–19	G
03–05	M	11–13	G	19–21	G
05–07	M	13–15	M	21–23	B

ADVICE FOR THE DAY

If you have worries on your mind, try to put time aside for prayer or reflection. There's a positive forecast for anyone beginning a new educational course, opening a business, signing a contract, and buying or selling goods. Lucky stars are shining on anyone moving to a new house or emigrating. Your social life is also well-starred so make the most of the opportunities that come your way, and anyone announcing an engagement can look forward to a happy and secure future. If you are expecting to receive a present today you could be in for a pleasant surprise. Finally it's an appropriate day for house maintenance or gardening.

WHAT TO AVOID TODAY

Although it's a positive day for DIY, avoid electrical repair work in the kitchen. This is also an unfortunate time to begin a period of mourning.

This is a day of setbacks and disappointments for anyone born in the following years of the Rat: 1924, 1936, 1948, 1960, 1972.

24TH DAY OF THE 4TH MONTH – THURSDAY, 6 JUNE

The period known as Mang Chung begins at 1.14 this afternoon. This is a traditional reminder to farmers that it is now time to clear weeds from the ground or pests off the crops.

THE HOURS OF FORTUNE

23–01	M	07–09	M	15–17	M
01–0	B	09–11	G	17–19	G
03–05	M	11–13	G	19–21	M
05–07	B	13–15	G	21–23	G

ADVICE FOR THE DAY

This is a good day to be creative, particularly if you're sewing, weaving or designing fabric. Don't allow social opportunities to slip by for you could miss the chance to renew contacts with old friends or begin a romance.

WHAT TO AVOID TODAY

It's an unlucky day for gardeners or farmers who are advised to avoid digging or ploughing. Postpone hairdressing appointments to avoid disappointment and, on a more sombre note, don't arrange or attend a funeral now.

You should be prepared for trouble where you least expect it if you were born in the following years of the Ox: 1925, 1937, 1949, 1961, 1973.

25TH DAY OF THE 4TH MONTH – FRIDAY, 7 JUNE

THE HOURS OF FORTUNE

23–01	B	07–09	G	15–17	G
01–03	G	09–11	G	17–19	M
03–05	B	11–13	M	19–21	M
05–07	M	13–15	G	21–23	M

ADVICE FOR THE DAY

You should take this opportunity to sort out travel plans and you can set off on journeys with confidence whether you're going on holiday, moving to a new house or a new country. This is an appropriate time to collect outstanding debts, and if you're opening a business you can look forward to a secure financial future. If you're spending time at home, turn your attention to gardening, needlework or DIY.

WHAT TO AVOID TODAY

Be careful if you're cleaning or working in your bedroom. You're also advised to seek further professional advice before you buy property.

This is an unlucky day for anyone born in the following years of the Tiger: 1926, 1938, 1950, 1962, 1974.

166

26TH DAY OF THE 4TH MONTH – SATURDAY, 8 JUNE

THE HOURS OF FORTUNE

23–01	B	07–09	G	15–17	G
01–03	B	09–11	G	17–19	M
03–05	M	11–13	G	19–21	M
05–07	G	13–15	G	21–23	B

ADVICE FOR THE DAY

Most of today's advice focuses on work around the house. Now is the time to give your house a thorough spring-cleaning, to decorate or to repair footpaths or walls in the garden. It's also an appropriate day to pay attention to your personal appearance and the forecast for getting your hair cut is excellent.

WHAT TO AVOID TODAY

Be sure to follow safety instructions if you're using electrical goods in the kitchen and beware of an accident if you're working near a cooker.

Be prepared for a day of disagreements if you were born in the following years of the Rabbit: 1927, 1939, 1951, 1963, 1975.

27TH DAY OF THE 4TH MONTH –
SUNDAY, 9 JUNE

THE HOURS OF FORTUNE

23–01	B	07–09	B	15–17	G
01–03	B	09–11	M	17–19	M
03–05	M	11–13	G	19–21	B
05–07	M	13–15	G	21–23	M

ADVICE FOR THE DAY

Make an effort to put some time aside to reflect on your problems or simply to find some peace and quiet. If you're thinking of furthering your education now is the time to sign up a full- or part-time course. This is a perfect day for social occasions so you can look forward to an enjoyable day whether you're meeting friends, beginning a romance, or getting married. The forecast is promising for anyone buying and selling goods and if you're opening a new business the financial prospects are excellent. If you're thinking of buying new clothes you should find exactly what you want, and if you're planning to make your own you'll be pleased with your handiwork. This is a day free of delays if you're travelling so you can set off on journeys with confidence.

WHAT TO AVOID TODAY

If you're a gardener or an angler take a rest from your hobby to avoid accident. There's likely to be hidden drawbacks if you're buying property so don't finalize the sale on a house or apartment. You should also avoid visiting an acupuncturist now: the treatment will be far more successful if you wait until tomorrow.

Don't take unnecessary risks today if you were born in the

following years of the Dragon: 1916, 1928, 1940, 1952, 1964, 1976.

28TH DAY OF THE 4TH MONTH – MONDAY, 10 JUNE

THE HOURS OF FORTUNE

23–01	B	07–09	M	15–17	M
01–03	B	09–11	B	17–19	B
03–05	G	11–13	G	19–21	G
05–07	G	13–15	G	21–23	M

ADVICE FOR THE DAY

Once again it's an opportune time to meet and make new friends or to begin a romance, so don't turn down social opportunities. The good fortune associated with travel also continues throughout the day. The future looks secure for anyone who is moving house today and the move itself should pass without a hitch. The rest of today's forecast focuses on domestic matters so if you're thinking of carrying out structural alterations, cleaning your house or gardening you will have a satisfying day.

WHAT TO AVOID TODAY

The gods of fortune are against you if you're getting married or making marriage plans. If you're celebrating now you should be careful not to over-indulge in alcohol, you'll only regret your actions.

This is an unlucky day for anyone born in the following years of the Snake: 1929, 1941, 1953, 1965, 1977.

29TH DAY OF THE 4TH MONTH –
TUESDAY, 11 JUNE

THE HOURS OF FORTUNE

23–01	B	07–09	G	15–17	B
01–03	B	09–11	G	17–19	M
03–05	G	11–13	B	19–21	M
05–07	G	13–15	G	21–23	M

ADVICE FOR THE DAY

Since this is a broken day within the month you shouldn't make commitments or plans. The day is best suited to minor demolition work around the house or garden and to clearing away rubble.

WHAT TO AVOID TODAY

There's misfortune associated with water so whether you're thinking of going swimming, watering your garden, or mending plumbing problems, wait until tomorrow.

Don't take any risks or make long-term commitments if you were born in the following years of the Horse: 1918, 1930, 1942, 1954, 1966, 1978.

FIFTH MONTH

There is fierce competition amongst the teams at the Dragon Boat festival as the competitors re-enact the race to save Ch'u Yuen, the legendary hero who sacrificed himself by drowning for the good of his country.

1ST DAY OF THE 5TH MONTH –
WEDNESDAY, 12 JUNE

THE HOURS OF FORTUNE

23–01	B	07–09	G	15–17	G
01–03	B	09–11	G	17–19	G
03–05	M	11–13	M	19–21	G
05–07	M	13–15	B	21–23	M

ADVICE FOR THE DAY

You should try to channel your energies into work around
the home. Concentrate on cleaning your bedroom and if
you've been intending to give the house a fresh coat of
paint, now is the time to do it.

WHAT TO AVOID TODAY

There's misfortune associated with legal matters today so
don't file a lawsuit or agree to a written or verbal contract.

This is a day of disappointment for anyone born in the
following years of the Ram: 1919, 1931, 1943, 1955,
1967.

2ND DAY OF THE 5TH MONTH –
THURSDAY, 13 JUNE

THE HOURS OF FORTUNE

23–01	B	07–09	G	15–17	B
01–03	B	09–11	M	17–19	G
03–05	G	11–13	B	19–21	G
05–07	M	13–15	G	21–23	M

ADVICE FOR THE DAY

This is a good day to put your plans into action or to take risks. There's good prospects in store for you if you're beginning a new educational course or waiting for results. This is an appropriate time to retrieve debts, finalize a business deal or open a new business. It's an ideal day to announce an engagement or to hold a party, and if you're on the receiving end of a party invitation you can look forward to an unexpected romantic surprise. If you've been thinking of treating yourself to some new clothes you can look forward to a successful day's shopping. There's also an optimistic forecast for anyone having medical treatment today. It's a positive day to attend a funeral so don't be afraid to turn to friends or relatives for support. Finally, if you're working at home it's a well-starred day for gardening and renovation.

WHAT TO AVOID TODAY

Don't be tempted to overspend or over-indulge now because there'll soon be unforeseen demands on your resources. You're specially advised not to buy jewellery or to lend money. On a more spiritual note, postpone religious ceremonies until another day.

Be prepared for personal problems throughout the day if you were born in the following years of the Monkey: 1920, 1932, 1944, 1956, 1968, 1980.

3RD DAY OF THE 5TH MONTH – FRIDAY, 14 JUNE

THE HOURS OF FORTUNE

23–01	B	07–09	M	15–17	G
01–03	B	09–11	B	17–19	B
03–05	G	11–13	M	19–21	G
05–07	G	13–15	G	21–23	G

ADVICE FOR THE DAY

The gods are on your side if you're attending a religious ceremony or asking for a favour. There's good news for sports enthusiasts, particularly if you're going hunting. If you're tied to the house today, focus your attention on getting rid of mice, rats, slugs or any other creatures that have infested your house or garden.

WHAT TO AVOID TODAY

If you want to avoid an accident, leave your gardening tools where they are and have a rest instead.

This is an unlucky day for anyone born in the following years of the Cock: 1921, 1933, 1945, 1957, 1969.

4TH DAY OF THE 5TH MONTH – SATURDAY, 15 JUNE

THE HOURS OF FORTUNE

23–01	B	07–09	B	15–17	G
01–03	B	09–11	G	17–19	G
03–05	M	11–13	M	19–21	B
05–07	M	13–15	M	21–23	G

ADVICE FOR THE DAY

This is still a good day for worship and your prayers may be unexpectedly answered. There's good news for anyone starting a new college or evening course and if you're waiting for exam results you're likely to hear good news. Take this opportunity to finalize travel plans or to set off on a special journey. Lucky stars are also shining on you if you're marrying or finalizing wedding arrangements. The forecast is promising for entrepreneurs so if you're opening a business or concluding a business deal there's a profitable year ahead. The rest of today's advice focuses on gardening and general maintenance around the house.

WHAT TO AVOID TODAY

Although the forecast for house maintenance is good be extra careful if you're working in the kitchen, particularly if you're thinking of repairing electrical appliances. There's also the threat of an accident if you're cutting wood or setting out on a hunting trip.

Don't make important decisions or commitments now if you were born in the following years of the Dog: 1922, 1934, 1946, 1958, 1970.

5TH DAY OF THE 5TH MONTH – SUNDAY, 16 JUNE

The Chinese celebrate the Dragon Boat festival today as a way of dispelling the disease and evil that is in the air. The festival is based on the legend of Ch'u Yuen, an honest official who lived during the reign of a corrupt emperor. His constant complaints against the emperor were overruled, so, in a desperate attempt to draw attention to the plight of the people, he threw himself into a lake. Local fishermen tried to save him but he was dead by the time they reached him. As they pulled his body out of the water they threw dumplings of rice into the river to ward off the dragons and evil spirits which were fighting to snatch Ch'u Yuen's body out of the river.

THE HOURS OF FORTUNE

23–01	B	07–09	M	15–17	M
01–03	B	09–11	G	17–19	G
03–05	M	11–13	G	19–21	G
05–07	B	13–15	G	21–23	B

ADVICE FOR THE DAY

For the second day running there's an excellent forecast for anyone on the move or channelling their energy into DIY around the house. If you have money to spare, treat yourself to some new clothes – you're sure to make a wise choice.

WHAT TO AVOID TODAY

If you're moving house or emigrating to a new country you can look forward to a day free of delays and setbacks. You should also postpone an appointment with the hairdresser until tomorrow.

Be prepared for problems at home and at work if you were born in the following years of the Pig: 1923, 1935, 1947, 1959, 1971.

6TH DAY OF THE 5TH MONTH –
MONDAY, 17 JUNE

THE HOURS OF FORTUNE

23–01	B	07–09	M	15–17	G
01–03	B	09–11	G	17–19	G
03–05	B	11–13	M	19–21	M
05–07	G	13–15	G	21–23	M

ADVICE FOR THE DAY

Don't make any important decisions or journeys now and make every attempt to keep out of trouble. You should, however, put some time aside to reflect on problems or simply to calm yourself down.

WHAT TO AVOID TODAY

Don't make hasty decisions now if you're thinking of buying property and check that you've been given sufficient background details before agreeing to the sale of a house.

This is an unlucky day for anyone born in the following years of the Rat: 1924, 1936, 1948, 1960, 1972.

7TH DAY OF THE 5TH MONTH –
TUESDAY, 18 JUNE

THE HOURS OF FORTUNE

23–01	B	07–09	M	15–17	G
01–03	B	09–11	G	17–19	M
03–05	G	11–13	G	19–21	M
05–07	G	13–15	G	21–23	B

ADVICE FOR THE DAY

This is still a positive day for prayer, worship and quiet reflection. But this is also an ideal day to make the most of social opportunities. Renew contacts with friends and an unexpected meeting could have a romantic outcome. Journeys by land, sea or air are blessed by good fortune and you can expect a smooth transition if you're moving house or emigrating. Don't worry about the future if you're signing contracts or finalizing a business deal. Now is the time to start maintenance or renovation work around the house and to spend some time clearing away weeds or planting seeds in the garden.

WHAT TO AVOID TODAY

Don't buy, make or mend clothes today. It's also an unlucky day to attend or arrange a funeral; try to keep your spirits up if you have lost a friend or relative – don't cut yourself off from the outside world.

This is a day of disappointments for anyone born in the following years of the Ox: 1925, 1937, 1949, 1961, 1973.

8TH DAY OF THE 5TH MONTH – WEDNESDAY, 19 JUNE

THE HOURS OF FORTUNE

23–01	B	07–09	G	15–17	G
01–03	B	09–11	G	17–19	M
03–05	B	11–13	G	19–21	B
05–07	M	13–15	G	21–23	M

ADVICE FOR THE DAY

This is still a promising day for quiet reflection so try to put some time aside for yourself. Lucky stars are still shining on you if you're on the move in your own country or abroad, but if you're spending the day at home it's still a good day to busy yourself with general DIY. On a more sombre note, it's an auspicious day to arrange or attend a funeral.

WHAT TO AVOID TODAY

There's misfortune associated with the bedroom today so spend as little time there as possible. There's also the possibility of an accident if you're thinking of going sailing today, so take extra care.

This is a day of misfortune for anyone born in the following years of the Tiger: 1926, 1938, 1950, 1962, 1974.

9TH DAY OF THE 5TH MONTH –
THURSDAY, 20 JUNE

THE HOURS OF FORTUNE

23–01	B	07–09	G	15–17	M
01–03	B	09–11	G	17–19	B
03–05	G	11–13	G	19–21	M
05–07	B	13–15	M	21–23	M

ADVICE FOR THE DAY

If you've been thinking of having your hair cut, do so today and you'll be more than satisfied with the results. The Almanac also offers a word of encouragement to anyone planning to spring-clean, re-decorate the home, or tidy up the garden.

WHAT TO AVOID TODAY

Watch out for accidents in the kitchen, particularly if you're making soups or organizing your own home-brew.

Don't make any hasty decisions or commitments if you were born in the following years of the Rabbit: 1927, 1939, 1951, 1963, 1965.

10TH DAY OF THE 5TH MONTH – FRIDAY, 21 JUNE

THE HOURS OF FORTUNE

23–01	B	07–09	B	15–17	B
01–03	B	09–11	G	17–19	M
03–05	G	11–13	M	19–21	G
05–07	G	13–15	G	21–23	G

ADVICE FOR THE DAY

You should channel your energies into spring-cleaning, but you should also try to put some time aside for prayer, worship or quiet reflection.

WHAT TO AVOID TODAY

Leave your gardening tools where they are for the time being and have a rest instead. You should also avoid clearing out drains or opening gutters.

This is an unlucky day for anyone born in the following years of the Dragon: 1916, 1928, 1940, 1952, 1964, 1976.

11TH DAY OF THE 5TH MONTH – SATURDAY, 22 JUNE

THE HOURS OF FORTUNE

23–01	B	07–09	G	15–17	M
01–03	B	09–11	B	17–19	M
03–05	G	11–13	G	19–21	G
05–07	G	13–15	B	21–23	G

ADVICE FOR THE DAY

Once again, this is a positive day for prayer and worship. Now is the time to begin the mending or darning that you've been delaying. It's also a day to pamper yourself and if you have the time you should treat yourself to a long, relaxing bath. Finally, on a more practical note, this is an appropriate time to lay down traps or insect repellent if you've been troubled by slugs, mice, ants or other vermin.

WHAT TO AVOID TODAY

Don't agree to legal contracts or file lawsuits today and you should, if possible, postpone court appearances.

Don't expect your plans to work out as you expected if you were born in the following years of the Snake: 1929, 1941, 1953, 1965, 1977.

12TH DAY OF THE 5TH MONTH – SUNDAY, 23 JUNE

Hsia Chi, the day that signals the arrival of summer, begins officially at 5.58 this morning.

THE HOURS OF FORTUNE

23–01	B	07–09	G	15–17	G
01–03	B	09–11	M	17–19	M
03–05	G	11–13	B	19–21	M
05–07	M	13–15	G	21–23	M

ADVICE FOR THE DAY

Since this is a broken day within the month, it is an appropriate time to demolish garden walls or sheds, and you should try to clear out cupboards or clear away rubble. If you've been feeling ill this is a promising time to receive treatment or start a period of convalescence.

WHAT TO AVOID TODAY

Be careful if you're wearing jewellery now and don't be tempted to overspend if you're buying jewellery. You should also avoid breaking into food supplies if you've been stocking up for a special occasion. Finally, don't lend money, even to friends; it may not be returned as quickly as promised.

This is a day of misfortune for anyone born in the following years of the Horse: 1930, 1942, 1954, 1966, 1978.

13TH DAY OF THE 5TH MONTH – MONDAY, 24 JUNE

THE HOURS OF FORTUNE

23–01	B	07–09	M	15–17	G
01–03	B	09–11	B	17–19	M
03–05	G	11–13	M	19–21	M
05–07	G	13–15	B	21–23	M

ADVICE FOR THE DAY

Put some time aside for quiet reflection and if you're upset over the death of a friend or relative you should accept help and support from outsiders. On a more practical note, if you have both energy and time on your hands it's a good time to repair faulty water pipes or clear out gutters.

WHAT TO AVOID TODAY

If you're a keen gardener you should concentrate on digging today but don't plant anything. You're also warned against cutting and arranging flowers.

This is an unlucky day for anyone born in the following years of the Ram: 1919, 1931, 1943, 1955, 1967, 1979.

14TH DAY OF THE 5TH MONTH – TUESDAY, 25 JUNE

THE HOURS OF FORTUNE

23–01	B	07–09	B	15–17	B
01–03	B	09–11	M	17–19	G
03–05	M	11–13	G	19–21	M
05–07	G	13–15	M	21–23	M

ADVICE FOR THE DAY

There's success in store if you're waiting for exam results or beginning a new college or evening course. Make every effort to accept social invitations since this is an ideal time to make friends or begin a romance. Travel is blessed by good fortune so don't worry if you're setting out on a journey now. Take a risk if you're thinking of investing money and if you're opening a new business you can look forward to a profitable year. This is also a fruitful day to buy, sell or work with animals. If you have time on your hands it would be well-spent on gardening or general DIY. Finally, this is an appropriate day to arrange or to attend a funeral.

WHAT TO AVOID TODAY

Although the forecast for DIY is good you're advised not to attempt renovation work in your kitchen and avoid repairing electrical kitchen appliances. You should try to keep yourself busy today so as not to spend time mulling over problems and, with the exception of funerals, you should postpone religious ceremonies until tomorrow.

This is a day of delays and disappointments for anyone born in the following years of the Monkey: 1920, 1932, 1944, 1956, 1968, 1980.

15TH DAY OF THE 5TH MONTH – WEDNESDAY, 26 JUNE

THE HOURS OF FORTUNE

23–01	B	07–09	M	15–17	M
01–03	B	09–11	M	17–19	B
03–05	G	11–13	G	19–21	M
05–07	B	13–15	G	21–23	G

ADVICE FOR THE DAY

Today is given over completely to spiritual matters. It's a perfect day for prayer or worship but it's also a suitable time to think problems through and to sort out personal matters.

WHAT TO AVOID TODAY

You're likely to be disappointed if you're getting your hair cut today so postpone an appointment until another day. There is also misfortune associated with water today and you're particularly warned not to repair drains or water pipes.

This is an unlucky day for anyone born in the following years of the Cock: 1921, 1933, 1945, 1957, 1969.

16TH DAY OF THE 5TH MONTH – THURSDAY, 27 JUNE

THE HOURS OF FORTUNE

23–01	B	07–09	M	15–17	G
01–03	B	09–11	G	17–19	G
03–05	B	11–13	M	19–21	B
05–07	G	13–15	G	21–23	M

ADVICE FOR THE DAY

There's an excellent forecast for travel, and you can journey at home or abroad with confidence. You can look forward to success in the months ahead if you're opening a business, starting a new job or beginning a new educational course. Don't be afraid if you're receiving medical treatment today, it should prove to be effective. There's good news for sports enthusiasts, particularly for sailors who can look forward to a safe and enjoyable day. The forecast is also good for creative and manual work, and carpentry, needlework, gardening and flower arranging are particularly highlighted. But this is also a day to think of others and your help will be gratefully received.

The forecast ends with good news for anyone thinking of getting a haircut.

WHAT TO AVOID TODAY

There's misfortune associated with funerals at the moment so try to avoid attending or arranging one. On a more practical note, don't agree to the sale of property or sign a final contract, even if you think you've found the house of your dreams.

Don't expect your plans to work out as you expected today if you were born in the following years of the Dog: 1922, 1934, 1946, 1958, 1970.

17TH DAY OF THE 5TH MONTH – FRIDAY, 28 JUNE

THE HOURS OF FORTUNE

23–01	B	07–09	M	15–17	G
01–03	B	09–11	M	17–19	M
03–05	G	11–13	G	19–21	M
05–07	M	13–15	G	21–23	B

ADVICE FOR THE DAY

This is a well-starred day for prayer, worship and quiet reflection. It's also a day to put your working clothes on and concentrate on home maintenance. So if the wallpaper needs sticking down, doors need securing, plugs need replacing or furniture mending, this is the day to do it.

WHAT TO AVOID TODAY

If you've suffered a period of loss this is an unlucky day to put the past behind you; give yourself a little more time to think things through.

Be prepared for delays and disappointments throughout the day if you were born in the following years of the Pig: 1923, 1935, 1947, 1959, 1971.

18TH DAY OF THE 5TH MONTH – SATURDAY, 29 JUNE

THE HOURS OF FORTUNE

23–01	B	07–09	M	15–17	G
01–03	B	09–11	M	17–19	G
03–05	G	11–13	G	19–21	B
05–07	M	13–15	G	21–23	M

ADVICE FOR THE DAY

Today's good fortune is channelled towards the house. Now is the time to start work on the maintenance problems that you may have been postponing for lack of time or enthusiasm. The forecast is particularly promising if you're plastering, painting or decorating.

WHAT TO AVOID TODAY

Be extra careful if you're darning or mending clothes. If you're an enthusiastic gardener you should also leave your garden tools where they are for now and have a rest instead.

This is an ill-fated day for anyone born in the following years of the Rat: 1924, 1936, 1948, 1960, 1972.

19TH DAY OF THE 5TH MONTH –
SUNDAY, 30 JUNE

THE HOURS OF FORTUNE

23–01	B	07–09	M	15–17	M
01–03	B	09–11	G	17–19	B
03–05	G	11–13	G	19–21	M
05–07	G	13–15	G	21–23	M

ADVICE FOR THE DAY

It's an ideal day to put some time aside for quiet reflection and if you have personal problems that need to be resolved, this is the day to sort them out. Bu this is also a day of activity and you can begin a new job or set off on a journey with confidence. Try to iron out problems with relationships and make the most of social opportunities because this is a well-starred day to meet friends or begin a romance. If you're celebrating today and hoping to receive presents you're in for a surprise.

Turn your attention to work at home because the forecast for gardening, cleaning and renovating the house is excellent. It should prove to be a fruitful day if you're working with animals and there's good news for farmers who plan to buy or sell livestock. Finally, it's an appropriate day to attend a funeral and if you are in mourning don't be afraid to turn to friends for support.

WHAT TO AVOID TODAY

Don't expect too much of yourself if you've been through a period of upheaval recently; give yourself longer to recover before you return to your normal routine.

This is an unlucky day for anyone born in the following years of the Ox: 1925, 1937, 1949, 1961, 1973.

20TH DAY OF THE 5TH MONTH – MONDAY, 1 JULY

THE HOURS OF FORTUNE

23–01	B	07–09	G	15–17	B
01–03	B	09–11	G	17–19	G
03–05	B	11–13	M	19–21	M
05–07	G	13–15	G	21–23	M

ADVICE FOR THE DAY

This is an excellent day for anyone on the move, whether you're setting off on a holiday or moving to a new house. Be prepared to take a business risk today because the gods of prosperity are on your side. If you have spare time on your hands it would be a good idea to concentrate on gardening or general repair and re-decoration work around your home. The advice for today ends with a word of encouragement for anyone arranging or attending a funeral.

WHAT TO AVOID TODAY

Beware of accidents if you're working in your bedroom today and avoid unblocking sinks or drains – call in an expert instead.

Be prepared for a day of disappointments if you were born in the following years of the Tiger: 1926, 1938, 1950, 1962, 1974.

21ST DAY OF THE 5TH MONTH –
TUESDAY, 2 JULY

THE HOURS OF FORTUNE

23–01	B		07–09	G		15–17	G
01–03	B		09–11	G		17–19	M
03–05	G		11–13	M		19–21	M
05–07	B		13–15	B		21–23	M

ADVICE FOR THE DAY

Today's advice focuses on your domestic life. There's an excellent forecast for enthusiastic painters and decorators and it's a positive time to repair or tidy up footpaths or roads. On a more general note, this is an appropriate time to finish roadworks and to open new roads so there could be good news in store for motorists. You should also put some time aside for yourself today and treat yourself to a haircut, a relaxing bath or a sauna.

WHAT TO AVOID TODAY

If you've recently received bad news try not to let it affect your day-to-day routine too much and don't cut yourself off from friends or family. There's also a word of warning for anyone thinking of initiating legal action or signing a contract; give yourself another day to think the matter through.

Don't take unnecessary risks or make any commitments today if you were born in the following years of the Rabbit: 1927, 1939, 1951, 1963, 1975.

22ND DAY OF THE 5TH MONTH –
WEDNESDAY, 3 JULY

THE HOURS OF FORTUNE

23–01	B	07–09	B	15–17	M
01–03	B	09–11	G	17–19	M
03–05	G	11–13	B	19–21	M
05–07	G	13–15	G	21–23	M

ADVICE FOR THE DAY

This is a well-starred day for friendship and romance so
don't refuse opportunities to meet new people or renew
contact with old friends. You can also look forward to
stability and happiness in the years ahead if you're
marrying today. There's good news in store if you're on
the move, whether it's to a new business, a new house or a
new country. Finally, there's a good forecast for gardening
or DIY, particularly for electrical repair work in your
kitchen.

WHAT TO AVOID TODAY

Don't be tempted to break into food supplies that you
have been saving for a special occasion, and make sure that
you have some extra food in case unexpected friends drop
by. Be careful if you're handling money or jewellery today
and think twice before you lend money even to friends.

This is an ill-fated day for anyone born in the following
years of the Dragon: 1916, 1928, 1940, 1952, 1964,
1976.

23RD DAY OF THE 5TH MONTH – THURSDAY, 4 JULY

THE HOURS OF FORTUNE

23–01	B	07–09	M	15–17	M
01–03	B	09–11	B	17–19	M
03–05	G	11–13	M	19–21	M
05–07	G	13–15	G	21–23	M

ADVICE FOR THE DAY

This is a good time to sort out personal problems so put some time aside to think through any worries on your mind. There's the prospect of good results in the future if you're beginning a new educational course or a new job. Make the most of social opportunities that come your way now since this is an excellent time to meet or make new friends, to begin a romance, or to solve romantic problems. You should be more than satisfied with the results of a shopping spree, a haircut or time spent on needlework. Finally, you should lay down traps or repellent now if you've been troubled by insects or vermin such as mice, cockroaches or mosquitoes.

WHAT TO AVOID TODAY

If you want to avoid accidents have a rest from gardening today. You should also postpone wedding arrangements until later in the week and if you are marrying now be prepared for arguments and disappointments in the years ahead.

This is an unlucky day if you were born in the following years of the Snake: 1917, 1929, 1941, 1953, 1965, 1977.

24TH DAY OF THE 5TH MONTH – FRIDAY, 5 JULY

THE HOURS OF FORTUNE

23–01	B	07–09	B	15–17	M
01–03	B	09–11	G	17–19	G
03–05	M	11–13	B	19–21	G
05–07	M	13–15	M	21–23	G

ADVICE FOR THE DAY

This is a broken day within the month so you should turn your attention to personal matters: it's a particularly good day for prayer or quiet reflection. If you feel that you have surplus energy today you should direct it to clearing away rubbish or to minor demolition work around the house or garden.

WHAT TO AVOID TODAY

There's a strong possibility of an accident in the kitchen so be extra cautious if you're cooking or cleaning there.

Be prepared for delays and disappointments throughout the day if you were born in the following years of the Horse: 1918, 1930, 1942, 1954, 1966, 1978.

25TH DAY OF THE 5TH MONTH – SATURDAY, 6 JULY

THE HOURS OF FORTUNE

23–01	B	07–09	M	15–17	M
01–03	B	09–11	G	17–19	G
03–05	M	11–13	G	19–21	M
05–07	B	13–15	B	21–23	G

ADVICE FOR THE DAY

This is a suitable day to sort out personal problems and to put some time aside for worship or quiet reflection. There's a promising forecast for renovation or repair work around the house, particularly in the bedroom, and it should be a satisfying day for gardeners.

WHAT TO AVOID TODAY

If you were thinking of having your hair cut now, postpone your appointment until another day. You're also advised not to end a period of mourning and if you've recently been upset don't expect too much of yourself; give yourself more time to recover.

This is an unlucky day for anyone born in the following years of the Ram: 1919, 1931, 1943, 1955, 1967, 1979.

26TH DAY OF THE 5TH MONTH – SUNDAY, 7 JULY

THE HOURS OF FORTUNE

23–01	B	07–09	G	15–17	B
01–03	B	09–11	G	17–19	M
03–05	B	11–13	G	19–21	M
05–07	G	13–15	G	21–23	M

ADVICE FOR THE DAY

This is an encouraging day to start new projects and to make decisions. You can look forward to a successful year if you're beginning a new job or opening a new business. If you're waiting for exam results you should receive good news and there's an optimistic forecast for anyone beginning an evening or full-time college course. Make the most of this opportunity to finalize travel plans or to make a special journey. You should also make every effort to meet friends or accept social invitations for you could be in for a pleasant surprise. This is also an ideal day to get married and to give or receive presents.

There's the prospect of a fruitful day on the home front so you should channel your spare energy into anything from brewing your own beer and wine to repairing garden fences. If you've been ill recently this is a good day to ease yourself back into work, but don't push yourself too far. If a close relative or friend has recently died this is a good day to arrange or to attend a funeral.

WHAT TO AVOID TODAY

There's misfortune associated with buying or selling property so give yourself at least another day before you make a binding agreement. If you've had worries on your mind, this is not a good time to resolve them. Wait until tomorrow; you should be able to see the solutions to your problems more clearly. With the exception of marriage and funerals, this is also an unlucky day for prayer or religious ceremony and you should wait until tomorrow to attend to spiritual matters.

Don't make any hasty decisions or commitments if you were born in the following years of the Monkey: 1920, 1932, 1944, 1956, 1968, 1980.

27TH DAY OF THE 5TH MONTH – MONDAY, 8 JULY

THE HOURS OF FORTUNE

23–01	G	07–09	M	15–17	M
01–03	B	09–11	M	17–19	B
03–05	G	11–13	G	19–21	M
05–07	G	13–15	G	21–23	B

ADVICE FOR THE DAY

There's still good fortune in store for anyone who is getting married, receiving presents, meeting friends, beginning a romance, or travelling. But it's not only journeys that are blessed by good luck – this is also an excellent day to move to a new house or to emigrate. The forecast is promising for finance and anyone who is finalizing a business deal or opening a new business can look forward to a prosperous future. Once again, this is a good day for recovery if you've been ill recently but if you're worried about your health and haven't consulted a doctor yet, do so today, the news may not be as bad as you expected. This is also a suitable time to stock up on food supplies. Today's forecast ends with a word of support for anyone considering DIY or gardening.

WHAT TO AVOID TODAY

There's misfortune associated with water today so take extra care if you're going swimming or sailing and don't attempt to unblock gutters or drains yourself. If you've recently been through an upheaval in your personal life this is not the right time to put the past behind you; give yourself more time to recover.

This is an unlucky day for anyone born in the following years of the Cock: 1921, 1933, 1945, 1957, 1969.

28TH DAY OF THE 5TH MONTH – TUESDAY, 9 JULY

THE HOURS OF FORTUNE

23–01	B	07–09	G	15–17	M
01–03	B	09–11	G	17–19	M
03–05	G	11–13	G	19–21	B
05–07	M	13–15	G	21–23	G

ADVICE FOR THE DAY

If you're owed money this is a good opportunity to collect it, and if you have lent personal belongings this is the right time to ask for their return. The forecast is excellent for gardeners or anyone else working on the land and you should be more than satisfied with the results of your efforts by the end of the day. There's a final word of advice for anyone who has been plagued by insects or vermin – lay down traps or repellent now or the problem may get out of hand if you leave it any longer.

WHAT TO AVOID TODAY

It's a bad day for needlework so take extra care if you're mending clothes, repairing home furnishings or using a sewing machine. You should also avoid repair work in your kitchen or garage, and you're advised to spend as little time as possible there.

This is a day of misfortune for anyone born in the following years of the Dog: 1922, 1934, 1946, 1958, 1970.

29TH DAY OF THE 5TH MONTH – WEDNESDAY, 10 JULY

THE HOURS OF FORTUNE

23–01	M	07–09	M	15–17	M
01–03	B	09–11	G	17–19	B
03–05	G	11–13	G	19–21	G
05–07	M	13–15	G	21–23	B

ADVICE FOR THE DAY

This is a good day for prayer and quiet reflection and you may find that your prayers are unexpectedly answered. There's good fortune associated with education so if you're beginning a new evening or full-time course there should be plenty of good opportunities in the months ahead. This is also an ideal day to make and meet friends and if you're going to a party you could be in for an unexpected romantic surprise. Lucky stars are shining on finance today so if you're opening a business or finalizing a business deal everything should run smoothly.

WHAT TO AVOID TODAY

Don't attempt elaborate recipes if you're cooking today and be extra careful if you're making sauces, soups, beer or wine.

This is a day of disappointments if you were born in the following years of the Pig: 1923, 1935, 1947, 1959, 1971.

30TH DAY OF THE 5TH MONTH –
THURSDAY, 11 JULY

THE HOURS OF FORTUNE

23–01	B	07–09	M	15–17	B
01–03	B	09–11	G	17–19	M
03–05	G	11–13	M	19–21	M
05–07	G	13–15	G	21–23	G

ADVICE FOR THE DAY

The emphasis today is on personal and domestic life. If you've been through a period of upheaval or loss this is an appropriate time to start thinking about the future and to develop new interests. If you have surplus energy you should channel it into repair or painting work around the house. If you've been thinking of brewing your own beer and wine you should stock up on supplies now and if you already have a supply of home-brew, this is an ideal time as any to sample it.

WHAT TO AVOID TODAY

Unless your house is in danger of flooding don't repair taps, unblock drains or clear out gutters.

This is an unlucky day for anyone born in the following years of the Rat: 1924, 1936, 1948, 1960, 1972.

SIXTH MONTH

Kaun Ti, a famous warrior in Chinese history, was once attacked by a bandit in the forest. He challenged his attacker to a duel on the condition that the loser would serve the victor as a servant for life. Kuan Ti won the duel and the bandit kept his promise.

1ST DAY OF THE 6TH MONTH –
FRIDAY, 12 JULY

THE HOURS OF FORTUNE

23–01	G	07–09	M	15–17	M
01–03	B	09–11	G	17–19	M
03–05	G	11–13	G	19–21	G
05–07	G	13–15	B	21–23	M

ADVICE FOR THE DAY

You should begin the day by sorting out personal matters and put some time aside for quiet reflection or prayer. If you're planning a special journey or are on the move to a new house or country, the gods of fortune are on your side. You can look forward to happiness and emotional stability in the years ahead if you're marrying today. There's also a promising forecast for anyone opening a business, buying stocks or shares or securing a business deal. Finally, there's a successful day in store for DIY enthusiasts, particularly if you're planning structural alterations.

WHAT TO AVOID TODAY

Stay well away from lawyers today and do not sign or agree to contracts unless you have read the small print carefully. This is also an unlucky day to arrange or to attend a funeral.

This is an unlucky day for anyone born in the following years of the Ox: 1925, 1937, 1949, 1961, 1973.

2ND DAY OF THE 6TH MONTH –
SATURDAY, 13 JULY

THE HOURS OF FORTUNE

23–01	G	07–09	G	15–17	G
01–03	B	09–11	G	17–19	G
03–05	B	11–13	B	19–21	M
05–07	M	13–15	G	21–23	M

ADVICE FOR THE DAY

You should try to put some time aside today for prayer, worship or quiet reflection. If you're getting married you can look forward to prosperity and happiness in the years ahead. Don't hesitate to accept social invitations, you could be in for an unexpected romantic surprise. The prospects are also excellent for anyone starting a new educational project or opening a business. If you're shopping today you should find exactly what you want, particularly if you're buying presents for others. There's good fortune associated with DIY at home and you should concentrate on work in the kitchen. On a more sombre note, this is a suitable time to arrange a funeral, and if you have recently lost someone close to you, don't be afraid to turn to friends or relatives for support.

WHAT TO AVOID TODAY

If you're thinking of treating yourself to expensive jewellery today, don't make a hasty decision and check that you're getting value for money. You're also advised not to lend money now, even to friends. If you've been saving food or drink for a special occasion don't be tempted to sample it, for unexpected visitors could be on the way. Finally, if you are cleaning or redecorating your bedroom be extra careful if you're climbing ladders or moving furniture.

This is a day of disappointments and setbacks for anyone born in the following years of the Tiger: 1926, 1938, 1950, 1962, 1974.

3RD DAY OF THE 6TH MONTH – SUNDAY, 14 JULY

THE HOURS OF FORTUNE

23–01	G	07–09	G	15–17	G
01–03	B	09–11	B	17–19	G
03–05	G	11–13	M	19–21	M
05–07	B	13–15	M	21–23	M

ADVICE FOR THE DAY

If you have worries on your mind this is a good day to resolve them and if you're feeling tense or stressed give yourself some time alone to sort things out. The gods of fortune are also with you if you are investing money or retrieving debts. The good fortune associated with house-work continues today so DIY enthusiasts can look forward to a fruitful day.

WHAT TO AVOID TODAY

There's the possibility of an accident in the garden today so channel your energy into another activity. You should also avoid health treatments today, particularly acupuncture.

Don't take risks or make any commitments now if you were born in the following years of the Rabbit: 1927, 1939, 1951, 1963, 1975.

4TH DAY OF THE 6TH MONTH –
MONDAY, 15 JULY

THE HOURS OF FORTUNE

23–01	G	07–09	B	15–17	G
01–03	B	09–11	G	17–19	G
03–05	G	11–13	M	19–21	G
05–07	G	13–15	M	21–23	G

ADVICE FOR THE DAY

Spend some time alone in prayer or quiet reflection. The rest of today's advice is centred on domestic matters and, if you've been thinking of painting or decorating, now is the time to do it.

WHAT TO AVOID TODAY

Beware of an accident if you're gardening and if you've been ill recently don't take any risks. You're also advised to do as little cooking as possible and be especially careful if you're handling hot pans or liquids.

This is a disappointing day for anyone born in the following years of the Dragon: 1928, 1940, 1952, 1964, 1976.

5TH DAY OF THE 6TH MONTH –
TUESDAY, 16 JULY

THE HOURS OF FORTUNE

23–01	M	07–09	M	15–17	M
01–03	B	09–11	B	17–19	G
03–05	G	11–13	G	19–21	G
05–07	B	13–15	G	21–23	G

ADVICE FOR THE DAY

Once again it's a good day for prayer and reflection but it's also a time to make the most of social opportunities; you could be in for an unexpected romantic surprise. This is also a successful day for anyone working with or caring for animals. Finally, there's the prospect of a fruitful day's work if you're planning general DIY around the house.

WHAT TO AVOID TODAY

Unless you're prepared for stormy months ahead, don't get married today and, to be on the safe side, postpone wedding arrangements until tomorrow. On a more immediate note, don't get your hair cut today, you're likely to be disappointed with the results.

Think carefully before you make important decisions today if you were born in the following years of the Snake: 1929, 1941, 1953, 1965, 1977.

6TH DAY OF THE 6TH MONTH – WEDNESDAY, 17 JULY

THE HOURS OF FORTUNE

23–01	M	07–09	G	15–17	G
01–03	B	09–11	G	17–19	G
03–05	B	11–13	B	19–21	M
05–07	G	13–15	M	21–23	M

ADVICE FOR THE DAY

This is an appropriate day for prayer or reflection and this could be the time that your prayers are unexpectedly answered. The forecast for travel is excellent so go ahead and organize business trips or holidays. If you're at home now you should make an effort to mend clothes or home furnishings that you've been intending to repair but have never found the time to do so. You should also take this opportunity to lay down traps or insect repellent in your home or garden. Finally, put some time aside for yourself: it's an excellent day to treat yourself to a little luxury without feeling guilty.

WHAT TO AVOID TODAY

Don't be tempted to agree to buy property today. Even if you think you've found the house of your dreams, you may not have been given enough background information on the property. If you've recently been through a period of personal upheaval you should try to renew contact with old friends and begin to make plans for your future.

This is an unlucky day for anyone born in the following years of the Horse: 1930, 1942, 1954, 1966, 1978.

7TH DAY OF THE 6TH MONTH – THURSDAY, 18 JULY

THE HOURS OF FORTUNE

23–01	G	07–09	M	15–17	G
01–03	B	09–11	G	17–19	G
03–05	G	11–13	M	19–21	M
05–07	G	13–15	B	21–23	B

ADVICE FOR THE DAY

Don't take any risks in your business or personal life because this is a broken day within the month. It's a good time for prayer and quiet reflection but if you do feel like

207

exerting yourself the Almanac advises you to clear away
rubble or throw away things that you've been holding
onto but no longer need.

WHAT TO AVOID TODAY

Try to avoid arranging or attending a funeral now. If
you've recently been upset, don't push yourself too far – it
may take longer to recover than you realized.

This is a day of disappointments for anyone born in the
following years of the Ram: 1919, 1931, 1943, 1955,
1967, 1979.

8TH DAY OF THE 6TH MONTH – FRIDAY, 19 JULY

THE HOURS OF FORTUNE

23–01	B	07–09	G	15–17	B
01–03	B	09–11	M	17–19	M
03–05	G	11–13	G	19–21	B
05–07	G	13–15	M	21–23	M

ADVICE FOR THE DAY

Lucky stars are shining on you now if you're waiting for
exam results or beginning an evening course. Make an
effort to accept social invitations because you could be in
for an unexpected romantic surprise. This is also a good
opportunity to meet old friends or to make new ones. You
can set off on journeys with confidence or finalize travel
arrangements that may have proved awkward in the past.
The time is right to negotiate a business deal and there's a
good financial forecast for anyone investing money. If
you're spending time at home you should concentrate on

shopping, gardening or work in your bedroom. On a more personal note, it's an ideal time to treat yourself to a haircut or to buy new jewellery.

WHAT TO AVOID TODAY

Beware of accidents in the kitchen, particularly if you're cooking. Don't attempt to make or mend clothes, you'll only be wasting your time. You're also advised not to mull over problems and to postpone religious ceremonies until tomorrow.

Be prepared for delays and accidents throughout the day if you were born in the following years of the Monkey: 1920, 1932, 1944, 1956, 1968, 1980.

9TH DAY OF THE 6TH MONTH – SATURDAY, 20 JULY

THE HOURS OF FORTUNE

23–01	M	07–09	M	15–17	M
01–03	B	09–11	G	17–19	B
03–05	G	11–13	G	19–21	G
05–07	G	13–15	M	21–23	M

ADVICE FOR THE DAY

The good fortune associated with educational projects, business negotiations and travel continues today. Don't turn down invitations to parties or to dinners; they could prove to be more enjoyable than you expected. Try to resolve personal differences today both in your private and business life. There's the prospect of a problem-free day if your travelling, moving house or emigrating. It's also an ideal day to concentrate on gardening or DIY around the house.

WHAT TO AVOID TODAY

Don't spend more time than you have to in the kitchen and be particularly careful if you're cooking soups or sauces and if you're brewing your own beer and wine. You should also be extra careful if you're using water, whether you're washing your hair, watering the garden or mending drains.

This is an unlucky day for anyone born in the following years of the Cock: 1921, 1933, 1945, 1957, 1969.

10TH DAY OF THE 6TH MONTH – SUNDAY, 21 JULY

THE HOURS OF FORTUNE

23–01	M	07–09	M	15–17	B
01–03	B	09–11	G	17–19	G
03–05	G	11–13	M	19–21	B
05–07	G	13–15	M	21–23	G

ADVICE FOR THE DAY

It's a good time for prayer, religious ceremony or quiet reflection. On a more wordly note, try to collect outstanding debts today. You can look forward to a successful day if you're working with animals or choosing a new pet. There's also a fruitful day in store for you if you're gardening.

WHAT TO AVOID TODAY

Once again there's misfortune associated with water so don't attempt to fix drains or gutters and postpone watering the garden until another day.

This is a day of disappointments for anyone born in the following years of the Dog: 1922, 1934, 1946, 1958, 1970.

11TH DAY OF THE 6TH MONTH – MONDAY, 22 JULY

THE HOURS OF FORTUNE

23–01	G	07–09	G	15–17	G
01–03	B	09–11	G	17–19	M
03–05	M	11–13	M	19–21	G
05–07	G	13–15	B	21–23	B

ADVICE FOR THE DAY

If you're willing to talk through your problems with other people they may be resolved today. The gods of fortune are on your side if you're marrying and you can look forward to stability and prosperity in the months ahead. This is also a fortunate day to meet and make friends and you should take this opportunity to begin a new romance or to iron out romantic problems.

If you've been feeling ill recently you should go to the doctor today: the news may not be as bad as you anticipated and you can expect a successful prognosis if you're having medical treatment. The day's forecast ends with a word of encouragement for anyone getting their hair cut.

WHAT TO AVOID TODAY

There's misfortune associated with lawyers, courts and contracts so avoid legal matters until tomorrow. You are also advised to take extra care if you're travelling and, if possible, postpone unnecessary journeys.

This is an unlucky day for anyone born in the following years of the Pig: 1923, 1935, 1947, 1959, 1971.

12TH DAY OF THE 6TH MONTH – TUESDAY, 23 JULY

Today is marked in the ancient Chinese agricultural calendar as the 'Great Heat' which begins officially at 4.51 in the afternoon. This is a reminder to farmers that the hottest time of the year is on its way.

THE HOURS OF FORTUNE

23–01	B	07–09	M	15–17	M
01–03	B	09–11	M	17–19	G
03–05	G	11–13	B	19–21	M
05–07	M	13–15	G	21–23	M

ADVICE FOR THE DAY

Try to put some time aside for quiet reflection or prayer; worries on your mind could be resolved now. Turn your attention to painting and decorating around the house or needlework that you've been avoiding. If you have money to spare and need new clothes, go shopping today, you're sure to make a wise buy. It's also a good day to buy wine or, if you're a home-brew enthusiast, to filter or sample your own wine. Finally, on a more sombre note, this is an appropriate time to arrange or attend a funeral.

WHAT TO AVOID TODAY

Don't break into food or drink supplies that you've been saving for a celebration or for unexpected guests. You should also handle money carefully – don't be persuaded to lend it to friends – and if you're thinking of buying expensive jewellery, make sure you get a second opinion before you buy. Finally, beware of an accident if you're cleaning or working in the bathroom.

This is a day of disappointments and setbacks for anyone born in the following years of the Rat: 1924, 1936, 1948, 1960, 1972.

13TH DAY OF THE 6TH MONTH – WEDNESDAY, 24 JULY

This is the festival of Lu Pan, the god of carpenters and joiners.

THE HOURS OF FORTUNE

23–01	G	07–09	M	15–17	G
01–03	B	09–11	B	17–19	M
03–05	G	11–13	M	19–21	G
05–07	G	13–15	M	21–23	G

ADVICE FOR THE DAY

For the next three days you should find time to discuss your problems with others, to ask advice, or to spend time in prayer. There's a good chance that you will find peace of mind. Anyone on the move can look forward to a day free of delays and accidents and there's excellent career prospects in store if you're beginning a new job. It's a promising day for DIY, particularly for structural work on ceilings or in your bedroom. Lucky stars are shining on you if you're getting married and you can expect stability in the months ahead. This is also an auspicious day for anyone working with animals and especially for farmers who are buying or selling cattle.

WHAT TO AVOID TODAY

Put your feet up and have a rest from gardening since there's misfortune associated with planting, digging or ploughing. It's also an unlucky time to mull over a recent loss or to attend a funeral — try to keep yourself busy with practical matters.

This is an unlucky day for anyone born in the following years of the Ox; 1925, 1937, 1949, 1961, 1973.

14TH DAY OF THE 6TH MONTH – THURSDAY, 25 JULY

THE HOURS OF FORTUNE

23–01	G	07–09	B	15–17	G
01–03	B	09–11	G	17–19	G
03–05	B	11–13	M	19–21	G
05–07	M	13–15	G	21–23	G

ADVICE FOR THE DAY

It's an excellent day for spring-cleaning, general DIY and gardening but remember to put some time aside to relax. The Almanac suggests that you treat yourself to a soothing bath or sauna. You can feel secure that you're making the right decision if you're signing a contract, finalizing a business deal or buying or selling goods. Don't be afraid to consult a doctor or other health advisor since this is an ideal time for recovery or healing. If you've been unhappy recently, don't mull over the past unnecessarily. Although it's a suitable day to arrange or to attend a funeral it's also the right time to put the past behind you.

WHAT TO AVOID TODAY

This is an unlucky day for anyone setting off on sea

journeys, so try to postpone your trip no matter how short it is. Although this is generally a promising day for DIY beware of accidents in the kitchen and bedroom.

Don't make hasty decisions or commitments now if you were born in the following years of the Tiger: 1926, 1938, 1950, 1962, 1974.

15TH DAY OF THE 6TH MONTH – FRIDAY, 26 JULY

THE HOURS OF FORTUNE

23–01	M	07–09	M	15–17	M
01–03	B	09–11	M	17–19	G
03–05	M	11–13	G	19–21	M
05–07	B	13–15	G	21–23	G

ADVICE FOR THE DAY

Most of today's advice focuses on home maintenance so you can be sure of a fruitful day's work whether you're fixing door handles, plastering ceilings or building a new house. If your job involves trading this is a lucky day for you and you can also feel secure of your commitment if you're signing a contract. If you're working with animals this should prove to be a successful day and if you've been thinking of buying a pet, now is the time to take action. Anyone troubled by personal problems in the last few weeks should put their sadness behind them and start making plans for the future.

WHAT TO AVOID TODAY

If you are planning to have your hair cut or have arranged other beauty treatments, postpone your appointment until tomorrow. Although it is an appropriate time to dig or plough land you are advised not to plant seeds or trees. Finally, you should avoid acupuncture treatment; the best time to see a specialist is on the seventeenth day of this month.

This is a day of setbacks and delays for anyone born in the following years of the Rabbit: 1927, 1939, 1951, 1963, 1975.

16TH DAY OF THE 6TH MONTH – SATURDAY, 27 JULY

THE HOURS OF FORTUNE

23–01	M	07–09	B	15–17	G
01–03	B	09–11	M	17–19	M
03–05	B	11–13	G	19–21	M
05–07	G	13–15	G	21–23	M

ADVICE FOR THE DAY

This is an appropriate day for manual work, particularly if you're making or mending fabric, painting or decorating and working on masonry or floors.

WHAT TO AVOID TODAY

Don't make a final commitment if you're buying property – it could prove to be more trouble than it's worth. You should also try to postpone funeral arrangements until another day.

Your plans will not work out as you expected today if you were born in the following years of the Dragon: 1916, 1928, 1940, 1952, 1964, 1976.

17TH DAY OF THE 6TH MONTH – SUNDAY, 28 JULY

THE HOURS OF FORTUNE

23–01	G	07–09	M	15–17	G
01–03	B	09–11	B	17–19	M
03–05	G	11–13	G	19–21	M
05–07	G	13–15	G	21–23	B

ADVICE FOR THE DAY

This is an ideal day for quiet reflection or prayer and you may find that your requests are unexpectedly answered. It's a good day to exercise your creative talents, particularly if you're skilled at needlework. Travel difficulties should be ironed out and you can look forward to punctual and safe journeys. Don't be afraid to take financial risks and be sure that loans will be returned without delays. You can look forward to a satisfying day if you're working with or buying animals. Gardeners or farmers should make use of the good fortune associated with the land and, finally, if you're concerned about your health, you should consult an acupuncturist.

WHAT TO AVOID TODAY

You should avoid buying or repairing kitchen goods and beware of an accident if you're cooking. Don't make wedding plans today and if you're getting married be prepared for romantic and financial problems in the months ahead.

This is an unlucky day for anyone born in the following years of the Snake: 1917, 1929, 1941, 1953, 1965, 1977.

18TH DAY OF THE 6TH MONTH –
MONDAY, 29 JULY

THE HOURS OF FORTUNE

23–01	B	07–09	M	15–17	G
01–03	B	09–11	M	17–19	G
03–05	M	11–13	B	19–21	B
05–07	M	13–15	G	21–23	M

ADVICE FOR THE DAY

Lucky stars are shining on anyone who is starting a full- or part-time college course and you can look forward to successful results in the future. There's also a promising career prospect in store if you're starting a new job. Anyone working at home should concentrate on needle-work or on cleaning the bedroom. It's a suitable day to attend a funeral but, if you have been through a period of upheaval recently, now is the time to forget the past and make plans for the future.

WHAT TO AVOID TODAY

Anglers are advised to handle fishing tackle carefully to avoid accident. This is also an unlucky time to ask others for advice or guidance; you may hear some unwelcome news.

This is a day of delays and disappointments for anyone born in the following years of the Horse: 1918, 1930, 1942, 1954, 1966, 1978.

19TH DAY OF THE 6TH MONTH –
TUESDAY, 30 JULY

This is the festival of Kuan Yin, the goddess of Mercy. She is seen as a compassionate figure by Buddhists and Taoists and through her kindness to others she attained the status of *bodhisattva*. This day commemorates that event. Although it is possible for her to attain Buddhahood, she has delayed this so she can work on earth to help those who are suffering.

THE HOURS OF FORTUNE

23–01	M	07–09	M	15–17	G
01–03	B	09–11	G	17–19	B
03–05	G	11–13	G	19–21	M
05–07	G	13–15	B	21–23	G

ADVICE FOR THE DAY

This is a broken day within the month and within the year and it's an ideal time for pulling down old walls or sheds but it's also a positive day for anyone who has been ill recently. Medical treatments begun today should prove to be successful and it's an encouraging time to begin a period of convalescence.

WHAT TO AVOID TODAY

Don't be too ambitious if you're cooking today and beware of a disaster if you're making sauces or soups. You're also advised not to over-indulge in alcohol or work on home-brewed beer or wine.

This is an unlucky day for anyone born in the following years of the Ram: 1919, 1931, 1943, 1955, 1967, 1979.

20TH DAY OF THE 6TH MONTH –
WEDNESDAY, 31 JULY

THE HOURS OF FORTUNE

23–01	M	07–09	M	15–17	B
01–03	B	09–11	M	17–19	M
03–05	G	11–13	M	19–21	G
05–07	G	13–15	G	21–23	M

ADVICE FOR THE DAY

This is a good opportunity to make a decision on an educational course and there could be good news in store if you're waiting for exam results. Travel is blessed by good fortune so you can make travel arrangements or set off on a journey with confidence. There's also a word of encouragement for anyone moving house or emigrating. There's promising financial prospects if you're opening a business, and good romantic prospects if you're announcing an engagement. Don't turn down social invitations because you could find an unexpected friend or romantic partner. If you do have the time and energy you should turn your attention to DIY. Finally, it's a suitable time to arrange a funeral and you should give yourself time to be sad if you've been through a period of loss.

WHAT TO AVOID TODAY

There's misfortune associated with water so don't attempt to solve plumbing problems, water your garden, or go swimming. This isn't a suitable time for prayer or worship so try to keep yourself busy with practical matters.

This is an unlucky day for anyone born in the following years of the Monkey: 1920, 1932, 1944, 1956, 1968.

21ST DAY OF THE 6TH MONTH – THURSDAY, 1 AUGUST

THE HOURS OF FORTUNE

23–01	G	07–09	M	15–17	M
01–03	B	09–11	M	17–19	B
03–05	G	11–13	M	19–21	G
05–07	G	13–15	B	21–23	M

ADVICE FOR THE DAY

Put some time aside to sort out personal problems and to think through worries that have been on your mind. There's an excellent forecast for anyone getting married now and this is also a promising time to begin a romance. Make the most of social invitations that come your way; you could be in for an unexpected surprise. If you've been feeling ill recently, try to consult a doctor, the news may not be as bad as you expected. This is an excellent day for travel and you can expect a smooth move if you're going on holiday, moving to a new house, or emigrating. There are positive financial and career prospects in store if you're starting a new job, opening your own business or investing money. You're safe to sign legal contracts today but think twice before you initiate legal action. There's also an encouraging forecast for gardeners, builders and DIY enthusiasts. Finally, if someone close to you has recently died this is a suitable day to attend a funeral and to make new plans for the future.

WHAT TO AVOID TODAY

If you're thinking of going on a fishing trip, postpone it until another day and take extra care if you're planning to unblock drains, repair gutters or fix anything that uses water.

This is a day of disappointments and setbacks if you were born in the following years of the Cock: 1921, 1933, 1945, 1957, 1969.

22ND DAY OF THE 6TH MONTH – FRIDAY, 2 AUGUST

THE HOURS OF FORTUNE

23–01	G	07–09	G	15–17	M
01–03	B	09–11	M	17–19	G
03–05	M	11–13	B	19–21	B
05–07	M	13–15	G	21–23	G

ADVICE FOR THE DAY

There's very little luck around today so don't do anything out of the ordinary. It's the right time to sort out personal problems and if you're owed money this is a good time to ask for it back again.

WHAT TO AVOID TODAY

If you've been stocking up on food or drink supplies for a celebration or for a rainy day don't be tempted to sample them now. While it's an ideal time to collect outstanding debts, beware of lending money for it may not be returned on time. You should also be especially cautious if you're thinking of investing money now.

This is an unlucky day for anyone born in the following years of the Dog: 1922, 1934, 1946, 1958, 1970.

23RD DAY OF THE 6TH MONTH – SATURDAY, 3 AUGUST

THE HOURS OF FORTUNE

23–01	G	07–09	M	15–17	G
01–03	B	09–11	B	17–19	G
03–05	M	11–13	M	19–21	G
05–07	M	13–15	M	21–23	B

ADVICE FOR THE DAY

Once again there isn't much good fortune around. Limit your activities to prayer and quiet reflection. If you've been feeling ill this is the appropriate time to visit the doctor: the diagnosis may not be as bad as you expected.

WHAT TO AVOID TODAY

Don't make long journeys now unless they are absolutely necessary. There's also the threat of an accident in the garden so handle garden tools carefully, particularly if you're planting trees or plants.

Be prepared for difficulties throughout the day if you were born in the following years of the Pig: 1923, 1935, 1947, 1959, 1971.

24TH DAY OF THE 6TH MONTH – SUNDAY, 4 AUGUST

This is the day when Kuan Ti, the god of Wealth and Justice is worshipped and honoured.

THE HOURS OF FORTUNE

23–01	B	07–09	B	15–17	G
01–03	B	09–11	G	17–19	G
03–05	M	11–13	G	19–21	G
05–07	M	13–15	M	21–23	G

ADVICE FOR THE DAY

Today's advice centres on domestic activities. It's an ideal time to paint, decorate or clean your house. If you've recently been through a period of upheaval you should try to renew contact with old friends and make plans for the coming months.

WHAT TO AVOID TODAY

Don't attempt to fix electrical kitchen goods and beware of an accident if you're cooking.

This is a day of disappointments for anyone born in the following years of the Rat: 1924, 1936, 1948, 1960, 1972.

25TH DAY OF THE 6TH MONTH – MONDAY, 5 AUGUST

THE HOURS OF FORTUNE

23–01	M	07–09	M	15–17	M
01–03	B	09–11	G	17–19	G
03–05	M	11–13	G	19–21	M
05–07	B	13–15	G	21–23	G

ADVICE FOR THE DAY

If you've been having difficulty arranging travel plans they should be resolved now and it's generally a positive time to set off on a journey by land, sea or air. You can look forward to good career and financial prospects if you're starting a new job today or arranging a business partnership. If you have spare time on your hands turn your attention to DIY around the home.

WHAT TO AVOID TODAY

Leave your gardening tools where they are today and have a rest instead. You're likely to be disappointed with the results if you get your hair cut so postpone your appointment until another day. Finally, if you're mourning the death of a friend or relative, this could be a particularly painful day for you so try to keep your mind on other things. You should try to avoid arranging or attending a funeral.

This is an unlucky day for anyone born in the following years of the Ox: 1925, 1937, 1949, 1961, 1973.

26TH DAY OF THE 6TH MONTH – TUESDAY, 6 AUGUST

THE HOURS OF FORTUNE

23–01	M	07–09	G	15–17	G
01–03	B	09–11	G	17–19	M
03–05	B	11–13	M	19–21	M
05–07	M	13–15	G	21–23	M

ADVICE FOR THE DAY

This is a good day for prayer, religious ceremony or quiet thought. The gods of fortune are on your side if you're announcing an engagement and you can look forward to happiness and stability in the years ahead if you're getting married now. It's a positive time to consult a doctor or to begin a health treatment and if you have been ill this is a good opportunity to ease yourself back into work. The forecast is excellent for anyone starting a new job or beginning a new project. Others may come to you for advice today so try to give them your time and support.

WHAT TO AVOID TODAY

You're strongly advised not to buy or sell property or land: give yourself at least another day to check all the relevant details.

Don't take unnecessary risks now if you were born in the following years of the Tiger: 1926, 1938, 1950, 1962, 1974.

27TH DAY OF THE 6TH MONTH – WEDNESDAY, 7 AUGUST

THE HOURS OF FORTUNE

23–01	G	07–09	G	15–17	G
01–03	B	09–11	G	17–19	M
03–05	M	11–13	G	19–21	M
05–07	B	13–15	G	21–23	B

ADVICE FOR THE DAY

Turn your attention to spring-cleaning around the house but put some time aside for yourself to sort out personal matters.

WHAT TO AVOID TODAY

This is a particularly upsetting day for anyone mourning

the death of a friend or relative. Try to avoid making funeral arrangements or attending a funeral. If you have already been through a period of upheaval or loss, don't keep mulling over the past, look to the future instead.

This is a day of disappointments if you were born in the following years of the Rabbit: 1927, 1939, 1951, 1963, 1975.

28TH DAY OF THE 6TH MONTH – THURSDAY, 8 AUGUST

According to the ancient calendar of China, this is Li Ch'iu – a reminder that the summer ends and the autumn begins at 9.20 this morning.

THE HOURS OF FORTUNE

23–01	B	07–09	B	15–17	G
01–03	B	09–11	M	17–19	M
03–05	M	11–13	G	19–21	B
05–07	M	13–15	G	21–23	M

ADVICE FOR THE DAY

Now is the time to spend time and energy at home. You should turn your attention to painting, decorating, plastering and cleaning. But this is also a day to enjoy yourself so make the most of social opportunities, you could be in for an unexpected and welcome surprise. If you've been thinking of having your hair cut, do so now and you'll be pleased with the result.

WHAT TO AVOID TODAY

Be extra careful if you're mending home furnishings,

sewing clothes or doing anything that involves using a
needle. You should, if possible avoid arranging or
attending a funeral.

This is a day of disappointments for anyone born in the
following years of the Dragon: 1928, 1940, 1952, 1964,
1976.

29TH DAY OF THE 6TH MONTH –
FRIDAY, 9 AUGUST

THE HOURS OF FORTUNE

23–01	M	07–09	M	15–17	M
01–03	B	09–11	B	17–19	B
03–05	B	11–13	G	19–21	G
05–07	G	13–15	G	21–23	M

ADVICE FOR THE DAY

The good fortune associated with painting, decorating and
general house maintenance continues over from yesterday.
This is also an appropriate time to start repair work on
garden paths or roads.

WHAT TO AVOID TODAY

Be prepared for a day of delays and setbacks if you were
born in the following years of the Snake: 1917, 1929,
1941, 1953, 1965, 1977.

SEVENTH MONTH

Once a year offerings of incense and food are made to the
Hungry Ghosts — the unsettled spirits of those who have died
without a family. Unless they are remembered at least once
a year by strangers, the Hungry Ghosts will cause trouble
wherever they can.

1ST DAY OF THE 7TH MONTH –
SATURDAY, 10 AUGUST

This is the birthday of the Chinese teacher and sage, Lao Tzu, also known as Tai Shung Lao-chun. In Taoist popular thought, Lao Tzu is one of the incarnations of the supreme force that created the world. He is believed to have lived in China over a thousand years ago, although his exact dates are unknown. Lao Tzu adapted and developed a philosophy called the Tao or the Way, which had existed in China long before his lifetime. Lao Tzu encouraged his followers and disciples to turn away from the world and to concentrate on meditation and other religious practices. This would enable them to escape from the human body and its limitations and become free in the spirit world. This path to immortality required years of dedicated practice, usually in remote places, so that the believers' attention could be turned to one or all of the following: fasting, deep breathing, meditation, elixirs, talismans, and secret formulae. In the search for immortality Taoist priests and monks experimented extensively with plants, minerals and animals and during centuries of trials and tests the formulae and their remedies were so carefully recorded that Taoist priests were as much respected for their healing powers as for their spiritual powers.

THE HOURS OF FORTUNE

23–01	G	07–09	G	15–17	B
01–03	B	09–11	G	17–19	M
03–05	B	11–13	B	19–21	M
05–07	G	13–15	G	21–23	M

ADVICE FOR THE DAY

Try to put some time aside for prayer or quiet reflection.

Educational projects are well-starred now, so there's good news in store if you're waiting for exam results or starting a new college course. Lucky stars are shining on anyone who is on the move so you can travel as far afield as you like. The long-term forecast is also positive for anyone who is emigrating or moving house.

Make the most of social opportunities that come your way because there could be an important and welcome meeting in store. Go ahead with wedding plans and if you are celebrating it's an ideal time to receive presents. Financial prospects are good for shopkeepers but it should also prove to be a profitable day for anyone investing in a new business. It's an appropriate time for gardening and DIY and you can expect satisfying results. The next two days are suitable for arranging or attending a funeral and if you have been through a period of loss or upheaval you should try to put the past behind you and concentrate on the future.

WHAT TO AVOID TODAY

There is misfortune associated with water so postpone plans to go swimming or sailing and if you have plumbing problems don't attempt to fix them yourself, call in a plumber instead. Try to sort out personal problems on your own and don't ask others for advice: you may hear some unwelcome news.

This is an unlucky day for anyone born in the following years of the Horse: 1930, 1942, 1954, 1966, 1978.

2ND DAY OF THE 7TH MONTH –
SUNDAY, 11 AUGUST

THE HOURS OF FORTUNE

23–01	G	07–09	G	15–17	G
01–03	B	09–11	G	17–19	G
03–05	B	11–13	M	19–21	G
05–07	M	13–15	B	21–23	M

ADVICE FOR THE DAY

Once again, it's an excellent time to meet friends, to make new ones or to begin a romance. The forecast is still good for anyone who is on the move at home or abroad. Lucky stars are shining on you if you're announcing an engagement and if you're giving presents now they are sure to be gratefully received. If you want to turn your attention to practical matters it's a positive day for gardening or DIY but it's also a day to spend some time on yourself, so go ahead and treat yourself to a little luxury.

WHAT TO AVOID TODAY

It's an unlucky day for sports enthusiasts, particularly if you're using heavy or potentially dangerous equipment, so make sure you follow the necessary safety procedures. There's also a disappointment in store if you're involved in a court case or other legal action.

This is a day of delays and disappointments for anyone born in the following years of the Ram: 1919, 1931, 1943, 1955, 1967.

3RD DAY OF THE 7TH MONTH –
MONDAY, 12 AUGUST

THE HOURS OF FORTUNE

23–01	M	07–09	G	15–17	B
01–03	B	09–11	M	17–19	G
03–05	B	11–13	B	19–21	G
05–07	M	13–15	G	21–23	M

ADVICE FOR THE DAY

Since this is a broken day within the month you should postpone important plans or decisions and concentrate on clearing away rubble or rubbish inside or outside the house.

WHAT TO AVOID TODAY

Concentrate on practical affairs, not spiritual ones: there's plenty of time tomorrow for personal reflection or prayer. You should also be wary of financial setbacks and don't squander your money on unnecessary items. If you've been saving food or drink for a special occasion don't be tempted to break into it now: you may need it sooner than you think.

Don't take unnecessary risks today if you were born in the following years of the Monkey: 1920, 1932, 1944, 1956, 1968.

4TH DAY OF THE 7TH MONTH –
TUESDAY, 13 AUGUST

THE HOURS OF FORTUNE

23–01	M	07–09	M	15–17	G
01–03	B	09–11	B	17–19	B
03–05	B	11–13	M	19–21	G
05–07	G	13–15	G	21–23	G

ADVICE FOR THE DAY

It's an appropriate day for religious celebration and the gods of fortune are on your side if you're getting married. You should find the emotional support you need if you're in a period of mourning or attending a funeral. If you're thinking of having acupuncture or other health treatments, they should prove to be successful. Now is the time to turn your attention to mending, cleaning or repair work in your bedroom and if you have the time and money on your hands you should treat yourself to a haircut or other beauty treatments.

WHAT TO AVOID TODAY

Beware of an accident if you're using heavy tools, particularly if you're moving soil or digging.

This is an unlucky day for anyone born in the following years of the Cock: 1921, 1933, 1945, 1957, 1969, 1971.

5TH DAY OF THE 7TH MONTH – WEDNESDAY, 14 AUGUST

THE HOURS OF FORTUNE

23–01	M	07–09	B	15–17	G
01–03	B	09–11	G	17–19	G
03–05	B	11–13	M	19–21	B
05–07	M	13–15	M	21–23	G

ADVICE FOR THE DAY

Go ahead and ask others for help or advice, your requests should be answered without hesitation. The future looks secure and prosperous for you if you're announcing an engagement, beginning a new educational course, or opening a business. If you've been planning to buy new clothes, do so today and you should find exactly what you need. Finally, it's a good time for repair or renovation work in your bedroom or on structural work around the house.

WHAT TO AVOID TODAY

Beware of an accident in the kitchen, especially if you're cooking, handling hot pans, or repairing electrical goods.

This is an unlucky day for anyone born in the following years of the Dog: 1922, 1934, 1946, 1958, 1970.

6TH DAY OF THE 7TH MONTH –
THURSDAY, 15 AUGUST

THE HOURS OF FORTUNE

23–01	M	07–09	M	15–17	M
01–03	B	09–11	G	17–19	G
03–05	B	11–13	G	19–21	G
05–07	B	13–15	G	21–23	B

ADVICE FOR THE DAY

Make every effort to accept social invitations that come your way and you could come across a meeting that will affect your plans in the months ahead. The gods of fortune are on your side if you're marrying and it's the perfect day to give or to receive presents. The financial forecast is excellent over the next two days for anyone who is setting up in business or negotiating a business deal. Building contractors and anyone working on house alterations can expect a productive day and if you're thinking of buying or selling animals this is the time to do it.

WHAT TO AVOID TODAY

You should try to postpone important journeys at home or abroad until tomorrow or until the 9th day of this month when the forecast for travel is improved. If you're thinking of having your hair cut, cancel your plans, at least for today, to avoid disappointment.

This is a day of emotional setbacks for anyone born in the following years of the Pig: 1923, 1935, 1947, 1959, 1971.

7TH DAY OF THE 7TH MONTH –
FRIDAY, 16 AUGUST

THE HOURS OF FORTUNE

23–01	B	07–09	M	15–17	G
01–03	B	09–11	G	17–19	G
03–05	B	11–13	M	19–21	M
05–07	G	13–15	G	21–23	M

ADVICE FOR THE DAY

Take this opportunity to sort out personal problems or to ask others for help – their advice should prove to be very helpful. If you've recently been through a period of upheaval or depression, you should try to forget the past and begin to make plans for the future. Lucky stars are also shining on you if you're marrying, moving to a new house or country, or putting your energies into building or renovation work. Now is the time to buy new clothes or to mend home furnishings. Finally, career prospects are excellent if you're starting a full- or part-time educational course.

WHAT TO AVOID TODAY

Although the forecast is positive for DIY, you should try to avoid general maintenance work in your bathroom. There could be unending problems in store if you buy property now without taking sufficient time to consider your move or take professional advice.

Don't take unnecessary risks today if you were born in the following years of the Rat: 1924, 1936, 1948, 1960, 1972.

8TH DAY OF THE 7TH MONTH –
SATURDAY, 17 AUGUST

THE HOURS OF FORTUNE

23–01	M	07–09	M	15–17	G
01–03	B	09–11	G	17–19	M
03–05	B	11–13	G	19–21	M
05–07	G	13–15	G	21–23	B

ADVICE FOR THE DAY

If you're announcing an engagement now you can look
forward to a secure and prosperous future. The rest of
today's forecast focuses on general maintenance work in
the house and garden.

WHAT TO AVOID TODAY

This is bad time to launch new projects, so don't try to be
too ambitious at the moment. You should also delay
making plans for the future if you've recently been
through a period of personal loss.

Be prepared for disappointments throughout the day if
you were born in the following years of the Ox: 1925,
1937, 1949, 1961, 1973.

9TH DAY OF THE 7TH MONTH –
SUNDAY, 18 AUGUST

THE HOURS OF FORTUNE

23–01	B	07–09	G	15–17	G
01–03	B	09–11	G	17–19	M
03–05	B	11–13	G	19–21	B
05–07	M	13–15	G	21–23	M

ADVICE FOR THE DAY

This is an ideal day to go shopping: if you've been thinking of buying new clothes you should find exactly what you need. Today and tomorrow are appropriate times to give your house a thorough clean and to sort out minor repairs that you've been delaying, particularly in the kitchen.

WHAT TO AVOID TODAY

Beware of an accident in the bedroom and don't attempt to move or mend furniture there. If you were planning to work in the garden, wait until tomorrow when the forecast is greatly improved.

This is a day of disappointments for anyone born in the following years of the Tiger: 1926, 1938, 1950, 1962, 1974.

10TH DAY OF THE 7TH MONTH – MONDAY, 19 AUGUST

THE HOURS OF FORTUNE

23–01	M	07–09	G	15–17	M
01–03	B	09–11	G	17–19	B
03–05	B	11–13	G	19–21	M
05–07	B	13–15	M	21–23	M

ADVICE FOR THE DAY

Be careful not to let your personal appearance slip if you're busy with practical matters. You should take this opportunity to treat yourself to a haircut or other beauty treatments. On a more serious note, this is an appropriate time to reflect on the events of the past if you have been through a period of loss or mourning.

WHAT TO AVOID TODAY

This could be a day of accidents in the kitchen and you're advised to be extra careful if you're cooking elaborate sauces or soups. Don't be tempted to over-indulge in alcohol; you could regret your actions tomorrow.

Be prepared for the unexpected today if you were born in the following years of the Rabbit: 1927, 1939, 1951, 1963, 1975.

11TH DAY OF THE 7TH MONTH – TUESDAY, 20 AUGUST

THE HOURS OF FORTUNE

23–01	M	07–09	B	15–17	B
01–03	B	09–11	G	17–19	M
03–05	B	11–13	M	19–21	G
05–07	G	13–15	G	21–23	G

ADVICE FOR THE DAY

This should be a day free of delays and accidents so you can set off on journeys at home or abroad with confidence. Make the most of social opportunities that come your way and you could be in for an unexpected and welcome surprise. If you're celebrating now this is an ideal time to choose, give or receive presents. The financial forecast is excellent for shopkeepers and anyone involved in trade or opening a business. The gods of fortune are also on your side if you're getting married and you can look forward to a secure future. The rest of today's forecast offers encouragement to gardening or DIY enthusiasts.

WHAT TO AVOID TODAY

Beware of an accident if you're handling or working near water. You're also advised to postpone funeral arrangements until the 16th day of this month.

This is an unlucky day for anyone born in the following years of the Dragon: 1928, 1940, 1952, 1964, 1976.

12TH DAY OF THE 7TH MONTH – WEDNESDAY, 21 AUGUST

THE HOURS OF FORTUNE

23–01	M	07–09	G	15–17	M
01–03	B	09–11	B	17–19	M
03–05	B	11–13	G	19–21	G
05–07	G	13–15	B	21–23	G

ADVICE FOR THE DAY

Try to put some time aside for quiet reflection or prayer. If you have time on your hands it would be a good idea to concentrate on painting and decorating around the house or general maintenance in the garden. This is also a suitable day to work on a creative project; you're likely to be more than pleased with your efforts by the end of the day.

WHAT TO AVOID TODAY

There could be a stormy future in store for you if you're getting married today; you're well advised to wait until tomorrow. Stay away from lawyers at the moment, and don't sign contracts or initiate legal action.

Don't take unnecessary risks today if you were born in the following years of the Snake: 1929, 1941, 1953, 1965, 1977.

13TH DAY OF THE 7TH MONTH – THURSDAY, 22 AUGUST

THE HOURS OF FORTUNE

23–01	G	07–09	G	15–17	G
01–03	B	09–11	M	17–19	M
03–05	B	11–13	B	19–21	M
05–07	M	13–15	G	21–23	M

ADVICE FOR THE DAY

This is a good day to concentrate on spiritual matters and don't be afraid to ask others for help with personal problems. This is a lucky time to renew contact with old friends or to make new ones and a chance meeting today could have a marked effect on you in the months ahead. If you've been having difficulties with travel plans they should be resolved now and you can set off on journeys with confidence. If you have money to spare this is a good time to treat yourself to some new clothes or to make your own. If you're working with animals or thinking of buying a new pet you can expect a satisfying day. If you're thinking of spending time on DIY or gardening, be ambitious with your plans and you could achieve more than you expected.

WHAT TO AVOID TODAY

Don't squander your savings, lend money or take unnecessary financial risks at the moment. If you have just been through a period of emotional upheaval try to keep your mind on practical matters; mulling over the past will not help you today.

This is an unlucky day for anyone born in the following years of the Horse: 1918, 1930, 1942, 1954, 1966, 1978.

14TH DAY OF THE 7TH MONTH – FRIDAY, 23 AUGUST

THE HOURS OF FORTUNE

23–01	G	07–09	M	15–17	G
01–03	B	09–11	B	17–19	M
03–05	B	11–13	M	19–21	M
05–07	G	13–15	B	21–23	M

ADVICE FOR THE DAY

There's still good fortune associated with social opportunities, so make the most of meetings or parties that come your way. If you're working with animals you can expect a satisfying day but this is also an appropriate time to get rid of insects, slugs, mice or vermin that have infested the house or garden.

WHAT TO AVOID TODAY

Don't attempt electrical repairs in the kitchen over the next two days and be especially careful if you're working near a cooker. Gardening enthusiasts are advised to avoid planting seeds, shrubs or trees.

This is an unlucky day for anyone born in the following years of the Ram: 1931, 1943, 1955, 1967, 1979.

15TH DAY OF THE 7TH MONTH – SATURDAY, 24 AUGUST

This is the festival of the Hungry Ghosts. These are the malignant spirits of those who have died without relatives or friends to make offerings in their memory. If the ghosts are angered they may strike the living so offerings are made today to placate them.

THE HOURS OF FORTUNE

23–01	G	07–09	B	15–17	B
01–03	B	09–11	M	17–19	G
03–05	B	11–13	G	19–21	M
05–07	G	13–15	M	21–23	M

ADVICE FOR THE DAY

Since this is a broken day within the month it is suited to minor demolition work around the house or garden and to clearing away rubble or rubbish.

WHAT TO AVOID TODAY

Focus your attention on practical, not spiritual matters. You won't achieve anything by mulling over your problems now.

Your plans may not turn out as you expected today if you

were born in the following years of the Monkey: 1920, 1932, 1944, 1956, 1968, 1980.

16TH DAY OF THE 7TH MONTH – SUNDAY, 25 AUGUST

THE HOURS OF FORTUNE

23–01	M	07–09	M	15–17	M
01–03	B	09–11	M	17–19	B
03–05	B	11–13	G	19–21	M
05–07	B	13–15	G	21–23	G

ADVICE FOR THE DAY

This is a good day for prayer or quiet reflection. If you're on the move you can look forward to punctual and comfortable travel. Lucky stars are shining on you if you're getting married, and it's an excellent time to give or to receive presents. Business plans and trading ventures should prove to be profitable so don't be afraid to take a risk. If you're planning to work on your house, you should concentrate on structural work or on DIY in your bedroom. If a close friend or relative has recently died these next two days are an appropriate time to make funeral arrangements or to attend a funeral.

WHAT TO AVOID TODAY

Be extra careful if you're showering or taking a bath, and if you have plumbing problems don't attempt to fix them yourself, call in an expert instead. If you're planning to have your hair cut, postpone your appointment until the 21st day of this month.

Be prepared for a day of disappointments if you were born in the following years of the Cock: 1921, 1933, 1945, 1957, 1969.

17TH DAY OF THE 7TH MONTH – MONDAY, 26 AUGUST

THE HOURS OF FORTUNE

23–01	M	07–09	M	15–17	G
01–03	B	09–11	G	17–19	G
03–05	B	11–13	M	19–21	B
05–07	G	13–15	G	21–23	M

ADVICE FOR THE DAY

You're advised to put time aside over these next two days to reflect on personal and spiritual affairs. The forecast for friendship and romance is excellent from now until the 19th day of this month so make the most of social opportunities. This period is also a suitable time to celebrate an engagement and to give or receive presents. This is also the time to treat yourself to new clothes – you should find exactly what you need. This is the right time to stock up liquid supplies if you are running low. If you're finalizing a business deal or setting up in business the gods of fortune should be on your side over the next few months. The day's forecast ends with a word of encouragement for anyone working on building projects or general maintenance around the house.

WHAT TO AVOID TODAY

This is an unlucky day to have acupuncture or to start a course of other health treatments. You should also think very carefully before you buy property — make sure that you have checked the background details thoroughly.

This is an unlucky day for anyone born in the following years of the Dog: 1922, 1934, 1946, 1958, 1970.

18TH DAY OF THE 7TH MONTH – TUESDAY, 27 AUGUST

THE HOURS OF FORTUNE

23–01	G	07–09	M	15–17	G
01–03	B	09–11	M	17–19	M
03–05	B	11–13	G	19–21	M
05–07	M	13–15	G	21–23	B

ADVICE FOR THE DAY

The future looks secure and bright if you're moving to a new house or thinking of setting up in business. The good fortune associated with DIY and gardening continues from yesterday as does the forecast for meeting friends and getting married. It's a suitable day to put your creative talents to good use; you could be surprised with your efforts.

WHAT TO AVOID TODAY

Make sure that you have taken all the necessary advice or precautions before you launch new projects — you should be prepared for a few setbacks at the beginning. Avoid making travel arrangements, and if you are setting off on a journey be prepared for delays or accidents. If you've been emotionally upset recently, don't expect a speedy recovery, give yourself a little longer to think your problems through.

Personal problems may come to the fore now if you were born in the following years of the Pig: 1923, 1935, 1947, 1959, 1971.

19TH DAY OF THE 7TH MONTH – WEDNESDAY, 28 AUGUST

THE HOURS OF FORTUNE

23–01	B	07–09	M	15–17	G
01–03	B	09–11	M	17–19	G
03–05	B	11–13	G	19–21	B
05–07	M	13–15	G	21–23	M

ADVICE FOR THE DAY

For the third day running the financial and social forecast is excellent. You can still expect satisfying results if you're concentrating on DIY or gardening. You can also feel confident of good results in the future as well as work satisfaction if you're starting a new educational course.

WHAT TO AVOID TODAY

Beware of an accident if you're using anything that involves needles. If you're working at home don't attempt repairs on ceilings or roofs. If a close relative or friend has died recently you should also postpone funeral arrangements until the 21st day of this month.

Don't make commitments or take risks now if you were born in the following years of the Rat: 1924, 1936, 1948, 1960, 1972.

20TH DAY OF THE 7TH MONTH – THURSDAY, 29 AUGUST

THE HOURS OF FORTUNE

23–01	M	07–09	M	15–17	G
01–03	B	09–11	G	17–19	B
03–05	B	11–13	G	19–21	M
05–07	G	13–15	M	21–23	M

ADVICE FOR THE DAY

This is a well-starred day for extending your social circle so make the most of social opportunities that come your way – you could be in for an unexpected romantic surprise. Journeys at home and abroad by any means of transport should pass off smoothly. The future is promising and secure if you're announcing an engagement or marrying. The financial forecast is excellent if you're opening a business or negotiating a business deal. Now is the time to turn your attention to your personal appearance so go ahead and buy yourself new clothes or treat yourself to a haircut. If you're at home you should concentrate on maintenance work in the kitchen, and on roofs or ceilings. Finally, the Almanac offers encouragement during the next two days to anyone who is in a period of mourning or attending a burial.

WHAT TO AVOID TODAY

If you're thinking of buying bedroom furniture or cleaning out your bedroom, wait until another day. There's the possibility of an accident in the garden, so have a rest from gardening for the moment. You should also beware of an accident if you're going swimming or working with water.

Be prepared for problems in your domestic life if you were born in the following years of the Ox: 1925, 1937, 1949, 1961, 1973.

21ST DAY OF THE 7TH MONTH – FRIDAY, 30 AUGUST

THE HOURS OF FORTUNE

23–01	G	07–09	G	15–17	B
01–03	B	09–11	G	17–19	G
03–05	B	11–13	M	19–21	M
05–07	G	13–15	G	21–23	M

ADVICE FOR THE DAY

Try to find some time alone today for quiet reflection or to think through worries on your mind. This is a perfect time to announce an engagement and to give or receive presents. On the domestic front, there's a good forecast for gardening and DIY. Anyone working with animals can also look forward to a successful day. Once again, it's a good time to pamper yourself, especially if you're getting your hair cut.

WHAT TO AVOID TODAY

Don't initiate legal action or sign contracts. Sports enthusiasts should also beware of an accident today, particularly if they're hunting, fishing or handling heavy equipment.

This is a day of delays and disagreements for anyone born in the following years of the Tiger: 1926, 1938, 1950, 1962, 1974.

22ND DAY OF THE 7TH MONTH –
SATURDAY, 31 AUGUST

This is a day when many Chinese make offerings to the
God of Wealth, give thanks for their existing wealth, and
pray for future riches.

THE HOURS OF FORTUNE

23–01	G	07–09	G	15–17	G
01–03	B	09–11	G	17–19	M
03–05	B	11–13	M	19–21	M
05–07	B	13–15	B	21–23	M

ADVICE FOR THE DAY

Be prepared to take a financial risk particularly if you're
planning to set up in your own business. It's also a
promising day to buy new clothes or to make your own:
you should be pleased with your choice. If you've been
thinking of decorating your house this is the time to start
work. This is still an appropriate day to arrange or attend
a funeral.

WHAT TO AVOID TODAY

Although this is an appropriate time to invest money,
don't be tempted to squander your savings on unnecessary
luxuries or to over-indulge in food or drink.

Be prepared for a day of disappointments if you were born
in the following years of the Rabbit: 1927, 1939, 1951,
1963, 1975.

23RD DAY OF THE 7TH MONTH – SUNDAY, 1 SEPTEMBER

THE HOURS OF FORTUNE

23–01	M	07–09	B	15–17	M
01–03	B	09–11	G	17–19	M
03–05	B	11–13	B	19–21	M
05–07	G	13–15	G	21–23	M

ADVICE FOR THE DAY

This is an ideal day to put your energies into general maintenance around the house or garden.

WHAT TO AVOID TODAY

Avoid marrying today or making wedding plans. You should also beware of an accident if you're working in the garden.

Don't take unnecessary risks today if you were born in the following years of the Dragon: 1928, 1940, 1952, 1964, 1976.

24TH DAY OF THE 7TH MONTH – MONDAY, 2 SEPTEMBER

THE HOURS OF FORTUNE

23–01	G	07–09	M	15–17	M
01–03	B	09–11	B	17–19	M
03–05	B	11–13	M	19–21	M
05–07	G	13–15	G	21–23	M

ADVICE FOR THE DAY

This is an excellent time for prayer or quiet reflection. Make the most of social opportunities that come your way, and if you're getting married the future looks bright. Any presents given today will be well received. Travel is well-starred whether you're travelling for business or pleasure, moving to a new house or to a new country. This should be a profitable day for shopkeepers and anyone else involved in trade; be prepared to take financial risks now. Practical domestic matters are well-starred and with the exception of DIY work in the kitchen, you can expect positive results whether you're attempting structural work or simply cleaning out the house. The forecast ends with a word of support for anyone arranging or attending a funeral.

WHAT TO AVOID TODAY

Although this is generally a good day for travel, there may be minor setbacks if you're travelling by sea.

Your plans may not work out as you expected now if you were born in the following years of the Snake: 1929, 1941, 1953, 1965, 1977.

25TH DAY OF THE 7TH MONTH – TUESDAY, 3 SEPTEMBER

THE HOURS OF FORTUNE

23–01	G	07–09	B	15–17	M
01–03	B	09–11	G	17–19	G
03–05	B	11–13	B	19–21	G
05–07	M	13–15	M	21–23	G

ADVICE FOR THE DAY

There's still good fortune in the air for anyone who is travelling, getting married, or working on DIY. If you've been feeling ill recently this is a good day to start a period of treatment or to consult a doctor – the news may not be as bad as you expected.

WHAT TO AVOID TODAY

Don't waste time or money on your personal appearance, concentrate on practical matters instead.

This is a day of disappointments for anyone born in the following years of the Horse: 1930, 1942, 1954, 1966, 1978.

26TH DAY OF THE 7TH MONTH – WEDNESDAY, 4 SEPTEMBER

THE HOURS OF FORTUNE

23–01	G	07–09	M	15–17	M
01–03	B	09–11	G	17–19	G
03–05	B	11–13	G	19–21	M
05–07	B	13–15	B	21–23	G

ADVICE FOR THE DAY

Since this is a broken day within the month you should concentrate on minor demolition work and try to clear away rubbish or rubble from the house or garden.

WHAT TO AVOID TODAY

Don't mull over personal problems or ask others for advice. You should also think twice before you agree to the sale of property; you may not have been given sufficient background information.

Be prepared for problems in your domestic life if you were born in the following years of the Ram: 1919, 1931, 1943, 1955, 1967, 1979.

27TH DAY OF THE 7TH MONTH – THURSDAY, 5 SEPTEMBER

THE HOURS OF FORTUNE

23–01	M		07–09	G		15–17	B
01–03	B		09–11	G		17–19	M
03–05	B		11–13	G		19–21	M
05–07	G		13–15	G		21–23	M

ADVICE FOR THE DAY

Since this is a broken day within the month you should concentrate on minor demolition work or on clearing away rubble or rubbish.

WHAT TO AVOID TODAY

Think twice before you invest money in property as you may not have been given sufficient background information. You should also try to concentrate on practical, not spiritual, matters for the time being.

Don't take unnecessary risks today if you were born in the following years of the Monkey: 1920, 1932, 1944, 1956, 1968.

28TH DAY OF THE 7TH MONTH – FRIDAY, 6 SEPTEMBER

THE HOURS OF FORTUNE

23–01	G	07–09	M	15–17	M
01–03	B	09–11	M	17–19	B
03–05	B	11–13	G	19–21	M
05–07	G	13–15	G	21–23	B

ADVICE FOR THE DAY

Today and tomorrow are ideal times for prayer and quiet reflection. If there are worries on your mind, confide in others to ease your worries. These last two days of the month are also excellent opportunities to meet old friends or make new ones, resolve romantic problems, announce an engagement, give or receive presents, or set up in business. Legal affairs should work in your favour and if you're owed outstanding debts now is the time to collect them. If you're thinking of getting your hair cut, do so now and you won't be disappointed with the results. Finally, it's an appropriate time to attend or arrange a funeral.

WHAT TO AVOID TODAY

This is an unlucky time to dig or plough land and beware of an accident if you're working with or near water.

Your plans may not work out as you expected now if you were born in the following years of the Cock: 1921, 1933, 1945, 1957, 1969.

29TH DAY OF THE 7TH MONTH – SATURDAY, 7 SEPTEMBER

THE HOURS OF FORTUNE

23–01	B	07–09	G	15–17	M
01–03	B	09–11	G	17–19	M
03–05	B	11–13	G	19–21	B
05–07	M	13–15	G	21–23	G

ADVICE FOR THE DAY

If you've been ill recently this is a positive time to ease back into your normal routine or to start a course of health treatment which should prove successful. If you're thinking of working at home concentrate on DIY particularly in the kitchen or bedroom.

WHAT TO AVOID TODAY

If you're gardening you should avoid planting trees, shrubs or seeds. Postpone creative plans until another day and be careful if you're using needles. Finally, this month ends with a warning not to invest money unless you fully trust your partners and feel secure with the terms of the agreement.

This is an unlucky day for anyone born in the following years of the Dog: 1922, 1934, 1946, 1958, 1970.

EIGHTH MONTH

*On the night of the brightest moon of the mid-autumn
festival, children parade through the streets with lanterns
that mirror the brilliance of the Harvest Moon.*

1ST DAY OF THE 8TH MONTH –
SUNDAY, 8 SEPTEMBER

The period known as 'Pei Lu' or 'White Dew', begins officially at 12.04 this afternoon. This is a traditional reminder in the agricultural calendar that heavy morning dews occur at this time of the year.

THE HOURS OF FORTUNE

23–01	M	07–09	M	15–17	M
01–03	B	09–11	G	17–19	B
03–05	B	11–13	G	19–21	G
05–07	M	13–15	G	21–23	B

ADVICE FOR THE DAY

This is an appropriate day for prayer or quiet reflection and you should try to put some time aside to think through worries that have been on your mind. Make the most of social opportunities that come your way and an unexpected meeting now could have a marked effect on your future. The gods of fortune are on your side if you're announcing an engagement, getting married, signing a contract or setting up in business. Now is the time to sort out financial problems and, if you are owed outstanding debts, now is the time to collect them. If you're planning to work at home you should put your energies into gardening or repairing electrical kitchen goods. The next two days are also suitable times to get rid of insects or vermin that may have infested your house or garden.

WHAT TO AVOID TODAY

If you've just been through a period of mourning or loss, give yourself more time to recover before you slip back into your normal routine. Journeys will be disrupted by delays or accidents today so don't travel more than necessary. You're advised to be careful if you're cooking, particularly if you're handling soups or making sauces.

This is a day of upheavals for anyone born in the following years of the Pig: 1923, 1935, 1947, 1959, 1971.

2ND DAY OF THE 8TH MONTH –
MONDAY, 9 SEPTEMBER

THE HOURS OF FORTUNE

23–01	B	07–09	M	15–17	B
01–03	B	09–11	G	17–19	M
03–05	G	11–13	M	19–21	M
05–07	B	13–15	G	21–23	G

ADVICE FOR THE DAY

You should pay some attention to your personal appearance since this is a favourable time to get your hair cut or to have other beauty treatments.

WHAT TO AVOID TODAY

There's misfortune associated with water so be careful whether you're going swimming, sailing, mending plumbing or even watering the garden.

Be prepared for problems in your domestic life if you were born in the following years of the Rat: 1924, 1936, 1948, 1960, 1972.

3RD DAY OF THE 8TH MONTH – TUESDAY, 10 SEPTEMBER

This is the birthday of the Kitchen God who protects and watches over the domestic affairs of each household. He remains in the kitchen until his effigy is burnt on the 24th night of the 12th month and then his spirit ascends to Heaven to report to the Jade Emperor.

THE HOURS OF FORTUNE

23–01	G	07–09	M	15–17	M
01–03	B	09–11	G	17–19	M
03–05	G	11–13	G	19–21	G
05–07	B	13–15	B	21–23	M

ADVICE FOR THE DAY

This is an ideal day for prayer or quiet reflection and you could find your personal worries resolved. You can set off on journeys, move to a new house, or begin an educational project with confidence. The future looks bright if you're getting married and if you're giving presents to others they are sure to be gratefully received. This should prove to be a satisfying day if you're working with animals and if you're considering spending time on DIY you should concentrate on structural repair work but avoid plastering.

WHAT TO AVOID TODAY

Stay well away from lawyers for the moment because you're likely to make a mistake that could have severe consequences in the future. You should also beware of an accident if you're digging land.

Be prepared for problems in your domestic life if you were born in the following years of the Ox: 1925, 1937, 1949, 1961, 1973.

4TH DAY OF THE 8TH MONTH – WEDNESDAY, 11 SEPTEMBER

THE HOURS OF FORTUNE

23–01	G		07–09	G		15–17	G
01–03	B		09–11	G		17–19	G
03–05	B		11–13	B		19–21	M
05–07	B		13–15	G		21–23	M

ADVICE FOR THE DAY

Travel arrangements that may have proved difficult in the past should be resolved now and you can set off on journeys with confidence. The future looks secure if you're getting married or setting up in business. If you have the money to spare it's an opportune day to treat yourself to new clothes or to have a haircut. If you've been thinking of carrying out minor repairs on the house or garden this is the day to do it. Finally, if someone close to you has recently died you should find the support and strength you need to cope with funeral arrangements.

WHAT TO AVOID TODAY

Handle money with care and don't be tempted to squander savings. If you have been saving food or drink for a special occasion, don't break into it now, you may need it for an unexpected visitor. Beware of an accident in your bedroom, and don't attempt to move furniture there.

Be prepared for disagreements throughout the day if you were born in the following years of the Tiger: 1926, 1938, 1950, 1962, 1974.

5TH DAY OF THE 8TH MONTH – THURSDAY, 12 SEPTEMBER

THE HOURS OF FORTUNE

23–01	G	07–09	G	15–17	G
01–03	B	09–11	B	17–19	G
03–05	G	11–13	M	19–21	M
05–07	B	13–15	M	21–23	M

ADVICE FOR THE DAY

The forecast is excellent for travel by land, sea or air, and the forecast for DIY is still positive. Find some time to unwind and the Almanac suggests that you treat yourself to a relaxing bath or sauna.

WHAT TO AVOID TODAY

There's the possibility of an accident for anyone who is planting or digging, so, if you're an enthusiastic gardener, have a rest from your hobby today.

Don't make commitments or take unnecessary risks now if you were born in the following years of the Rabbit: 1927, 1939, 1951, 1963, 1975.

6TH DAY OF THE 8TH MONTH – FRIDAY, 13 SEPTEMBER

THE HOURS OF FORTUNE

23–01	G	07–09	B	15–17	G
01–03	B	09–11	G	17–19	G
03–05	G	11–13	M	19–21	G
05–07	B	13–15	M	21–23	G

ADVICE FOR THE DAY

Pay some attention to spiritual matters and don't be afraid to ask others for support or advice. If you've been through a difficult emotional period you should come to terms with the past and look forward to the future. There are good career possibilities in store if you're starting a new job or initiating a new business venture. If you've been ill recently this is a good day for recovery, and if you're thinking of taking health treatments they should prove to be very successful. Anyone working with animals or planning to spend time gardening can expect a satisfying day.

WHAT TO AVOID TODAY

Spend as little time as possible in your kitchen, don't attempt to fix faulty electrical goods, and handle crockery and hot pans with care.

This is a day of disagreements and delays for anyone born in the following years of the Dragon: 1928, 1940, 1952, 1964, 1976.

7TH DAY OF THE 8TH MONTH –
SATURDAY, 14 SEPTEMBER

THE HOURS OF FORTUNE

23–01	M	07–09	M	15–17	M
01–03	B	09–11	B	17–19	G
03–05	G	11–13	G	19–21	G
05–07	B	13–15	G	21–23	G

ADVICE FOR THE DAY

The financial prospects are excellent if you're thinking of

setting up in business. The forecast for legal affairs is also excellent and you can sign contracts with confidence. You can feel secure that you're doing the right thing if you're lending money. Now is the time to have acupuncture or other medical treatments for they should prove to be effective. Finally, it's a good opportunity to mend furnishings or carry out repair work around the house.

WHAT TO AVOID TODAY

The future looks bleak if you're getting married now, so try to postpone your arrangements until the 12th day of this month. This is also an inappropriate time to get a haircut, so if you did have an appointment you should at least wait until tomorrow.

This is an unlucky day for anyone born in the following years of the Snake: 1929, 1941, 1953, 1965, 1977.

8TH DAY OF THE 8TH MONTH – SUNDAY, 15 SEPTEMBER

THE HOURS OF FORTUNE

23–01	M	07–09	G	15–17	G
01–03	B	09–11	G	17–19	G
03–05	B	11–13	B	19–21	M
05–07	B	13–15	M	21–23	M

ADVICE FOR THE DAY

Concentrate on manual work since the forecast is excellent for maintenance work around the house and garden.

WHAT TO AVOID TODAY

If you're thinking of buying property make sure that you

266

have been given sufficient background details before you agree to the sale. You should also avoid asking others for help or advice; their reply may not be welcome.

This is a day of upheavals for anyone born in the following years of the Horse: 1930, 1942, 1954, 1966, 1978.

9TH DAY OF THE 8TH MONTH – MONDAY, 16 SEPTEMBER

THE HOURS OF FORTUNE

23–01	G	07–09	M	15–17	G
01–03	B	09–11	G	17–19	G
03–05	G	11–13	M	19–21	M
05–07	B	13–15	B	21–23	B

ADVICE FOR THE DAY

Since this is a broken day within the year, you should put some time aside to deal with personal or spiritual matters. On a practical note, this is an appropriate time to carry out minor demolition work or clear away rubble.

WHAT TO AVOID TODAY

This is an unlucky day for builders or anyone attempting construction work. You should also avoid planting, buying or arranging flowers.

This is a day of setbacks and quarrels for anyone born in the following years of the Ram: 1919, 1931, 1943, 1955, 1967, 1979.

10TH DAY OF THE 8TH MONTH – TUESDAY, 17 SEPTEMBER

THE HOURS OF FORTUNE

23–01	B	07–09	G	15–17	B
01–03	B	09–11	M	17–19	M
03–05	G	11–13	G	19–21	B
05–07	B	13–15	M	21–23	M

ADVICE FOR THE DAY

Educational projects should prove to be successful and if you've been thinking about further education you should make a firm decision now. Journeys by land, sea or air are blessed by good fortune and the gods of fortune are also on your side if you're announcing an engagement. The bad luck associated with building work has now changed direction and you can expect a successful day if you're making alterations or building extensions. The day's forecast ends with a word of encouragement for anyone making funeral arrangements: the support of others will help to carry you through this period.

WHAT TO AVOID TODAY

Although this is a suitable day to concentrate on funeral arrangements, this is not the right time to reflect on your spiritual well-being or to mull over problems.

This is an unlucky day for anyone born in the following years of the Monkey: 1920, 1932, 1944, 1956, 1968, 1980.

11TH DAY OF THE 8TH MONTH –
WEDNESDAY, 18 SEPTEMBER

THE HOURS OF FORTUNE

23–01	M		07–09	M		15–17	M
01–03	B		09–11	G		17–19	B
03–05	G		11–13	G		19–21	G
05–07	B		13–15	M		21–23	M

ADVICE FOR THE DAY

This is a broken day within the month and is a positive day for demolition workers or for anyone planning to knock down old walls or dilapidated buildings.

WHAT TO AVOID TODAY

Beware of an accident in the kitchen when you're handling liquids and avoid making soups or sauces. You should also drink alcohol in moderation, if at all, because you may regret your words or actions tomorrow.

This is a day of upheavals for anyone born in the following years of the Cock: 1921, 1933, 1945, 1957, 1969.

12TH DAY OF THE 8TH MONTH –
THURSDAY, 19 SEPTEMBER

THE HOURS OF FORTUNE

23–01	M		07–09	M		15–17	B
01–03	B		09–11	G		17–19	G
03–05	G		11–13	M		19–21	B
05–07	B		13–15	M		21–23	G

ADVICE FOR THE DAY

Luck is on your side today and tomorrow if you're beginning a new educational project, opening a business, or getting married. Journeys are likely to pass off smoothly and punctually and, if you're thinking of making holiday arrangements, now is the time to do it. If you have time on your hands you should channel your energy into gardening or general DIY, particularly in the bedroom. If a friend or relative has just died this is an appropriate time to make funeral arrangements or to attend a funeral.

WHAT TO AVOID TODAY

Be careful of an accident if you're working near or handling water and don't attempt to mend drains or gutters – call in an expert instead.

Be prepared for problems in your personal life if you were born in the following years of the Dog: 1922, 1934, 1946, 1958, 1970.

13TH DAY OF THE 8TH MONTH – FRIDAY, 20 SEPTEMBER

THE HOURS OF FORTUNE

23–01	G	07–09	G	15–17	G
01–03	B	09–11	G	17–19	M
03–05	M	11–13	M	19–21	G
05–07	B	13–15	B	21–23	B

ADVICE FOR THE DAY

This is an ideal day for religious ceremony, prayer or quiet reflection. This is likely to be a day free of delays and breakages if you're moving to a new house or emigrating. Make the most of parties or dinners that come your way because you could be in for a welcome reunion. If you need to buy presents for friends you should find exactly what you need and your gifts will be gratefully received. The financial forecast is excellent for anyone buying or selling goods, and it's a safe time to commit yourself to contracts. Anyone working with animals or concentrating on DIY should be more than satisfied with their efforts by the end of the day. Finally, it's a suitable day to buy alcohol or to brew your own.

WHAT TO AVOID TODAY

Although this is a safe day to sign contracts you should think twice before you initiate legal action. Local journeys could be hit by delays so don't travel more than you have to. If you've been through a period of upheaval, don't push yourself too far, you may need more time to recover than you think.

This is an unlucky day for anyone born in the following years of the Pig: 1923, 1935, 1947, 1959, 1971.

14TH DAY OF THE 8TH MONTH – SATURDAY, 21 SEPTEMBER

THE HOURS OF FORTUNE

23–01	B	07–09	M	15–17	M
01–03	B	09–11	M	17–19	G
03–05	G	11–13	B	19–21	M
05–07	B	13–15	G	21–23	M

ADVICE FOR THE DAY

This is an excellent time for reflection or prayer and you could find that your requests are unexpectedly answered. Lucky stars are shining on you if you're getting married and you can look forward to a secure relationship. If you've been thinking of getting your hair cut now is the time to make an appointment and, on a more mundane note, lay down traps or repellent if you've been troubled by insects or vermin.

WHAT TO AVOID TODAY

Handle your finances carefully and don't be tempted to waste money on unnecessary luxuries. You should even think twice before you lend money to friends. You should also avoid using up food or drink that you may have been saving for a special occasion.

Don't take unnecessary risks now if you were born in the following years of the Rat: 1924, 1936, 1948, 1960, 1972.

15TH DAY OF THE 8TH MONTH – SUNDAY, 22 SEPTEMBER

This is the festival of Tai Yin, the day when the moon is at its brightest and the mid-autumn festival can begin. Offerings are made to the Moon Goddess throughout the day and the celebrations continue into the night, when the streets are thronged with children and adults carrying lanterns.

THE HOURS OF FORTUNE

23–01	G	07–09	M	15–17	G
01–03	B	09–11	B	17–19	M
03–05	G	11–13	M	19–21	G
05–07	B	13–15	M	21–23	G

ADVICE FOR THE DAY

Since this is the day preceding Ch'iu Fen, the festival of the Monkey King, you should give your house a thorough clean. This is a way of sweeping away the misfortune that may have accumulated during the past months. You should also try to find some time for prayer or reflection.

WHAT TO AVOID TODAY

According to the Almanac this is an unlucky day to begin or end a period of mourning. You should also beware of an accident if you're digging earth or if you're planting trees, plants or seeds.

This is a day of arguments and setbacks for anyone born in the following years of the Ox: 1925, 1937, 1949, 1961, 1973.

16TH DAY OF THE 8TH MONTH – MONDAY, 23 SEPTEMBER

Celebrations are held today in commemoration of the Monkey King who has a role as a trickster and guardian of justice. According to legend, he was born from stone and gained access to Heaven through trickery. Once in Heaven, he caused havoc amongst the residents. After many adventures he was expelled from Heaven and was eventually redeemed through Buddhist teachings.

273

THE HOURS OF FORTUNE

23–01	G	07–09	B	15–17	G
01–03	B	09–11	G	17–19	G
03–05	B	11–13	M	19–21	G
05–07	B	13–15	G	21–23	G

ADVICE FOR THE DAY

Now is the time to concentrate on your personal appearance and on domestic matters. Put your energy into cleaning the house or into mending woodwork. But you should also find some time for yourself to relax and treat yourself to a little luxury. On a more sombre note, this is an appropriate time to arrange or attend a funeral.

WHAT TO AVOID TODAY

Don't arrange to get your hair cut, you're likely to be disappointed with the result. If you're a keen gardener you should avoid digging or lifting earth.

This is an unlucky day for anyone born in the following years of the Tiger: 1926, 1938, 1950, 1962, 1974.

17TH DAY OF THE 8TH MONTH – TUESDAY, 24 SEPTEMBER

THE HOURS OF FORTUNE

23–01	M	07–09	M	15–17	M
01–03	B	09–11	M	17–19	G
03–05	M	11–13	G	19–21	M
05–07	B	13–15	G	21–23	G

ADVICE FOR THE DAY

Today's advice focuses on domestic matters. It's an ideal

day to give your house a thorough clean or to turn your attention to carpentry. You should also try to find time to relax with a sauna or hot bath. On a sadder note, this is an appropriate time to arrange or attend a funeral.

WHAT TO AVOID TODAY

To avoid disappointment, postpone having your hair cut until tomorrow. Anyone working in the garden should beware of accidents if they're digging or moving earth.

You're likely to encounter problems throughout the day if you were born in the following years of the Rabbit: 1927, 1939, 1951, 1963, 1975.

18TH DAY OF THE 8TH MONTH – WEDNESDAY, 25 SEPTEMBER

THE HOURS OF FORTUNE

23–01	M	07–09	B	15–17	G
01–03	B	09–11	M	17–19	M
03–05	B	11–13	G	19–21	M
05–07	B	13–15	G	21–23	M

ADVICE FOR THE DAY

This is a demanding and successful day for anyone beginning a new job, travelling at home or abroad or working in the construction industry. It's an opportune time for prayer or worship and give yourself time to work through worries that have been on your mind. If you've been ill, don't be afraid to consult a doctor or other health practitioner, you should be reassured by their advice. Once again it's an ideal day for cleaning the house, gardening, buying or moving bedroom furniture and for repairing electrical goods in your kitchen. It's also important that you find time to relax and don't feel guilty about pampering yourself.

WHAT TO AVOID TODAY

You're likely to make a bad investment if you buy property now. Give yourself a few more days to consider your decision. This is also an unlucky day for funerals or for mourning so try to keep yourself busy with day-to-day demands.

Don't make any binding commitments now if you were born in the following years of the Dragon: 1928, 1940, 1952, 1964, 1976.

19TH DAY OF THE 8TH MONTH – THURSDAY, 26 SEPTEMBER

THE HOURS OF FORTUNE

23–01	G	07–09	M	15–17	G
01–03	B	09–11	B	17–19	M
03–05	G	11–13	G	19–21	M
05–07	B	13–15	G	21–23	B

ADVICE FOR THE DAY

The gods of fortune are still on your side if you're travelling, moving house or emigrating. Don't be afraid to take legal action, the outcome should be in your favour. It's a promising day to shop for clothes or food and if you've been saving food or drink for a special occasion you should treat yourself to it now. If you've been thinking of going to see an acupuncturist, do so today and the results should be beneficial. The rest of the day's advice focuses on domestic matters and you should take this opportunity to garden or to carry out structural repair work around the house.

WHAT TO AVOID TODAY

Don't make wedding plans or marry today. This is also an unlucky day to end a period of mourning. Wait a few days more before you return to your normal routine.

Be prepared for problems in your domestic life if you were born in the following years of the Snake: 1929, 1941, 1953, 1965, 1977.

20TH DAY OF THE 8TH MONTH – FRIDAY, 27 SEPTEMBER

THE HOURS OF FORTUNE

23–01	B	07–09	M	15–17	G
01–03	B	09–11	M	17–19	G
03–05	M	11–13	B	19–21	B
05–07	B	13–15	G	21–23	M

ADVICE FOR THE DAY

The day's advice is given over completely to practical domestic matters. You should channel your energy into maintenance work around the house and into painting and decorating inside.

WHAT TO AVOID TODAY

Beware of an accident in the kitchen if you're cooking, and make sure that you handle pans and crockery with care.

You should also beware of an accident if you're sewing or mending furnishings.

This is a day of delays and disagreements for anyone born in the following years of the Horse: 1930, 1942, 1954, 1966, 1978.

21ST DAY OF THE 8TH MONTH – SATURDAY, 28 SEPTEMBER

THE HOURS OF FORTUNE

23–01	M	07–09	M	15–17	G
01–03	B	09–11	G	17–19	B
03–05	G	11–13	G	19–21	M
05–07	B	13–15	B	21–23	G

ADVICE FOR THE DAY

Since this is a broken day within the year you should try to spend some time cleaning your house and clearing out cupboards. If you've been planning to have your hair cut this is an appropriate day to make an appointment. But this is also a day to focus on spiritual matters and problems that have been on your mind may well be resolved now.

WHAT TO AVOID TODAY

Handle liquids with care, particularly if you're drinking alcohol or making soups and sauces. If someone close to you has died recently or if you have been through a period of upheaval, don't dwell on your loss — try to keep busy with day-to-day practical matters.

Be prepared for the unexpected now if you were born in

the following years of the Ram: 1931, 1943, 1955, 1967, 1979.

22ND DAY OF THE 8TH MONTH – SUNDAY, 29 SEPTEMBER

THE HOURS OF FORTUNE

23–01	M	07–09	M	15–17	B
01–03	B	09–11	M	17–19	M
03–05	G	11–13	M	19–21	G
05–07	B	13–15	G	21–23	M

ADVICE FOR THE DAY

Educational projects are blessed by good fortune and you can look forward to positive results from your efforts if you're beginning a full- or part-time course now. Lucky stars are shining on anyone who is on the move so you can travel as far afield as you like. Don't hesitate to accept social invitations, they could prove to be more interesting than you thought. There's an excellent reading for gardeners, builders and DIY enthusiasts.

WHAT TO AVOID TODAY

Don't attempt to mend plumbing problems today, however small; call in an expert instead. With the exception of funerals you should avoid religious ceremonies for the moment. Concentrate on practical matters instead.

This is an unlucky day for anyone born in the following years of the Monkey: 1920, 1932, 1944, 1956, 1968, 1980.

23RD DAY OF THE 8TH MONTH –
MONDAY, 30 SEPTEMBER

THE HOURS OF FORTUNE

23–01	G	07–09	M	15–17	M
01–03	B	09–11	M	17–19	B
03–05	G	11–13	M	19–21	G
05–07	B	13–15	B	21–23	M

ADVICE FOR THE DAY

Since this is a broken day within the month you should try to clear away rubble or rubbish and if there is masonry that needs knocking down, now is the time to do it. This is also an excellent time to consider your health, so don't be afraid to visit a doctor or to start a course of medical treatment.

WHAT TO AVOID TODAY

Legal affairs are marred by difficulties now so don't take risks unless you are sure of your facts. You should also beware of an accident if you're gardening, particularly if you're digging.

Personal problems may come to the fore now if you were born in the following years of the Cock: 1921, 1933, 1945, 1957, 1969.

24TH DAY OF THE 8TH MONTH –
TUESDAY, 1 OCTOBER

THE HOURS OF FORTUNE

23–01	G	07–09	G	15–17	M
01–03	B	09–11	M	17–19	G
03–05	M	11–13	B	19–21	B
05–07	B	13–15	G	21–23	G

ADVICE FOR THE DAY

This is an excellent day for religious ceremony or prayer: you could find that your requests are unexpectedly answered. If you're celebrating this is the right time to give or receive presents. Shopkeepers and anyone else involved in trade can look forward to a profitable day's business, and if you're committing yourself to a contract you should feel confident in your decision.

WHAT TO AVOID TODAY

Try to be thrifty today and don't be tempted to waste your money on unnecessary luxuries. You're also advised not to lend money even to friends.

This is an unlucky day for anyone born in the following years of the Dog: 1922, 1934, 1946, 1958, 1970.

25TH DAY OF THE 8TH MONTH –
WEDNESDAY, 2 OCTOBER

This is the festival of Tai Yang, the sun festival. Yin and yang are the two forces that keep the universe in balance. Yin is cold, moist and dark, yang is hot, fiery and light.

Since this is the day to remember the forces of yang, the power of the sun is particularly celebrated.

THE HOURS OF FORTUNE

23–01	G	07–09	M	15–17	G
01–03	B	09–11	B	17–19	G
03–05	M	11–13	M	19–21	G
05–07	B	13–15	M	21–23	B

ADVICE FOR THE DAY

Give yourself time to sort out personal problems; if you put time aside for prayer or reflection you could find peace of mind. Be careful not to neglect your health and if you are feeling ill you should visit a doctor now; the diagnosis may not be as bad as you expected. If you have been through a period of illness this is a positive day for recovery and you can begin to re-adjust to your normal routine.

WHAT TO AVOID TODAY

Journeys are likely to be plagued by delays and accidents now so don't travel unless it is necessary. If you were planning to garden you should postpone planting until another day.

Your plans may not work out as you expected today if you were born in the following years of the Pig: 1923, 1935, 1947, 1959, 1971.

26TH DAY OF THE 8TH MONTH – THURSDAY, 3 OCTOBER

THE HOURS OF FORTUNE

23–01	B	07–09	B	15–17	G
01–03	B	09–11	G	17–19	G
03–05	M	11–13	G	19–21	G
05–07	B	13–15	M	21–23	G

ADVICE FOR THE DAY

The gods of fortune are on your side if you're getting married now and you can look forward to a secure future. This is also a positive day to attend to health matters or to start a course of medical treatment. Hunters and fishermen can expect a successful day's catch today but, on a more mundane note, this is the right time to lay down traps or insect repellent if you've been troubled by insects or vermin.

WHAT TO AVOID TODAY

Beware of an accident in the kitchen and don't attempt to repair electrical goods.

This is a day of delays and disagreements if you were born in the following years of the Rat: 1924, 1936, 1948, 1960, 1972.

27TH DAY OF THE 8TH MONTH – FRIDAY, 4 OCTOBER

Today Chinese people remember the birthday of Confucius, or K'ung Fu-tzu (551–479 BC). During his life he had a varied career as government official, minister and teacher, but it is for his writings that he is now remembered. He believed that obedience and filial duty were the cornerstones of a successful society and he taught a way of life based on concepts of duty and responsibility.

THE HOURS OF FORTUNE

23–01	M	07–09	M	15–17	M
01–03	B	09–11	G	17–19	G
03–05	M	11–13	G	19–21	M
05–07	B	13–15	G	21–23	G

ADVICE FOR THE DAY

If you've been waiting for exam results you may hear good news and now is the time to make a decision if you're thinking of starting a new educational course. Lucky stars are shining on you if you're on the move so you can set off on journeys at home or abroad with confidence. You can look forward to a secure future if you're announcing an engagement and if you're celebrating this is a good time to give and receive presents. If repair work is needed on the ceilings, roof or walls of your house you should call in an expert today or tomorrow before it is too late. Finally, this should prove to be a successful day for anyone working with animals.

WHAT TO AVOID TODAY

If you're thinking of having your hair cut, wait until tomorrow to avoid disappointment. Gardeners are also advised to have a rest from their hobby to avoid accident.

Be prepared for problems in your domestic life if you were born in the following years of the Ox: 1925, 1937, 1949, 1961, 1973.

30TH DAY OF THE 8TH MONTH – MONDAY, 7 OCTOBER

THE HOURS OF FORTUNE

23–01	B	07–09	B	15–17	G
01–03	B	09–11	M	17–19	M
03–05	M	11–13	G	19–21	B
05–07	B	13–15	G	21–23	M

ADVICE FOR THE DAY

Don't hesitate to accept social invitations, you could be in for an unexpected romantic surprise. This is also an appropriate time to renew contact with old friends. If you're on the move to a new house or country or setting off on a holiday you can expect a safe journey. Lucky stars are shining on anyone who is announcing an engagement or getting married and it's a perfect time to give or receive presents. Career prospects are excellent for anyone who is beginning a new job and promotion may come your way sooner than you expected. If you're owed money this is an appropriate time to retrieve your debts. On the domestic front, it's the right time to turn your attention to DIY, gardening or caring for pets. The day's advice ends with a word of support for anyone who is arranging or attending a funeral, but it is an unlucky time to begin a period of mourning.

WHAT TO AVOID TODAY

Avoid work that involves using needles and you're particularly warned against darning, weaving or sewing.

This is an unlucky day for anyone born in the following years of the Dragon: 1928, 1940, 1952, 1964, 1976.

NINTH MONTH

In the ninth month of the year Chinese families climb to the summit of the highest nearby hill in remembrance of a family saved from death by one of the Immortals.

1ST DAY OF THE 9TH MONTH – TUESDAY, 8 OCTOBER

THE HOURS OF FORTUNE

23–01	M	07–09	M	15–17	M
01–03	B	09–11	B	17–19	B
03–05	G	11–13	G	19–21	G
05–07	B	13–15	G	21–23	M

ADVICE FOR THE DAY

The month starts off on an encouraging note for anyone travelling by land, sea or air. You can also feel secure that you have made the right decision if you're moving to a new house or emigrating. This is an opportune day to initiate new ventures in your career or in your personal life. There's generally a good forecast for buying clothes, mending home furnishings and for manual work whether it's creative or practical.

WHAT TO AVOID TODAY

To avoid arguments in the months ahead, try to postpone wedding plans until the 8th day of this month. Be careful that you don't scald or cut yourself if you're cooking and don't consume too much alcohol at the moment – there could be painful consequences.

This is a day of upheaval and disappointment for anyone born during the following years of the Snake: 1929, 1941, 1953, 1965, 1977.

2ND DAY OF THE 9TH MONTH –
WEDNESDAY, 9 OCTOBER

The period known as Han Lu begins at 3.28 this morning. This time of the year is also known as 'deep autumn' and it is a traditional reminder that heavy dews appear at this time of the year, a sign of the oncoming winter.

THE HOURS OF FORTUNE

23–01	G	07–09	B	15–17	B
01–03	B	09–11	G	17–19	M
03–05	G	11–13	B	19–21	M
05–07	G	13–15	G	21–23	M

ADVICE FOR THE DAY

Lucky stars are still shining on you if you're on the move. Your career prospects are excellent if you're starting a new educational course and the prospects are good for anyone beginning a romance or meeting new friends. Sports enthusiasts can expect an enjoyable day and anglers in particular can expect a good catch. Try to put some time aside now to pamper yourself with a sauna, haircut or other beauty treatment. If someone close to you has recently died or you've been through a period of loss, you should make the necessary arrangements now or simply give yourself time for reflection or mourning.

WHAT TO AVOID TODAY

It's a bad time to ask others for help or advice; you may hear some unwelcome suggestions. You should also handle water carefully, and don't attempt to mend plumbing problems yourself.

Don't take unnecessary risks now if you were born in the

following years of the Horse: 1918, 1930, 1942, 1954, 1966, 1978.

3RD DAY OF THE 9TH MONTH – THURSDAY, 10 OCTOBER

THE HOURS OF FORTUNE

23–01	G	07–09	B	15–17	G
01–03	B	09–11	G	17–19	G
03–05	M	11–13	M	19–21	G
05–07	M	13–15	B	21–23	M

ADVICE FOR THE DAY

Don't make important plans or commitments because this is a broken day within the year. You should turn your attention to clearing away rubble or debris around the house or garden.

WHAT TO AVOID TODAY

Legal affairs are likely to be beset by disappointments so check your facts before you commit yourself. Anyone planning a fishing trip should postpone it for a few days to avoid accident.

This is a day of unexpected personal problems for anyone born in the following years of the Ram: 1919, 1931, 1943, 1955, 1967, 1979.

4TH DAY OF THE 9TH MONTH – FRIDAY, 11 OCTOBER

THE HOURS OF FORTUNE

23–01	M	07–09	B	15–17	B
01–03	B	09–11	M	17–19	G
03–05	G	11–13	B	19–21	G
05–07	M	13–15	G	21–23	M

ADVICE FOR THE DAY

Don't turn down social invitations because you could be in for an unexpected and pleasant surprise. If you have been delaying painting and decorating around the house now is the time to do it. You should also turn your attention to carpentry that needs completing. On a more sombre note, today and tomorrow are appropriate days to arrange or attend a funeral.

WHAT TO AVOID TODAY

If you're wearing jewellery, make sure that it is securely fastened and if you're thinking of buying jewellery don't be persuaded to buy something beyond your means. Try to restrain yourself if you're tempted to break into food or drink supplies that you've been saving for a special occasion – you may need it sooner than you think. Finally, this is an inappropriate time for personal reflection; concentrate on practical matters instead.

Don't expect plans to work out as you expected if you were born in the following years of the Monkey: 1920, 1932, 1944, 1956, 1968, 1980.

5TH DAY OF THE 9TH MONTH –
SATURDAY, 12 OCTOBER

THE HOURS OF FORTUNE

23–01	M	07–09	B	15–17	G
01–03	B	09–11	B	17–19	B
03–05	G	11–13	M	19–21	G
05–07	G	13–15	G	21–23	G

ADVICE FOR THE DAY

Now is the time to reflect on personal matters or to ask others for advice; don't be afraid to let your feelings show. If you've been planning to buy new clothes, choose some now and you won't be disappointed with your choice.

This is an excellent day for domestic matters, whether you're thinking of doing anything from mending torn furnishings to building an extension. If you're planning to have medical treatment it should prove to be effective.

WHAT TO AVOID TODAY

There's misfortune associated with water so avoid going swimming and don't attempt to repair or build anything involving water. Gardeners should also avoid planting seeds, shrubs or trees; whatever you plant is unlikely to take root today.

This is a day of delays and disagreements for anyone born in the following years of the Cock: 1921, 1933, 1945, 1957, 1969.

6TH DAY OF THE 9TH MONTH – SUNDAY, 13 OCTOBER

THE HOURS OF FORTUNE

23–01	M	07–09	B	15–17	G
01–03	B	09–11	G	17–19	G
03–05	M	11–13	M	19–21	B
05–07	M	13–15	M	21–23	G

ADVICE FOR THE DAY

Since this is a broken day within the month it is best suited to minor demolition work and to clearing away debris or rubbish.

WHAT TO AVOID TODAY

Handle hot pans and kitchen utensils with care because there is likely to be an accident in or near the cooker. You should also avoid repairing electrical kitchen goods.

This is an unlucky day for anyone born in the following years of the Dog: 1922, 1934, 1946, 1958, 1970.

7TH DAY OF THE 9TH MONTH – MONDAY, 14 OCTOBER

THE HOURS OF FORTUNE

23–01	M	07–09	B	15–17	M
01–03	B	09–11	G	17–19	G
03–05	M	11–13	G	19–21	G
05–07	B	13–15	G	21–23	B

ADVICE FOR THE DAY

Lucky stars are shining on you if you're announcing an engagement and you shouldn't let social opportunities slip by because a chance meeting could have a positive effect on your future. On a sadder note, this is a suitable time to make funeral arrangements if someone close to you has recently died.

WHAT TO AVOID TODAY

If you are thinking of getting your hair cut wait until tomorrow and you won't be disappointed with the results. Try to avoid making long and unnecessary journeys because travel will be plagued by delays throughout the day.

Be prepared for a day of disappointments for anyone born in the following years of the Pig: 1923, 1935, 1947, 1959, 1971.

8TH DAY OF THE 9TH MONTH – TUESDAY, 15 OCTOBER

THE HOURS OF FORTUNE

23–01	B	07–09	B	15–17	G
01–03	B	09–11	G	17–19	G
03–05	B	11–13	M	19–21	M
05–07	G	13–15	G	21–23	M

ADVICE FOR THE DAY

Try to renew contact with old friends or make new ones; it will be worth the effort. If you're waiting for exam results you're likely to hear good news, and the prospects are bright if you're beginning a new educational course. You can travel with confidence whether you're going on holiday or moving to a new house. The forecast is excellent if you're announcing an engagement or getting married and now is the time to give or receive presents. If you feel like turning your attention to practical matters, this is a promising day for building, gardening and general maintenance, including electrical repair work, around the house.

WHAT TO AVOID TODAY

Make sure that you have taken sufficient professional or safety advice before you launch into new projects, and if you're thinking of buying property, wait until tomorrow before you make a final decision. If you have recently had problems in your personal life you should try to put them behind you and concentrate on the future.

Personal problems may come to the fore now if you were born in the following years of the Rat: 1924, 1936, 1948, 1960, 1972.

9TH DAY OF THE 9TH MONTH – WEDNESDAY, 16 OCTOBER

Today is known as the Double Nine Festival since it always falls on the 9th day of the 9th month. It commemorates the story of a family who met an immortal upon a lonely road near their house. The immortal gathered the family around him and told them to climb the highest mountain in that area on the 9th day of the 9th month. Then he disappeared. When the day arrived the family did as they had been told: they climbed the highest hill in that area. Just as they reached the top a

297

river broke its banks and the water came flooding through the valley, drowning everyone except the family who had followed the immortal's advice. In memory of this event, each year on this day families celebrate with a picnic on the highest hill or mountain near their home.

THE HOURS OF FORTUNE

23–01	M	07–09	B	15–17	G
01–03	B	09–11	G	17–19	M
03–05	G	11–13	G	19–21	M
05–07	G	13–15	G	21–23	G

ADVICE FOR THE DAY

This is an unlucky day for animals since the Almanac gives a positive forecast to hunters or to anyone who is planning to get rid of insects, slugs, mosquitoes or vermin that have infested the house or garden.

WHAT TO AVOID TODAY

Don't cut yourself off from the world if you have personal worries on your mind, try to face up to day-to-day demands. If you have recently been bereaved this is not the right time to make funeral arrangements, wait until tomorrow.

This is a day of setbacks and disappointments for anyone born in the following years of the Ox: 1925, 1937, 1949, 1961, 1973.

10TH DAY OF THE 9TH MONTH –
THURSDAY, 17 OCTOBER

THE HOURS OF FORTUNE

23–01	B	07–09	B	15–17	G
01–03	B	09–11	G	17–19	M
03–05	B	11–13	G	19–21	B
05–07	M	13–15	G	21–23	M

ADVICE FOR THE DAY

This is an ideal day for prayer, worship or quiet reflection. If you've been thinking about taking up an evening course or a full-time educational course, you should make a final decision now. The gods of fortune are on your side if you're travelling by land, sea or air so you can journey as far afield as you like. Business dealings should pass off smoothly and it's a profitable day for traders and anyone setting up in business. Now is the time to stock up on food supplies or to concentrate on gardening or DIY but avoid maintenance work in the bedroom. Don't forget to pay attention to your personal appearance and now is the time to have your hair cut or arrange for other beauty treatments.

WHAT TO AVOID TODAY

This is not an appropriate time to be creative, particularly if you were thinking of making or designing clothes. You should also beware of an accident if you're using needles or heavy sports equipment.

This could be a day of unhappiness and arguments for anyone born in the following years of the Tiger: 1926, 1938, 1950, 1962, 1974.

11TH DAY OF THE 9TH MONTH – FRIDAY, 18 OCTOBER

THE HOURS OF FORTUNE

23–01	M	07–09	B	15–17	M
01–03	B	09–11	G	17–19	B
03–05	G	11–13	G	19–21	M
05–07	B	13–15	M	21–23	M

ADVICE FOR THE DAY

Try to put some time aside for reflection or prayer and you could find that your worries are resolved or your requests are answered. There's still good fortune associated with business negotiations, travel and general house-cleaning and DIY. Once again you should find time to pamper yourself and to take care of your personal appearance. If you're working with animals or thinking of buying a pet, this should prove to be a satisfying day. If you've been through a period of mourning or emotional trauma this would be a reasonable time to face reality and make plans for the future.

WHAT TO AVOID TODAY

Avoid visiting an acupuncturist or other health practitioner; your treatment is likely to be more effective if you wait until later in the week. You should also beware of an accident in the kitchen if you're making soups or sauces, brewing or consuming alcohol.

Personal problems could come to the fore now if you were born in the following years of the Rabbit: 1927, 1939, 1951, 1963, 1975.

12TH DAY OF THE 9TH MONTH –
SATURDAY, 19 OCTOBER

THE HOURS OF FORTUNE

23–01	M	07–09	B	15–17	B
01–03	B	09–11	G	17–19	M
03–05	G	11–13	M	19–21	G
05–07	G	13–15	G	21–23	G

ADVICE FOR THE DAY

There is still a positive forecast for spiritual matters and
for travel. The gods of fortune are on your side if you're
announcing an engagement and you could be in for an
unexpected and welcome surprise if you're meeting
friends. These next two days are good opportunities to
begin a period of convalescence or to recover from illness.
Time at home could be well spent on DIY or on clearing
out cupboards.

WHAT TO AVOID TODAY

Make sure that you have taken precautions and advice if
you are launching new projects and avoid taking unnecessary risks. If you are responsible for making funeral
arrangements or contacting anyone who has been through
a period of upheaval, wait at least another day before you
take action.

Be prepared for emotional upheavals throughout the day if
you were born in the following years of the Dragon: 1928,
1940, 1952, 1964, 1976.

13TH DAY OF THE 9TH MONTH –
SUNDAY, 20 OCTOBER

THE HOURS OF FORTUNE

23–01	M	07–09	B	15–17	M
01–03	B	09–11	B	17–19	M
03–05	G	11–13	G	19–21	G
05–07	G	13–15	B	21–23	G

ADVICE FOR THE DAY

The good fortune associated with spiritual matters, social affairs, travel and finance is still in the air. The future looks bright if you are on the move to a new house or to a new country and you are unlikely to regret your decision. On a more mundane note, now is the time to lay down traps or repellent if you've been plagued by insects, mosquitoes or vermin.

WHAT TO AVOID TODAY

Unless you're prepared for arguments in the months to come you should postpone wedding arrangements until the 17th day of this month. The Almanac also advises you to avoid digging or ploughing today so if you were thinking of gardening, have a rest instead.

This is an unlucky day for anyone born in the following years of the Snake: 1929, 1941, 1953, 1965, 1977.

14TH DAY OF THE 9TH MONTH – MONDAY, 21 OCTOBER

THE HOURS OF FORTUNE

23–01	G	07–09	B	15–17	G
01–03	B	09–11	M	17–19	M
03–05	G	11–13	B	19–21	M
05–07	M	13–15	G	21–23	M

ADVICE FOR THE DAY

If you have personal problems on your mind put some time aside today to get to the root of them but if you have already been through a period of personal upheaval this is a positive time to face the world again. Make the most of social invitations since this is an opportune time to meet and make friends or to begin a romance. Educational projects and travel at home or abroad should run smoothly and if you're owed outstanding debts, now is the time to collect them. This is also an appropriate day to care for animals or to work on masonry.

WHAT TO AVOID TODAY

Don't be tempted to break into food or drink that you have been saving for a special occasion and don't squander your money on unnecessary luxuries. You should avoid asking other people for advice about your future: you may get an unwelcome or upsetting reply.

This is a day of delays and disagreements for anyone born in the following years of the Horse: 1930, 1942, 1954, 1966, 1978.

15TH DAY OF THE 9TH MONTH – TUESDAY, 22 OCTOBER

THE HOURS OF FORTUNE

23–01	G	07–09	B	15–17	G
01–03	B	09–11	B	17–19	M
03–05	G	11–13	M	19–21	M
05–07	G	13–15	B	21–23	M

ADVICE FOR THE DAY

Since this is a broken day within the year you should put your energies into knocking down old walls or sheds and into clearing away rubble or rubbish.

WHAT TO AVOID TODAY

This is an unlucky day for anything connected with plants or flowers so it's best not to garden, buy or arrange flowers.

This is an unlucky day for anyone born in the following years of the Ram: 1931, 1943, 1955, 1967, 1979.

16TH DAY OF THE 9TH MONTH – WEDNESDAY, 23 OCTOBER

THE HOURS OF FORTUNE

23–01	G	07–09	B	15–17	B
01–03	B	09–11	M	17–19	G
03–05	M	11–13	G	19–21	M
05–07	G	13–15	M	21–23	M

ADVICE FOR THE DAY

If you've been thinking of gardening, this is an ideal day to do it, particularly if you're digging or moving earth. If you've been through a period of loss or upheaval, put time aside to think through your worries or simply to recover. If you have recently been bereaved this is also a suitable time to arrange or attend a funeral.

WHAT TO AVOID TODAY

With the exception of funerals, you're advised to avoid all other religious ceremonies. On a more practical note, don't attempt to repair electrical kitchen goods, and handle hot pans or kitchen utensils with care.

Personal problems could come to the fore now if you were born in the following years of the Monkey: 1920, 1932, 1944, 1956, 1968, 1980.

17TH DAY OF THE 9TH MONTH – THURSDAY, 24 OCTOBER

Sheng Kan begins at 6.17 this morning. It is a reminder to farmers that the frosts of winter are on their way.

THE HOURS OF FORTUNE

23–01	M	07–09	B	15–17	M
01–03	B	09–11	M	17–19	B
03–05	G	11–13	G	19–21	M
05–07	B	13–15	G	21–23	G

ADVICE FOR THE DAY

Try to put some time aside now for worship or quiet

reflection. Anyone travelling at home or abroad can look forward to a safe and punctual journey, and if you have had difficulties finalizing travel plans they should be resolved now. This is an ideal day to announce an engagement, to get married, to meet new friends and to resolve romantic difficulties. There's an excellent forecast for gardening and general DIY and you should make the most of this opportunity to sort out domestic problems. Your plans should work out well if you're thinking of buying a new pet or if you're working with animals. Finally, it's a suitable time to reflect on personal difficulties, to begin a period of mourning or to attend a funeral.

WHAT TO AVOID TODAY

Beware of an accident if you're thinking of going swimming or if you're handling water. If you are planning to have your hair cut, wait until tomorrow to avoid disappointment.

This is an unlucky day for anyone born in the following years of the Cock: 1921, 1933, 1945, 1957, 1969.

18TH DAY OF THE 9TH MONTH – FRIDAY, 25 OCTOBER

THE HOURS OF FORTUNE

23–01	M	07–09	B	15–17	G
01–03	B	09–11	G	17–19	G
03–05	B	11–13	M	19–21	B
05–07	G	13–15	G	21–23	M

ADVICE FOR THE DAY

Since this is a broken day within the month you should

put your energies into clearing out rubbish or clearing away rubble and if you've been considering knocking down old masonry, sheds or walls, this is the day to do it.

WHAT TO AVOID TODAY

Be prepared for domestic problems if you were born in the following years of the Dog: 1922, 1934, 1946, 1958, 1970.

19TH DAY OF THE 9TH MONTH – SATURDAY, 26 OCTOBER

Kuan Yin's departure from earth and release from all earthly ties and desires is celebrated in Chinese homes and temples today. Although she is free from the cycles of birth and death she comes to earth many times to help those in need and is commonly known as the Goddess of Mercy.

THE HOURS OF FORTUNE

23–01	G	07–09	B	15–17	G
01–03	B	09–11	M	17–19	M
03–05	G	11–13	G	19–21	M
05–07	M	13–15	G	21–23	B

ADVICE FOR THE DAY

Lucky stars are shining on you if you're announcing an engagement, getting married or receiving presents. If you're owed money, don't be afraid to ask for its return —it should be repaid in full. Anyone working at home should concentrate on gardening, needlework and darning, or repair work in your bedroom. Today's reading ends with a word of encouragement for anyone involved in outdoor sports.

WHAT TO AVOID TODAY

Be prepared for delays throughout the day if you're travelling by land, sea or air. Don't push yourself too far if you've recently been through an emotional upheaval; you may need more time than you realized to get back to your normal routine.

This is a day of disappointments for anyone born in the following years of the Pig: 1923, 1935, 1947, 1959, 1971.

20TH DAY OF THE 9TH MONTH – SUNDAY, 27 OCTOBER

THE HOURS OF FORTUNE

23–01	B	07–09	B	15–17	G
01–03	B	09–11	M	17–19	G
03–05	G	11–13	G	19–21	B
05–07	M	13–15	G	21–23	M

ADVICE FOR THE DAY

This is an an appropriate day to reflect on personal difficulties or to put time aside for prayer. Lucky stars are shining on anyone who is starting a new educational project, opening a business or emigrating. This should also prove to be a profitable day for anyone buying or selling goods. Now is the time to buy or make new clothes or to turn your attention to gardening or general DIY. If a close relative or friend has recently died you should channel your energies into taking care of funeral matters.

WHAT TO AVOID TODAY

If you're planning DIY you should avoid work in the

bathroom or on ceilings and beware of an accident if you're using needles or scissors. If you're involved in competitive sports you should check your equipment carefully before using it or postpone your activities until tomorrow.

Don't rush into commitments now if you were born in the following years of the Rat: 1924, 1936, 1948, 1960, 1972.

21ST DAY OF THE 9TH MONTH – MONDAY, 28 OCTOBER

THE HOURS OF FORTUNE

23–01	M	07–09	B	15–17	G
01–03	B	09–11	G	17–19	B
03–05	G	11–13	G	19–21	M
05–07	G	13–15	M	21–23	M

ADVICE FOR THE DAY

Start the day with a few moments to yourself for reflection or prayer; the problems that have been on your mind may fade as the day passes. The gods of fortune are on your side if you're marrying and you can look forward to a safe and secure future. On the domestic front, it's a suitable time to clean and if you've been troubled by insects or vermin in your house or garden, this is a suitable time to lay down traps or repellent.

WHAT TO AVOID TODAY

There's the possibility of an accident in the kitchen and you're advised to be extra careful if you're cooking soups or sauces. Don't be tempted to over-indulge if you're drinking alcohol, you're likely to regret your actions.

This is an unlucky day for anyone born in the following years of the Ox: 1925, 1937, 1949, 1961, 1973.

22ND DAY OF THE 9TH MONTH – TUESDAY, 29 OCTOBER

THE HOURS OF FORTUNE

23–01	G	07–09	B	15–17	B
01–03	B	09–11	G	17–19	G
03–05	B	11–13	M	19–21	M
05–07	G	13–15	G	21–23	M

ADVICE FOR THE DAY

These next three days are excellent times for quiet reflection or to sort out worries that have been on your mind. If you've been thinking of starting a full- or part-time educational course try to make a final decision now, and if you're on the move to a new house or if you're simply travelling for pleasure you can look forward to a day free of delays and accidents. The financial forecast is good for anyone who is opening a business or investing money. If you've been feeling ill recently this is a positive day to begin a period of convalescence or begin a course of health treatments. If you're at home you should turn your attention to gardening or DIY, but you should avoid plastering walls.

WHAT TO AVOID TODAY

There could be an accident in your bedroom now so spend the minimum amount of time there and don't attempt to move bedroom furniture. Watch out for a mishap if you're working with water and postpone swimming or sailing trips.

Be prepared for a day of disappointments if you were born in the following years of the Tiger: 1926, 1938, 1950, 1962, 1974.

23RD DAY OF THE 9TH MONTH – WEDNESDAY, 30 OCTOBER

THE HOURS OF FORTUNE

23–01	G	07–09	B	15–17	G
01–03	B	09–11	G	17–19	M
03–05	G	11–13	M	19–21	M
05–07	B	13–15	B	21–23	M

ADVICE FOR THE DAY

There's still good fortune associated with travel and general DIY and you should have a particularly satisfying day if you're cooking or working in the kitchen. You can look forward to happiness and security in the months ahead if you're getting married or making wedding plans. If you have been through a period of personal loss, don't be afraid to express your feelings, and if you're mourning the death of a friend or relative this is an appropriate time to arrange or to attend a funeral.

WHAT TO AVOID TODAY

Stay well away from lawyers now because you're likely to find yourself in deeper trouble than you imagined. You're also advised not to sign legal contracts or to make final decisions on a legal case. If you're planning to have acupuncture or other health treatments, postpone your visit until tomorrow.

This is a day of delays and disagreements for anyone born

in the following years of the Rabbit: 1927, 1939, 1951, 1963, 1975.

24TH DAY OF THE 9TH MONTH – THURSDAY, 31 OCTOBER

THE HOURS OF FORTUNE

23–01	M	07–09	B	15–17	M
01–03	B	09–11	G	17–19	M
03–05	G	11–13	B	19–21	M
05–07	G	13–15	G	21–23	M

ADVICE FOR THE DAY

It's a positive time to concentrate on spiritual matters but if you feel you have excess energy you should channel it into creative or practical manual work.

WHAT TO AVOID TODAY

You could be in for financial disappointments so don't lend or invest money, and don't be tempted to squander your savings on unnecessary buys.

This is a day of upheavals for anyone born in the following years of the Dragon: 1928, 1940, 1952, 1964, 1976.

25TH DAY OF THE 9TH MONTH – FRIDAY, 1 NOVEMBER

THE HOURS OF FORTUNE

23–01	G	07–09	B	15–17	M
01–03	B	09–11	B	17–19	M
03–05	G	11–13	M	19–21	M
05–07	G	13–15	G	21–23	M

ADVICE FOR THE DAY

Make the most of social opportunities that come your way and you could be in for an unexpected and welcome surprise. If you're feeling ill don't be afraid to visit a doctor or to begin a course of treatment; you should feel well on the way to recovery soon. Don't be afraid to take risks and you can sign contracts or set up new projects with confidence. Now is the time to give your house a thorough clean and to concentrate on structural repair work, particularly in your bedroom or kitchen.

WHAT TO AVOID TODAY

There's misfortune associated with gardening so if you're a gardening enthusiast put your feet up and have a rest instead. This is also an inappropriate time to get married so, unless you're prepared for romantic problems in the months ahead, postpone your marriage until another time.

Don't expect your plans to work out as you expected if you were born in the following years of the Snake: 1929, 1941, 1953, 1965, 1977.

26TH DAY OF THE 9TH MONTH –
SATURDAY, 2 NOVEMBER

THE HOURS OF FORTUNE

23–01	G	07–09	B	15–17	M
01–03	B	09–11	G	17–19	G
03–05	M	11–13	B	19–21	G
05–07	M	13–15	M	21–23	G

ADVICE FOR THE DAY

Put some time aside today to concentrate on spiritual matters and you should feel more relaxed by the end of the day. Make the most of social opportunities that come your way: you could be in for an unexpected surprise. This is also an excellent time to make wedding arrangements or to get married. If you've been having problems finalizing travel plans they should be resolved now and you can set off on journeys with confidence. The forecast for business is excellent and you can afford to take financial risks. This should prove to be a fruitful day for builders and anyone planning general maintenance around the house or garden. Finally, this is an appropriate time to arrange or attend a funeral.

WHAT TO AVOID TODAY

If you're spending time in the kitchen, handle hot pans, sharp utensils and electrical goods with care. If you have problems on your mind, don't ask others for advice, you may hear some unwelcome news. This is also an inappropriate time to make or buy new clothes.

This is an unlucky day for anyone born in the following years of the Horse: 1918, 1930, 1942, 1954, 1966, 1978.

27TH DAY OF THE 9TH MONTH – SUNDAY, 3 NOVEMBER

THE HOURS OF FORTUNE

23–01	G	07–09	B	15–17	M
01–03	B	09–11	G	17–19	G
03–05	M	11–13	G	19–21	M
05–07	B	13–15	B	21–23	G

ADVICE FOR THE DAY

Since this is a broken day within the month you should channel your energies into domestic matters. It's an opportune time to give your house a thorough clean and get rid of belongings that you no longer need. If you're working outside it's a suitable time to pull down old masonry.

WHAT TO AVOID TODAY

If you were planning to buy or make new clothes wait until tomorrow to avoid making the wrong choice.

Don't take unnecessary risks if you were born in the following years of the Ram: 1919, 1931, 1943, 1955, 1967, 1979.

28TH DAY OF THE 9TH MONTH – MONDAY, 4 NOVEMBER

This is the festival of Wah Kwong, the god worshipped by musicians, singers and actors.

THE HOURS OF FORTUNE

23–01	M	07–09	B	15–17	B
01–03	B	09–11	G	17–19	M
03–05	B	11–13	G	19–21	M
05–07	G	13–15	G	21–23	M

ADVICE FOR THE DAY

This is a good day to be creative, particularly if you're sewing or weaving. The forecast is excellent for sports enthusiasts and for fishermen in particular who can look forward to a successful day's catch.

WHAT TO AVOID TODAY

Try to concentrate on practical not spiritual matters and don't try to resolve emotional problems now. If you're thinking of buying property give yourself more time to seek professional advice before you agree to a sale.

Be prepared for the unexpected today if you were born in the following years of the Monkey: 1920, 1932, 1944, 1956, 1968, 1980.

29TH DAY OF THE 9TH MONTH – TUESDAY, 5 NOVEMBER

THE HOURS OF FORTUNE

23–01	G	07–09	B	15–17	M
01–03	B	09–11	M	17–19	B
03–05	G	11–13	G	19–21	M
05–07	G	13–15	G	21–23	B

ADVICE FOR THE DAY

This is an ideal day for prayer or quiet reflection and don't be afraid to share your problems with others — they could be solved sooner than you expected. This is a good day to renew contact with old friends, to make new ones or to begin a romance. The gods of fortune are on your side if you're getting married and it's a perfect opportunity to give or receive presents. If you're feeling ill don't be afraid to consult a doctor; the news may not be as bad as you expected. Anyone working with animals can look forward to a satisfying day and if you're thinking of buying a pet this is the day to do so. If you have time on your hands you should focus your attention on domestic matters, whether it's cleaning or mending household goods. On a more sombre note, it's an appropriate time to arrange or attend a funeral.

WHAT TO AVOID TODAY

This is a day of disappointments and setbacks for anyone born in the following years of the Cock: 1921, 1933, 1945, 1957, 1969.

TENTH MONTH

The Monkey King is renowned as the protector of Tripitaka, the monk who brought the Buddha's scriptures to China. The Monkey King is gifted in magic and the martial arts, but he is also renowned as a trickster.

1ST DAY OF THE 10TH MONTH – WEDNESDAY, 6 NOVEMBER

THE HOURS OF FORTUNE

23–01	B	07–09	B	15–17	M
01–03	B	09–11	G	17–19	M
03–05	G	11–13	G	19–21	B
05–07	M	13–15	G	21–23	G

ADVICE FOR THE DAY

Since this is a broken day within the month you should postpone important meetings or decisions until tomorrow. The Almanac suggests that you turn your attention to clearing away rubbish or rubble in or around the house.

WHAT TO AVOID TODAY

Steer clear of financial dealings and investments – the element of risk is too great at the moment. There's also the possibility of an accident if you're sewing, darning or weaving.

This is a day of disappointments for anyone born in the following years of the Dog: 1922, 1934, 1946, 1958, 1970.

2ND DAY OF THE 10TH MONTH – THURSDAY, 7 NOVEMBER

THE HOURS OF FORTUNE

23–01	M	07–09	B	15–17	M
01–03	B	09–11	G	17–19	B
03–05	G	11–13	G	19–21	G
05–07	M	13–15	G	21–23	B

ADVICE FOR THE DAY

Since this is the day that precedes Li Tung you shouldn't take unnecessary risks or begin new projects. Concentrate on domestic matters today, particularly on cleaning the house.

WHAT TO AVOID TODAY

There's the possibility of an accident in the kitchen particularly if you're cooking soups or sauces and brewing your own beer and wine.

This is a day of upheavals for anyone born in the following years of the Pig: 1923, 1935, 1947, 1959, 1971.

3RD DAY OF THE 10TH MONTH –
FRIDAY, 8 NOVEMBER

Li Tung, the beginning of winter, officially starts at 6.23 this morning.

THE HOURS OF FORTUNE

23–01	B	07–09	M	15–17	B
01–03	B	09–11	B	17–19	M
03–05	G	11–13	M	19–21	M
05–07	G	13–15	G	21–23	G

ADVICE FOR THE DAY

Make the most of social opportunities that come your way now because an unexpected meeting could prove to be fruitful in the future. You should also try to resolve disagreements with friends or with romantic partners. If you're thinking of getting married this would also be an ideal time to announce an engagement. This should be a satisfying day for DIY or gardening enthusiasts so you should try to begin work on domestic jobs that you have been ignoring or postponing. Finally, if you're buying clothes you will be more than happy with your purchases, or if you're having your hair cut you should be pleased with the results.

WHAT TO AVOID TODAY

There's misfortune associated with water today so you should be extra careful around the house whether you're taking a shower, watering plants or unblocking drains. If you've recently been through a period of upheaval or loss don't push yourself too far – give yourself time to rest and sort out the worries on your mind.

This is an unlucky day for anyone born in the following years of the Rat: 1924, 1936, 1948, 1960, 1972.

4TH DAY OF THE 10TH MONTH –
SATURDAY, 9 NOVEMBER

THE HOURS OF FORTUNE

23–01	G	07–09	M	15–17	M
01–03	B	09–11	B	17–19	M
03–05	G	11–13	G	19–21	G
05–07	G	13–15	B	21–23	M

ADVICE FOR THE DAY

Your prayers may be unexpectedly granted now; don't be afraid to ask others for help. There's good prospects in store if you're starting a new college or evening course and if you're planning to open a business you can look forward to financial success. Take this opportunity to invest money, particularly if you're involved in any sort of trading venture. Now is the time to turn your attention to general maintenance around the house or garden, and if you've been thinking of brewing your own beer and wine you should set to work on it today. Today's advice ends with a word of support for anyone who is in mourning or making funeral arrangements.

WHAT TO AVOID TODAY

Don't pursue legal action today, your case may not be as watertight as you imagine. You should also handle electrical kitchen goods with care and avoid electrical repairs. It's also an unlucky day for fishermen or hunters so postpone your trip if you want to avoid accidents.

Don't take unnecessary risks now if you were born in the following years of the Ox: 1925, 1937, 1949, 1961, 1973.

5TH DAY OF THE 10TH MONTH –
SUNDAY, 10 NOVEMBER

THE HOURS OF FORTUNE

23–01	G	07–09	G	15–17	G
01–03	B	09–11	B	17–19	G
03–05	B	11–13	B	19–21	M
05–07	M	13–15	G	21–23	M

ADVICE FOR THE DAY

Good fortune favours sportsmen now, particularly hunters. But on a more mundane level this is the appropriate time to set traps or lay down poison if you've been troubled by insects or vermin.

WHAT TO AVOID TODAY

If you've been saving money, food or drink for a special occasion, don't be tempted to break into it now. If you're wearing expensive jewellery, make sure it is securely fastened, and if you're thinking of buying jewellery, don't make a hasty decision.

Personal problems may come to the fore today if you were born in the following years of the Tiger: 1926, 1938, 1950, 1962, 1974.

6TH DAY OF THE 10TH MONTH –
MONDAY, 11 NOVEMBER

THE HOURS OF FORTUNE

23–01	G	07–09	G	15–17	G
01–03	B	09–11	B	17–19	G
03–05	G	11–13	M	19–21	M
05–07	B	13–15	M	21–23	M

ADVICE FOR THE DAY

Try to put some time aside today for quiet reflection or prayer. There are good career prospects in store if you're starting a full- or part-time educational course. If you're getting married the years ahead promise to be prosperous and stable and the future looks secure if you're on the move to a new house or to a new country. Don't be afraid to take financial risks; it's a particularly lucky day for anyone opening a business or finalizing a business deal.

WHAT TO AVOID TODAY

Don't buy, cut or plant flowers, seeds or shrubs today — you should even avoid arranging flowers although this is a safe day for digging or ploughing. There's an unlucky reading for work around the house and you should stay well away from plastering or painting.

This is a day of disappointments for anyone born in the following years of the Rabbit: 1927, 1939, 1951, 1963, 1975.

7TH DAY OF THE 10TH MONTH – TUESDAY, 12 NOVEMBER

THE HOURS OF FORTUNE

23–01	G	07–09	B	15–17	G
01–03	B	09–11	B	17–19	G
03–05	G	11–13	M	19–21	G
05–07	G	13–15	M	21–23	G

ADVICE FOR THE DAY

This is a good day to sort out personal problems or to put some time aside for quiet reflection. If you're going shopping for new clothes now you should find exactly what you're looking for; if you're planning to do needlework you should be pleased with your efforts. The Almanac also offers encouragement to builders or DIY enthusiasts who are starting work on structural repairs.

WHAT TO AVOID TODAY

Don't attempt electrical repair work in the kitchen and handle hot pans or dishes with care since there's the likelihood of an accident when you are cooking. On a more sombre note, this is an inappropriate time to make funeral arrangements or to attend a funeral.

This is a day of upheavals for anyone born in the following years of the Dragon: 1928, 1940, 1952, 1964, 1976.

8TH DAY OF THE 10TH MONTH – WEDNESDAY, 13 NOVEMBER

THE HOURS OF FORTUNE

23–01	M		07–09	M		15–17	M
01–03	B		09–11	B		17–19	G
03–05	G		11–13	G		19–21	G
05–07	B		13–15	G		21–23	G

ADVICE FOR THE DAY

Once again the Almanac advises you to put some time aside for religious ceremony or simply for quiet thought. Today's advice focuses on domestic matters and it's a particularly appropriate time to give your house a thorough clean. Don't forget to put some time aside to relax, however: you shouldn't feel guilty about treating yourself to a little luxury.

WHAT TO AVOID TODAY

Don't get your hair cut now because you'll only be disappointed with the results. You should also postpone wedding arrangements; if it is too late to do this you should be prepared for recriminations in the months ahead.

Don't take unnecessary risks now if you were born in the following years of the Snake: 1929, 1941, 1953, 1965, 1977.

9TH DAY OF THE 10TH MONTH –
THURSDAY, 14 NOVEMBER

THE HOURS OF FORTUNE

23–01	M	07–09	G	15–17	G
01–03	B	09–11	B	17–19	G
03–05	B	11–13	B	19–21	M
05–07	G	13–15	M	21–23	M

ADVICE FOR THE DAY

If you're waiting for exam results you're likely to hear good news today and the future also looks bright for anyone starting a new educational course. Journeys are blessed by good fortune now so you can travel as far afield as you like. If you've been feeling under the weather this is a positive time to have treatment or begin a period of convalescence. If you're at home today you should turn your attention to clearing ground, planting seeds and to DIY work in your kitchen or bathroom, or on ceilings.

WHAT TO AVOID TODAY

There's misfortune linked to property so don't agree to the sale of a house, flat or farm – you may be letting yourself in for unexpected and expensive problems.

This is an unlucky day for anyone born in the following years of the Horse: 1930, 1942, 1954, 1966, 1978.

10TH DAY OF THE 10TH MONTH –
FRIDAY, 15 NOVEMBER

THE HOURS OF FORTUNE

23–01	G	07–09	M	15–17	G
01–03	B	09–11	B	17–19	G
03–05	G	11–13	M	19–21	M
05–07	G	13–15	B	21–23	B

ADVICE FOR THE DAY

Since this is a broken day within the year you should find some time to focus on spiritual matters. On a practical note, this is an opportune moment to demolish old walls or buildings and to clear away rubble or rubbish.

WHAT TO AVOID TODAY

Try to keep yourself occupied with practical matters so you don't dwell on personal disappointments. It's an unsuitable time to mull over a loss or to cut yourself off from others.

Be prepared for disappointments throughout the day if you were born in the following years of the Ram: 1931, 1943, 1955, 1967, 1979.

11TH DAY OF THE 10TH MONTH – SATURDAY, 16 NOVEMBER

THE HOURS OF FORTUNE

23–01	B	07–09	G	15–17	B
01–03	B	09–11	B	17–19	M
03–05	G	11–13	G	19–21	B
05–07	G	13–15	M	21–23	M

ADVICE FOR THE DAY

This is an ideal time to meet old friends and make new ones; don't turn down party invitations, there could be new romance in the air. The gods of fortune are on your side if you're getting married and you can look forward to happiness and security in the years ahead. This is also a suitable time to give or receive presents. You can feel secure that you've made the right decision if you're moving house, emigrating or opening a new business. If you're at home today and have energy to spare you should concentrate on structural repair work or on gardening. Finally, it's an appropriate time to arrange a funeral.

WHAT TO AVOID TODAY

Try to concentrate on practical matters now; personal worries are unlikely to be resolved today. You should handle knives and scissors with extra care and if you are thinking of sewing or darning, wait until tomorrow.

This is a day of arguments and delays for anyone born in the following years of the Monkey: 1920, 1932, 1944, 1956, 1968, 1980.

12TH DAY OF THE 10TH MONTH –
SUNDAY, 17 NOVEMBER

THE HOURS OF FORTUNE

23–01	M	07–09	M	15–17	M
01–03	B	09–11	B	17–19	B
03–05	G	11–13	G	19–21	G
05–07	G	13–15	M	21–23	M

ADVICE FOR THE DAY

Make the most of today by starting a new educational course, making travel plans, meeting friends or beginning a romance. There's a secure future in store if you're getting married, moving to a new house or emigrating. It will prove to be a satisfying and fruitful day for builders, DIY enthusiasts, farmers and gardeners. Be prepared to take a financial risk if you're investing money or opening a business. If you're thinking of having your hair cut, make an appointment in the next two days and you won't be disappointed with the results. If you've been through a period of loss give yourself time to mourn and to rest. The Almanac also suggests that funeral arrangements should be made now.

WHAT TO AVOID TODAY

Be careful if you're working with water and beware of an accident if you're near swimming pools, ponds or lakes. It's also an unlucky day in the kitchen and you're advised to avoid making soups and sauces and to be restrained if you're drinking or buying alcohol.

Be prepared for disappointments now if you were born in the following years of the Cock: 1921, 1933, 1945, 1957, 1969.

13TH DAY OF THE 10TH MONTH –
MONDAY, 18 NOVEMBER

THE HOURS OF FORTUNE

23–01	M	07–09	M	15–17	B
01–03	B	09–11	B	17–19	G
03–05	G	11–13	M	19–21	B
05–07	G	13–15	M	21–23	G

ADVICE FOR THE DAY

Once again it's a suitable time to make educational plans
or to get married. Now is the time to lay down traps or
insect repellent if the house or garden has been infested by
insects, slugs, mice or other vermin.

WHAT TO AVOID TODAY

There's still misfortune associated with water and you're
advised not to repair gutters or clean out drains.
Gardeners are also advised to rest from their work for the
day to avoid accident.

This is an unlucky day for anyone born in the following
years of the Dog: 1922, 1934, 1946, 1958, 1970.

14TH DAY OF THE 10TH MONTH –
TUESDAY, 19 NOVEMBER

THE HOURS OF FORTUNE

23–01	G	07–09	G	15–17	G
01–03	B	09–11	B	17–19	M
03–05	M	11–13	M	19–21	G
05–07	G	13–15	B	21–23	B

ADVICE FOR THE DAY

Since this is a broken day within the month you should turn your attention to clearing away rubbish and to minor demolition work that needs doing in the garden. But this is also a positive day for anyone who has been feeling ill recently; so if you've been thinking of trying a health treatment or consulting a doctor, do so now.

WHAT TO AVOID TODAY

If you've been feeling depressed or have just been through a period of loss, give yourself more time to recover before you face the world again. On a practical note, this is an unlucky day to travel by land, sea or air.

Be prepared for a day of disappointments if you were born in the following years of the Pig: 1923, 1935, 1947, 1959, 1971.

15TH DAY OF THE 10TH MONTH – WEDNESDAY, 20 NOVEMBER

THE HOURS OF FORTUNE

23–01	B	07–09	M	15–17	M
01–03	B	09–11	B	17–19	G
03–05	G	11–13	B	19–21	M
05–07	M	13–15	G	21–23	M

ADVICE FOR THE DAY

Try to put some time aside for quiet reflection or prayer, your requests may be answered. Don't turn down social invitations because you could be in for an unexpected and welcome surprise. Travel difficulties that you may have had should be resolved and you can set off on journeys with confidence. This is a particularly good day for moving house or for foreign travel. If you're announcing an engagement or getting married you can look forward to happiness and financial security in the years ahead, and now is the time to choose or accept presents. If there are repairs that need attention on the house you should set to work now. If someone close to you has died recently you shouldn't be afraid to show your grief or to ask others for help. This is also an appropriate day to arrange or attend a funeral.

WHAT TO AVOID TODAY

Don't take financial risks now, avoid spending money on unnecessary luxuries, and don't be persuaded to lend money, even to friends. Although this is a good day for DIY around the house, be careful if you're working in the bathroom or on ceilings.

This is a day of upheavals for anyone born in the following years of the Rat: 1924, 1936, 1948, 1960, 1972.

16TH DAY OF THE 10TH MONTH – THURSDAY, 21 NOVEMBER

THE HOURS OF FORTUNE

23–01	G	07–09	M	15–17	G
01–03	B	09–11	B	17–19	M
03–05	G	11–13	M	19–21	G
05–07	G	13–15	M	21–23	G

ADVICE FOR THE DAY

This is a positive day for prayer or quiet reflection. If you're waiting for exam results or are thinking of beginning a full- or part-time course you can look forward to successful results. Make every effort to attend parties or other social events because this is a good opportunity to make new friends or to begin a romance. If you're celebrating now it's an ideal time to give or receive presents and it's the perfect time to announce an engagement. It's a promising day to open a business and shopkeepers and other traders can expect a profitable day. Anyone working with electrical goods or attempting DIY should be more than happy with the results of their work and there's a final word of encouragement for anyone working with animals.

WHAT TO AVOID TODAY

This is an unlucky day for gardeners and you're advised to avoid planting crops, seeds or trees, and to beware of an accident or a breakage if you're cutting or arranging flowers. Don't sign binding contracts and don't initiate legal action: your case is unlikely to succeed.

Don't take unnecessary risks now if you were born in the following years of the Ox: 1925, 1937, 1949, 1961, 1973.

17TH DAY OF THE 10TH MONTH –
FRIDAY, 22 NOVEMBER

Hsiao Hsueh, the traditional reminder that the first snows are coming, begins at 3.39 this morning.

THE HOURS OF FORTUNE

23–01	G	07–09	B	15–17	G
01–03	B	09–11	B	17–19	G
03–05	B	11–13	M	19–21	G
05–07	M	13–15	G	21–23	G

ADVICE FOR THE DAY

Today's advice focuses on work at home. Put your energies into spring-cleaning or needlework and if you've had problems with vermin or insects now is the time to lay down traps or repellent.

WHAT TO AVOID TODAY

Spend the minimum amount of time in the kitchen to avoid accidents and if you're handling hot liquids or pans be extra careful. You should also avoid moving beds, changing bed linen and, if you had plans to clean your bedroom, postpone them until tomorrow.

Be prepared for problems in your domestic life if you were born in the following years of the Tiger: 1926, 1938, 1950, 1962, 1974.

18TH DAY OF THE 10TH MONTH –
SATURDAY, 23 NOVEMBER

THE HOURS OF FORTUNE

23–01	M	07–09	M	15–17	M
01–03	B	09–11	B	17–19	G
03–05	M	11–13	G	19–21	M
05–07	B	13–15	G	21–23	G

ADVICE FOR THE DAY

Now is the time to sort out personal problems and to ask others for advice. There's good luck in store for anyone starting a new educational course or initiating a business venture. The gods of fortune are on your side if you're on the move, whether it is to a new house or to a new country. If you're at home it would be a good idea to spend some time and energy on DIY or gardening.

WHAT TO AVOID TODAY

This is an unlucky day for beauty treatments so if you're thinking of having your hair cut or treating yourself to other beauty treatments wait until tomorrow. If you are working at home today avoid plastering or repairs to roofs.

This is a day of arguments and setbacks for anyone born in the following years of the Rabbit: 1927, 1939, 1951, 1963, 1975.

19TH DAY OF THE 10TH MONTH – SUNDAY, 24 NOVEMBER

THE HOURS OF FORTUNE

23–01	M	07–09	B	15–17	G
01–03	B	09–11	B	17–19	M
03–05	B	11–13	G	19–21	M
05–07	G	13–15	G	21–23	M

ADVICE FOR THE DAY

If you're at home today you should channel your energy into gardening and general maintenance work, particularly in your bathroom. If you have fabric or house furnishings that need mending, now is the time to do it.

WHAT TO AVOID TODAY

If you've been looking for property and think you've found the ideal home, don't commit yourself to a sale or lease until tomorrow.

This is an unlucky day for anyone born in the following years of the Dragon: 1928, 1940, 1952, 1964, 1976.

20TH DAY OF THE 10TH MONTH – MONDAY, 25 NOVEMBER

THE HOURS OF FORTUNE

23–01	G	07–09	M	15–17	G
01–03	B	09–11	B	17–19	M
03–05	G	11–13	G	19–21	M
05–07	G	13–15	G	21–23	B

ADVICE FOR THE DAY

If you have been having difficulty with travel arrangements they should be sorted out and journeys at home or abroad are blessed with good fortune. You shouldn't miss this opportunity to widen your social circle or meet new business contacts. If you are meeting friends today you could hear good news and this is the time to resolve romantic difficulties.

WHAT TO AVOID TODAY

Try to postpone wedding plans until the 23rd day of this month because the gods of fortune have deserted you for the moment. Farmers and gardeners are also advised to have a rest from ploughing or light digging.

Personal relationships could prove difficult today if you were born in the following years of the Snake: 1929, 1941, 1953, 1965, 1977.

21ST DAY OF THE 10TH MONTH – TUESDAY, 26 NOVEMBER

THE HOURS OF FORTUNE

23–01	B	07–09	M	15–17	G
01–03	B	09–11	B	17–19	G
03–05	M	11–13	B	19–21	B
05–07	M	13–15	G	21–23	M

ADVICE FOR THE DAY

This is a positive day for prayer or quiet reflection and you may find that your prayers are unexpectedly answered. Try to make travel arrangements now and you can set off on journeys at home or abroad with confidence. This good fortune also extends to anyone moving house or emigrating. If you're celebrating today you can expect to receive some unexpected and welcome presents, and it's an excellent day to marry or make wedding arrangements. The future looks bright for anyone starting a new job or opening a business. This is also an opportune day to have your hair cut and to put some effort into gardening or structural alterations around the house. Finally, it's an appropriate time to arrange or attend a funeral.

WHAT TO AVOID TODAY

Be careful if you're working with or handling needles or knives. There's a particular note of caution for anyone planning a hunting trip. If you've been thinking of asking others for advice or guidance about the future, wait until tomorrow.

Don't take unnecessary risks now if you were born in the following years of the Horse: 1918, 1930, 1942, 1954, 1966, 1978.

22ND DAY OF THE 10TH MONTH – WEDNESDAY, 27 NOVEMBER

THE HOURS OF FORTUNE

23–01	M	07–09	M	15–17	G
01–03	B	09–11	B	17–19	B
03–05	G	11–13	G	19–21	M
05–07	G	13–15	B	21–23	G

ADVICE FOR THE DAY

Since this is a broken day within the year you should turn

your attention to minor demolition work and to tidying up your house or garden.

WHAT TO AVOID TODAY

If you're cooking today try to keep your meals as simple as possible and avoid making sauces or soups and brewing your own beer and wine.

Plans or projects may not work out as you expected now if you were born in the following years of the Ram: 1931, 1943, 1955, 1967, 1979.

23RD DAY OF THE 10TH MONTH – THURSDAY, 28 NOVEMBER

THE HOURS OF FORTUNE

23–01	M	07–09	M	15–17	B
01–03	B	09–11	B	17–19	M
03–05	G	11–13	M	19–21	G
05–07	G	13–15	G	21–23	M

ADVICE FOR THE DAY

Make the most of social opportunities that come your way now and you could be in for an unexpected romantic surprise. This is the perfect time to open a business and you can look forward to financial security in the months to come. The future is also promising for anyone getting married. Everything should run smoothly if you're moving to a new house, to a new country or simply travelling for pleasure. If you're spending time at home it's an opportune day to work in the garden or to carry out structural repair on the house.

WHAT TO AVOID TODAY

Don't take unnecessary risks if you're near water and you should avoid clearing out drains and gutters; call in a plumber instead.

Don't make long-term commitments today if you were born in the following years of the Monkey: 1920, 1932, 1944, 1956, 1968, 1980.

24TH DAY OF THE 10TH MONTH – FRIDAY, 29 NOVEMBER

THE HOURS OF FORTUNE

23–01	G	07–09	M	15–17	M
01–03	B	09–11	B	17–19	B
03–05	G	11–13	M	19–21	G
05–07	G	13–15	B	21–23	M

ADVICE FOR THE DAY

Once again the gods of fortune are shining on you if you're on the move, meeting friends or beginning a romance. There's still good fortune associated with opening a business and with general DIY around the house. You shouldn't face any difficulties if you're signing a contract, concluding a business deal or selling goods, and there's excellent career prospects if you're starting a new job. Finally, it's a suitable time to arrange or attend a funeral if someone close to you has died recently.

WHAT TO AVOID TODAY

Even if you are sure you are in the right, don't be persuaded to initiate legal action. You should also be careful if you're gardening and there's still misfortune associated with water.

This is an unlucky day for anyone born in the following years of the Cock: 1921, 1933, 1945, 1957, 1969.

25TH DAY OF THE 10TH MONTH – SATURDAY, 30 NOVEMBER

THE HOURS OF FORTUNE

23–01	G	07–09	G	15–17	M
01–03	B	09–11	B	17–19	G
03–05	M	11–13	B	19–21	B
05–07	M	13–15	G	21–23	G

ADVICE FOR THE DAY

This is an excellent time to meet old friends or find new ones, so make the most of your free time. If you've been feeling ill the Almanac suggests that you visit an acupuncturist today. The forecast is also positive for anyone setting off on a hunting trip and, on a less adventurous level, this is the time to lay down traps or repellent if you've been troubled by insects, cockroaches, mice or other vermin. If you've been through a period of sadness recently you should now try to forget what has happened and start making new plans.

WHAT TO AVOID TODAY

There's still bad luck associated with gardening, particularly if you're digging. To be on the safe side you should postpone gardening until the 28th day of this month.

Be prepared for problems in your domestic life if you were

born in the following years of the Dog: 1922, 1934, 1946, 1958, 1970.

26TH DAY OF THE 10TH MONTH – SUNDAY, 1 DECEMBER

THE HOURS OF FORTUNE

23–01	G	07–09	M	15–17	G
01–03	B	09–11	B	17–19	G
03–05	M	11–13	M	19–21	G
05–07	M	13–15	M	21–23	B

ADVICE FOR THE DAY

This is a broken day within the month so you're advised to put your energies into clearing away rubble. However, this is also a constructive time for anyone who has been ill recently and medical consultations or treatments should have positive results.

WHAT TO AVOID TODAY

Travel is likely to be plagued by delays and minor accidents so, if possible, postpone important travel arrangements until tomorrow. You're also advised not to plant seeds, crops or trees.

This is a day of upheavals if you were born in the following years of the Pig: 1923, 1935, 1947, 1959, 1971.

27TH DAY OF THE 10TH MONTH –
MONDAY, 2 DECEMBER

This is the festival of the Tzu Wei god, the god of the Purple Star, the largest star in the Chinese astrological charts. It is not a widely celebrated festival, but it is popular amongst astrologers.

THE HOURS OF FORTUNE

23–01	B	07–09	B	15–17	G
01–03	B	09–11	B	17–19	G
03–05	M	11–13	G	19–21	G
05–07	M	13–15	M	21–23	G

ADVICE FOR THE DAY

Don't try to deal with problems alone; if you ask others for advice they may have the solution. It's also a good time to turn your attention to spiritual matters and you could find renewed peace of mind. On a more practical note, it's an ideal time for cleaning, gardening and house maintenance, particularly if you're working with wood. The forecast ends on an encouraging note for sports enthusiasts.

WHAT TO AVOID TODAY

Handle kitchen utensils with care and beware of an accident if you're mending electrical kitchen goods.

Be prepared for unwelcome surprises if you were born in the following years of the Rat: 1924, 1936, 1948, 1960, 1972.

28TH DAY OF THE 10TH MONTH – TUESDAY, 3 DECEMBER

THE HOURS OF FORTUNE

23–01	M	07–09	M	15–17	M
01–03	B	09–11	B	17–19	G
03–05	M	11–13	G	19–21	M
05–07	B	13–15	G	21–23	G

ADVICE FOR THE DAY

This is the perfect time to announce an engagement and to give or receive presents. Don't worry about the future if you're starting a new educational course; the course will turn out to be more useful than you imagine. This is an opportune day to open a business and shopkeepers or anyone else involved in trade can expect a profitable day. If you have time and energy on your hands you should concentrate on DIY in the house and in the garden. This is also a suitable day to reflect on a loss in your life or to attend a funeral.

WHAT TO AVOID TODAY

Don't make legal commitments and don't pursue legal action – the judgement may not work in your favour. This is an unlucky day for sports enthusiasts and hunters and anglers are advised to take extra care or, better still, postpone their trip for at least three days.

Be prepared for problems in your domestic life if you were born in the following years of the Ox: 1925, 1937, 1949, 1961, 1973.

29TH DAY OF THE 10TH MONTH –
WEDNESDAY, 4 DECEMBER

THE HOURS OF FORTUNE

23–01	M	07–09	G	15–17	G
01–03	B	09–11	B	17–19	M
03–05	B	11–13	M	19–21	M
05–07	M	13–15	G	21–23	M

ADVICE FOR THE DAY

Today's forecast is limited to work around the house. Now is the time to clean your home thoroughly or to lay down traps or repellents if you've been troubled by mice, mosquitoes, insects or other vermin.

WHAT TO AVOID TODAY

Don't buy, sell or move beds; you should even avoid changing your bed linen. If you've been looking for property don't agree to a sale today even if you think you've found the ideal accommodation.

Be prepared for a day of disappointments if you were born in the following years of the tiger: 1926, 1938, 1950, 1962, 1974.

30TH DAY OF THE 10TH MONTH –
THURSDAY, 5 DECEMBER

THE HOURS OF FORTUNE

23–01	G	07–09	G	15–17	G
01–03	B	09–11	B	17–19	M
03–05	M	11–13	G	19–21	M
05–07	B	13–15	G	21–23	B

ADVICE FOR THE DAY

This is a promising day for prayer or quiet reflection and don't be afraid to talk your problems through with friends. There's good news in store if you're waiting for exam results or beginning a part- or full-time educational course. The financial prospects are excellent for anyone opening a new business and if you're moving to a new house or emigrating everything should run smoothly. If you've been thinking of gardening or carrying out maintenance work on ceilings, this is the day to do it.

WHAT TO AVOID TODAY

Joiners or carpenters should take extra precautions to avoid accidents and you should postpone plans to repair roofs or plaster walls.

Personal problems may come to the fore now if you were born in the following years of the Rabbit: 1927, 1939, 1951, 1963, 1975.

ELEVENTH MONTH

The Jade Emperor is the supreme ruler of Heaven. He controls gods, spirits, immortals and humans and nothing that happens on Heaven or Earth escapes his notice.

1ST DAY OF THE 11TH MONTH –
FRIDAY, 6 DECEMBER

THE HOURS OF FORTUNE

23–01	B	07–09	B	15–17	G
01–03	B	09–11	B	17–19	M
03–05	M	11–13	G	19–21	B
05–07	M	13–15	G	21–23	M

ADVICE FOR THE DAY

The month begins with a word of encouragement for anyone planning to mend home furnishings or to carry out DIY. If you have been postponing minor repair work you should do it now and you'll be surprised how much can be achieved in a short space of time.

WHAT TO AVOID TODAY

If you're working on or near a cooker be extra careful that you don't burn or scald yourself. You should also try to keep your mind on practical rather than creative matters. Finally, beware of an accident if you're weaving, darning or sewing.

This is an unlucky day for anyone born in the following years of the Dragon: 1928, 1940, 1952, 1964, 1976.

2ND DAY OF THE 11TH MONTH –
SATURDAY, 7 DECEMBER

Today is known as Ta Hsueh and it is a reminder that the heavy winter snows are on their way. It begins officially at 11.05 this evening.

THE HOURS OF FORTUNE

23–01	M	07–09	M	15–17	M
01–03	B	09–11	B	17–19	B
03–05	G	11–13	G	19–21	G
05–07	G	13–15	G	21–23	M

ADVICE FOR THE DAY

This is a good opportunity for prayer or quiet reflection; you could find that your problems are resolved or prayers answered. You can look forward to the day with confidence if you're travelling or meeting friends, and you could be in store for an unexpected meeting or a welcome reunion. The financial forecast is excellent for business negotiation so be prepared to take risks. There's also a positive forecast for anyone who is spending time on DIY or gardening.

WHAT TO AVOID TODAY

Watch out for an accident if you're cooking sauces or soups and make sure that you handle hot pans with care. Avoid drinking too much alcohol – you're likely to regret your actions tomorrow – and if you were thinking of brewing your own beer and wine, wait until tomorrow. You're also advised to postpone wedding plans until the 7th day of this month.

This is a day of disappointments for anyone born in the following years of the Snake: 1929, 1941, 1953, 1965, 1977.

3RD DAY OF THE 11TH MONTH –
SUNDAY, 8 DECEMBER

THE HOURS OF FORTUNE

23–01	G	07–09	G	15–17	B
01–03	B	09–11	G	17–19	M
03–05	G	11–13	B	19–21	M
05–07	G	13–15	G	21–23	M

ADVICE FOR THE DAY

Try to concentrate on spiritual matters and the worries that are on your mind may be eased by the end of the day. This is not only a good day for painting and decorating the house but it's also a suitable time to put your creative talents to good use, particularly if you enjoy painting.

WHAT TO AVOID TODAY

There's misfortune associated with water throughout the day so be careful if you're swimming, sailing, working with or near water. Although it's a good idea to concentrate on personal matters, don't ask others for advice – you may receive an unwelcome reply.

Don't make long term commitments now if you were born in the following years of the Horse: 1930, 1942, 1954, 1966, 1978.

4TH DAY OF THE 11TH MONTH –
MONDAY, 9 DECEMBER

This is the 2nd day in the year dedicated to the popular sage and writer, Confucius (see 27th day of the 8th month).

THE HOURS OF FORTUNE

23–01	G	07–09	G	15–17	G
01–03	B	09–11	G	17–19	G
03–05	M	11–13	B	19–21	G
05–07	M	13–15	B	21–23	M

ADVICE FOR THE DAY

Since this is a broken day within the year it's an ideal time to put your energies into cleaning your house but you should also put some time aside for prayer or quiet reflection.

WHAT TO AVOID TODAY

Don't file a lawsuit or become involved in legal wranglings, your case may not be as strong as you imagined. There could be more problems ahead of you than you bargained if you're planning funeral arrangements; postpone them until tomorrow.

This is a disappointing day for anyone born in the following years of the Ram: 1919, 1931, 1943, 1955, 1967, 1979.

5TH DAY OF THE 11TH MONTH – TUESDAY, 10 DECEMBER

THE HOURS OF FORTUNE

23–01	M	07–09	G	15–17	B
01–03	B	09–11	M	17–19	G
03–05	G	11–13	B	19–21	G
05–07	M	13–15	G	21–23	M

ADVICE FOR THE DAY

Lucky stars are shining on anyone beginning a new educational project or setting off on a journey at home or abroad. This is a profitable day for buying or selling and, if you're owed money now is the time to collect it. There could be a fruitful meeting in store so make every effort to contact old friends or make new ones. This is also the time to resolve romantic problems. If you've been thinking of buying new clothes, you should go shopping today and you're likely to find exactly what you need. Work should run smoothly if you're planning DIY or gardening and you'll be more than pleased with your efforts by the end of the day.

This is also a good opportunity to put the past behind you and look to the future if you've just been through a period of upheaval. You should also find the support you need if you're making funeral arrangements or attending a funeral.

WHAT TO AVOID TODAY

Although this is a good day for financial negotiations, don't be tempted to squander your money. You're particularly advised to think twice before you pay out for an expensive piece of jewellery. You should also be wary of lending money unless you're sure it can be returned on time. Keep your mind on practical not spiritual matters and be wary of asking others for advice on emotional problems.

This is an unlucky day for anyone born in the following years of the Monkey: 1920, 1932, 1944, 1956, 1968.

6TH DAY OF THE 11TH MONTH –
WEDNESDAY, 11 DECEMBER

Today is Tung Chi, the Jade Emperor's festival, on which the ruler of Heaven is remembered with prayers and offerings.

THE HOURS OF FORTUNE

23–01	M	07–09	M	15–17	G
01–03	B	09–11	B	17–19	B
03–05	G	11–13	B	19–21	G
05–07	G	13–15	G	21–23	G

ADVICE FOR THE DAY

This is a positive day for manual work whether you're laying a footpath, decorating the house or putting your creative talents to use.

WHAT TO AVOID TODAY

Beware of an accident if you're boiling water or taking a shower. You should also handle flowers and plants with care and should avoid cutting or arranging flowers.

Personal problems could come to the fore now if you were born in the following years of the Cock: 1921, 1933, 1945, 1957, 1969.

7TH DAY OF THE 11TH MONTH –
THURSDAY, 12 DECEMBER

THE HOURS OF FORTUNE

23–01	M	07–09	B	15–17	G
01–03	B	09–11	G	17–19	G
03–05	M	11–13	B	19–21	B
05–07	M	13–15	M	21–23	G

ADVICE FOR THE DAY

This is an ideal time for prayer, worship or quiet reflection. Try to find time to sort out travel arrangements and if you're setting off of an important journey you can do so with confidence. You can expect good results from meetings whether they are for business or pleasure and the future prospects are bright for anyone who is announcing an engagement or getting married. Whatever it is that you're celebrating at the moment, the time is right to give or to receive presents. This should prove to be a fruitful day for anyone who is working with animals or planning to buy a new pet. If you have the time to spare it's also an opportune day to put your energies into general DIY. You should find the support you need if you're making funeral arrangements and if you have been through a period of loss, don't be afraid to show your feelings.

WHAT TO AVOID TODAY

If you are spending time on house maintenance you should avoid DIY in the kitchen; be particularly cautious if you're working on or near a cooker.

There's misfortune in the air now if you were born in the following years of the Dog: 1922, 1934, 1946, 1958, 1970.

8TH DAY OF THE 11TH MONTH – FRIDAY, 13 DECEMBER

THE HOURS OF FORTUNE

23–01	M	07–09	M	15–17	M
01–03	B	09–11	G	17–19	G
03–05	M	11–13	B	19–21	G
05–07	B	13–15	G	21–23	B

ADVICE FOR THE DAY

This is still a positive time for religious ceremony or to reflect on personal matters. If you've been postponing general house maintenance, this is the time to start work. You should also take the necessary precautions to get rid of insects or vermin that have infested your house or garden.

WHAT TO AVOID TODAY

If you were thinking of getting your hair cut, postpone your appointment until the 10th day of this month. You may have difficulty finalizing travel plans and you should postpone long journeys unless they are absolutely necessary.

Don't take risks today if you were born in the following years of the Pig: 1923, 1935, 1947, 1959, 1971.

9TH DAY OF THE 11TH MONTH –
SATURDAY, 14 DECEMBER

THE HOURS OF FORTUNE

23–01	B	07–09	M	15–17	G
01–03	B	09–11	G	17–19	G
03–05	B	11–13	B	19–21	M
05–07	G	13–15	G	21–23	M

ADVICE FOR THE DAY

Since this is a broken day within the month you should channel your energy into clearing away rubble or rubbish. You should also pay attention to your health since this is an ideal day to consult a doctor or begin a period of convalescence.

WHAT TO AVOID TODAY

If you're planning DIY you should avoid maintenance work in the bathroom. There's also a strong possibility that you're making a serious mistake if you're buying property so make sure that you take the necessary professional advice before you agree to the sale of property.

This is a day of delays and disappointments for anyone born in the following years of the Rat: 1924, 1936, 1948, 1960, 1972.

10TH DAY OF THE 11TH MONTH – SUNDAY, 15 DECEMBER

THE HOURS OF FORTUNE

23–01	M	07–09	M	15–17	G
01–03	B	09–11	G	17–19	M
03–05	G	11–13	B	19–21	M
05–07	G	13–15	G	21–23	B

ADVICE FOR THE DAY

This is a good day to ask others for advice, or for personal prayer: you could find that your requests are answered. If you've been thinking of getting your hair cut or having other beauty treatments you should do so now and you'll be pleased with the results. Now is the time to stock up on fuel supplies or to check heating systems. Weather permitting, it's a suitable day for gardening and don't worry about accidents if you're thinking of going sailing, swimming or working near water.

WHAT TO AVOID TODAY

Avoid needlework and be wary of an accident if you're using needles for any other reason.

This could be a day of personal problems for anyone born in the following years of the Ox: 1925, 1937, 1949, 1961, 1973.

11TH DAY OF THE 11TH MONTH –
MONDAY, 16 DECEMBER

THE HOURS OF FORTUNE

23–01	B	07–09	G	15–17	G
01–03	B	09–11	G	17–19	M
03–05	B	11–13	B	19–21	B
05–07	M	13–15	G	21–23	M

ADVICE FOR THE DAY

If you're waiting for exam results you could hear good news now, and if you've been thinking about starting a full- or part-time educational course, you should make a final decision. Travel by land, sea or air is blessed by good fortune and you're advised to make the most of social opportunities that come your way; they could prove to have a marked effect in the months to come. You can feel secure that you've made the right decision if you're moving to a new house or emigrating and the journey should pass off safely. The financial prospects are excellent for anyone opening a business or working in trade.

If you're planning to give someone a surprise or a present, it should be more than welcome. Now is the time to consider taking health treatments, and if you've been ill recently this is a good day for recovery. The forecast is promising for structural or alteration work on the house, particularly in the kitchen, and if you're thinking of brewing your own wine or stocking up on supplies, you should do so now. If you have the time on your hands you should treat yourself to a haircut or find time to care for your personal appearance. On a more sombre note, this is an appropriate time to arrange or attend a funeral.

WHAT TO AVOID TODAY

Don't move bedroom furniture now or clear out cupboards, and beware of an accident if you're using needles. Although the forecast for travel is positive, you should avoid wind-surfing, canoeing, or setting to sea in small vessels.

Be prepared for setbacks throughout the day if you were born in the following years of the Tiger: 1926, 1938, 1950, 1962, 1974.

12TH DAY OF THE 11TH MONTH – TUESDAY, 17 DECEMBER

THE HOURS OF FORTUNE

23–01	M	07–09	G	15–17	M
01–03	B	09–11	G	17–19	B
03–05	G	11–13	B	19–21	M
05–07	B	13–15	M	21–23	M

ADVICE FOR THE DAY

It would be a good idea to put some time aside for prayer or quiet reflection; the worries on your mind are likely to be eased. If you're owed money, don't worry about asking for its return – it should be repaid in full. Now is the time to mend clothes or home furnishings, but it is also a good opportunity to put your creative talents to effective use, particularly for intricate work. For the second day running you're advised to pay attention to your personal appearance. Sports enthusiasts can expect a satisfying day, particularly if they're hunting or fishing. On a more mundane note, you should lay down traps or repellent now if you've been troubled by insects, mice or other vermin.

WHAT TO AVOID TODAY

There could be an accident in the garden so, if you were thinking of spending time there, have a rest instead. You should also handle liquids carefully in the kitchen and avoid making soups or sauces. Make sure that you don't over-indulge with alcohol, or you could regret your actions tomorrow.

This is an unlucky day for anyone born in the following years of the Rabbit: 1927, 1939, 1951, 1963, 1975.

13TH DAY OF THE 11TH MONTH – WEDNESDAY, 18 DECEMBER

THE HOURS OF FORTUNE

23–01	M	07–09	B	15–17	B
01–03	B	09–11	G	17–19	M
03–05	G	11–13	B	19–21	G
05–07	G	13–15	G	21–23	G

ADVICE FOR THE DAY

Educational projects that you begin now should reap rewards in the future and lucky stars are shining on you if you're getting married. Try to renew contact with old friends and make an effort to resolve romantic problems, but, if you're just beginning a romance, good luck is on your side. If you're gardening or spending time on house maintenance your efforts will be rewarded and now is the time to stock up on alcohol supplies or to begin brewing your own. If you've been thinking about getting your hair cut, do so now and you'll be pleased with the results.

WHAT TO AVOID TODAY

There's misfortune associated with water so make sure that you take necessary safety precautions if you're doing anything from mending plumbing to going swimming.

Don't take unnecessary risks now if you were born in the following years of the Dragon: 1928, 1940, 1952, 1964, 1976.

14TH DAY OF THE 11TH MONTH – THURSDAY, 19 DECEMBER

THE HOURS OF FORTUNE

23–01	M	07–09	G	15–17	M
01–03	B	09–11	B	17–19	M
03–05	G	11–13	B	19–21	G
05–07	G	13–15	B	21–23	G

ADVICE FOR THE DAY

The day's forecast focuses on practical and creative manual work inside and outside the house. Whether you're making or mending furniture, repairing electrical goods or working on a piece of art, you can expect successful results. You should also try to find some time in the day to unwind with a relaxing bath or just spend some time on your own.

WHAT TO AVOID TODAY

Legal action will be plagued by bad luck so think twice before you waste time or money. You're also advised to postpone wedding plans until the 17th day of this month unless you're prepared for arguments and setbacks in the months ahead.

Don't make long term commitments today if you were born in the following years of the Snake: 1929, 1941, 1953, 1965, 1977.

15TH DAY OF THE 11TH MONTH – FRIDAY, 20 DECEMBER

THE HOURS OF FORTUNE

23–01	G	07–09	G	15–17	G
01–03	B	09–11	M	17–19	M
03–05	G	11–13	B	19–21	M
05–07	M	13–15	G	21–23	M

ADVICE FOR THE DAY

If you have worries on your mind this is an ideal time to think them through, and if you ask others for help you could find that your request is answered. Journeys at home or abroad should pass off smoothly and the financial prospects are excellent for anyone who is buying or selling goods. Go ahead and take a risk if you've been asked to lend money, it should be returned as agreed. If you're working at home now is the time to concentrate on repair work in your kitchen, and it's also a suitable day to make a decision about buying a kitchen appliance. Finally, take some time over your personal appearance and having your hair cut or a beauty treatment should make you feel more confident.

WHAT TO AVOID TODAY

If you've been saving food or drink for a special occasion,

don't be tempted to break into it now because you may need it sooner than you expected. If you were planning to spend some time in the garden you should avoid digging or lifting earth.

This is an unlucky day for anyone born in the following years of the Horse: 1930, 1942, 1954, 1966, 1978.

16TH DAY OF THE 11TH MONTH – SATURDAY, 21 DECEMBER

THE HOURS OF FORTUNE

23–01	G	07–09	M	15–17	G
01–03	B	09–11	B	17–19	M
03–05	G	11–13	B	19–21	M
05–07	G	13–15	B	21–23	M

ADVICE FOR THE DAY

Since this is a broken day within the year you should channel your energy into giving your house a thorough clean. But this is also a positive day for dealing with spiritual matters and you should try to spend some time in prayer or in quiet reflection.

WHAT TO AVOID TODAY

If you were thinking of gardening, put your feet up and have a rest instead – you could avoid an accident. If you've been through an upsetting emotional period you should try to keep your mind off the past and don't cut yourself off from the world. This is also an unlucky day to make funeral arrangements or to attend a funeral.

Be prepared for disagreements at home and at work if you were born in the following years of the Ram: 1919, 1931, 1943, 1955, 1967, 1979.

17TH DAY OF THE 11TH MONTH – SUNDAY, 22 DECEMBER

Today is Tung Chi, the day that marks the winter solstice which begins at 4.52 this afternoon. This is also the festival of A Ni To Fu, also known as the Amida Buddha. It is believed that his compassion for the universe is boundless and anyone who calls on his name will be released from some, if not all, of their rebirths. Those who are saved through Amida Buddha's compassion can attain the Pure Land ruled by Amida Buddha.

THE HOURS OF FORTUNE

23–01	G	07–09	B	15–17	B
01–03	B	09–11	M	17–19	G
03–05	M	11–13	B	19–21	M
05–07	G	13–15	M	21–23	M

ADVICE FOR THE DAY

There's good fortune in store if you're getting married and it's an ideal time to give or to receive presents. This is a positive day for recovery if you've been ill recently and it's also an opportune day to begin health treatments. You can feel secure that you've made the right decision if you're signing a contract and anyone buying or selling goods can expect brisk business. Now is the time to stock up on food supplies that may be running low or to begin structural work on your house. If you have been through a period of upheaval you should try to make plans for the future; but if someone close to you has recently died this is an appropriate day to arrange or to attend a funeral.

WHAT TO AVOID TODAY

Handle hot pans or liquids with care and beware of an accident if you're working on or near a cooker. If you have worries on your mind wait at least another day before you ask others for help or advice.

This is a day of disappointments for anyone born in the following years of the Monkey: 1920, 1932, 1944, 1956, 1968.

18TH DAY OF THE 11TH MONTH – MONDAY, 23 DECEMBER

THE HOURS OF FORTUNE

23–01	M	07–09	M	15–17	M
01–03	B	09–11	M	17–19	B
03–05	G	11–13	B	19–21	M
05–07	B	13–15	G	21–23	G

ADVICE FOR THE DAY

Now is the time to put your energies into general maintenance work inside and outside the house. You should find that the tasks ahead of you may not seem as difficult as you first imagined.

WHAT TO AVOID TODAY

If you were planning to go to the hairdresser, postpone your trip until tomorrow to avoid disappointment. You should also beware of an accident if you're near water, particularly if you're sailing or swimming.

Be prepared for domestic disagreements throughout the day if you were born in the following years of the Cock: 1921, 1933, 1945, 1957, 1969.

19TH DAY OF THE 11TH MONTH – TUESDAY, 24 DECEMBER

THE HOURS OF FORTUNE

23–01	M	07–09	M	15–17	G
01–03	B	09–11	G	17–19	G
03–05	B	11–13	B	19–21	B
05–07	G	13–15	G	21–23	M

ADVICE FOR THE DAY

Put some time aside for quiet reflection or prayer and you could find that your worries are resolved or your prayers answered. Lucky stars are shining on anyone who is getting married, giving or receiving presents or beginning a new educational project. Your social life is blessed by good fortune now, so make the most of your free time and you could be in for an unexpected surprise. The financial prospects are promising for anyone opening a business or negotiating a business deal, and if you're concentrating on practical domestic matters you can expect a satisfying day. Remember to spend time on your appearance and this is a particularly good day to treat yourself to a haircut. On a more sombre note, this is an approppriate time to arrange or attend a funeral.

WHAT TO AVOID TODAY

This is an unlucky time to set to sea whether it's in an ocean-going liner or a dinghy. You're advised to postpone trips by sea until later in the month. You should also think twice before you agree to buy property, you may not have been given sufficient information to make an informed decision.

Don't expect your plans to work out as you expected if you were born in the following years of the Dog: 1922, 1934, 1946, 1958, 1970.

20TH DAY OF THE 11TH MONTH – WEDNESDAY, 25 DECEMBER

THE HOURS OF FORTUNE

23–01	G	07–09	M	15–17	G
01–03	B	09–11	M	17–19	M
03–05	G	11–13	B	19–21	M
05–07	M	13–15	G	21–23	B

ADVICE FOR THE DAY

Once again, this is a positive day for prayer or quiet reflection. Good luck is now on your side if you're thinking of buying property and you can feel secure that you have made the right decision. The remainder of the day's forecast concentrates on domestic matters so if you've been thinking of gardening, DIY or cleaning out your house, this is the day to do it.

WHAT TO AVOID TODAY

Travel at home and abroad is likely to be plagued by delays or accidents so try to avoid unnecessary journeys. If you have recently been through a period of upheaval this is an appropriate time to put the past behind you and make new plans for the future.

Don't take unnecessary risks today if you were born in the following years of the Pig: 1923, 1935, 1947, 1959, 1971.

21ST DAY OF THE 11TH MONTH – THURSDAY, 26 DECEMBER

THE HOURS OF FORTUNE

23–01	B	07–09	M	15–17	G
01–03	B	09–11	M	17–19	G
03–05	G	11–13	B	19–21	B
05–07	M	13–15	G	21–23	M

ADVICE FOR THE DAY

Since this is a broken day within the month you shouldn't make important plans or commitments. Turn your attention to clearing away rubble or rubbish and to minor demolition work in the house or garden.

WHAT TO AVOID TODAY

Beware of an accident in the bathroom and don't attempt DIY there. You should also postpone sewing clothes or mending home furnishings until tomorrow.

You're likely to meet with problems throughout the day if you were born in the following years of the Rat: 1924, 1936, 1948, 1960, 1972.

22ND DAY OF THE 11TH MONTH – FRIDAY, 27 DECEMBER

THE HOURS OF FORTUNE

23–01	M	07–09	M	15–17	G
01–03	B	09–11	G	17–19	B
03–05	G	11–13	B	19–21	M
05–07	G	13–15	M	21–23	M

ADVICE FOR THE DAY

This is a good day to finalize business deals and to sign legal contracts. Shopkeepers and anyone else involved in trade can look forward to a successful day's work. If you've been thinking of buying bedroom furniture or decorating your bedroom, do so now – tomorrow will be too late.

WHAT TO AVOID TODAY

This is a day of accidents in the kitchen and you're advised to be extra careful if you're making soups or sauces or if you're brewing your own wine. Don't over-indulge in alcohol now, you may regret your actions.

This is an unlucky day for anyone born in the following years of the Ox: 1925, 1937, 1949, 1961, 1973.

23RD DAY OF THE 11TH MONTH – SATURDAY, 28 DECEMBER

This is the day that the Southern Dipper, a star in the Tzu Wei (Purple or Pole star) group, descends to earth. If he is worshipped now he will grant long life in return.

THE HOURS OF FORTUNE

23–01	G	07–09	G	15–17	B
01–03	B	09–11	G	17–19	G
03–05	B	11–13	B	19–21	M
05–07	G	13–15	G	21–23	M

ADVICE FOR THE DAY

This is a positive day for prayer or quiet reflection and you could find that your personal problems are resolved now. If you have been through a period of loss this is an appropriate time to put the past behind you; if someone close to you has recently died you should arrange or attend a funeral. Career prospects are excellent if you're starting a new job and the forecast is also very good for anyone who is on the move, whether it is to a new house or to a new country. It's a lucky day to give or receive presents and if you're celebrating you may receive an unexpected surprise. Now is the time to turn your attention to carpentry around the house and to repairing or buying electrical kitchen goods. Finally, don't let your personal appearance slip – these next two days are lucky times to treat yourself to a haircut.

WHAT TO AVOID TODAY

If you're an enthusiastic gardener put your feet up and have a rest from gardening for the day.

This is a day of disappointment for anyone born in the following years of the Tiger: 1926, 1938, 1950, 1962, 1974.

24TH DAY OF THE 11TH MONTH –
SUNDAY, 29 DECEMBER

THE HOURS OF FORTUNE

23–01	G	07–09	G	15–17	G
01–03	B	09–11	G	17–19	M
03–05	G	11–13	B	19–21	M
05–07	B	13–15	B	21–23	M

ADVICE FOR THE DAY

Now is the time to concentrate on domestic matters. If you've been thinking of cleaning the house do so now, and if you've been infested by insects or vermin in your house or garden you should lay down traps or repellent. If you're owed money don't be afraid to ask for it back; this is an ideal time to retrieve debts.

WHAT TO AVOID TODAY

This is an unlucky day to arrange or to attend a funeral and if you have recently been through a period of personal upheaval concentrate on personal matters instead of mulling over the past.

You're likely to find problems at home and at work if you were born in the following years of the Rabbit: 1927, 1939, 1951, 1963, 1975.

25TH DAY OF THE 11TH MONTH –
MONDAY, 30 DECEMBER

THE HOURS OF FORTUNE

23–01	M	07–09	B	15–17	M
01–03	B	09–11	G	17–19	M
03–05	G	11–13	B	19–21	M
05–07	G	13–15	G	21–23	M

ADVICE FOR THE DAY

This is an ideal day to sort out personal problems or to put some time aside for prayer; you may find that your requests are answered. There's good news in store if you're starting a new college course or waiting for exam results. Don't turn down social opportunities because this is an excellent time to meet or make new friends and to begin a romance. Lucky stars are shining on you if you are announcing an engagement and you can look forward to a stable marriage. The rest of today's advice focuses on domestic matters so whether you're buying property, building extensions, or repairing electrical faults you can look forward to a fruitful day's work.

WHAT TO AVOID TODAY

You're likely to make a mistake if you're negotiating financial matters or investing money. Don't be tempted to spend your savings on unnecessary luxuries. Although this is an excellent day for DIY, avoid plastering or painting walls.

This is a day of disappointments for anyone born in the following years of the Dragon: 1928, 1940, 1952, 1964, 1976.

26TH DAY OF THE 11TH MONTH –
TUESDAY, 31 DECEMBER

THE HOURS OF FORTUNE

23–01	G	07–09	M	15–17	M
01–03	B	09–11	B	17–19	M
03–05	G	11–13	B	19–21	M
05–07	G	13–15	G	21–23	M

ADVICE FOR THE DAY

It's still an opportune day to resolve personal difficulties and, on the domestic front, to concentrate on DIY. If you're thinking of buying a pet, now is the time to make a decision and if you're working with animals you should have a successful day.

WHAT TO AVOID TODAY

Take care if you're planning to work in the garden and avoid repotting plants or arranging flowers.

This is an unlucky day for anyone born in the following years of the Snake: 1929, 1941, 1953, 1965, 1977.

27TH DAY OF THE 11TH MONTH –
WEDNESDAY, 1 JANUARY

THE HOURS OF FORTUNE

23–01	G	07–09	B	15–17	M
01–03	B	09–11	G	17–19	G
03–05	M	11–13	B	19–21	G
05–07	M	13–15	M	21–23	G

ADVICE FOR THE DAY

If you've been thinking of painting or decorating your house you should do so now and this is also a good day for anyone to put their creative skills to effective use.

WHAT TO AVOID TODAY

Beware of an accident in the kitchen now, particularly if you're cooking and if you were thinking of digging in the garden, postpone it until tomorrow.

This is a day of upheavals for anyone born in the following years of the Horse: 1930, 1942, 1954, 1966, 1978.

28TH DAY OF THE 11TH MONTH – THURSDAY, 2 JANUARY

THE HOURS OF FORTUNE

23–01	G	07–09	M	15–17	M
01–03	B	09–11	G	17–19	G
03–05	M	11–13	B	19–21	M
05–07	B	13–15	B	21–23	G

ADVICE FOR THE DAY

Don't be afraid to ask others for advice or to put time aside to think your problems through. This is a good day to concentrate on spiritual matters. Make the most of social opportunities that come your way and you could be in for an unexpected and welcome surprise. Now is the time to choose presents for others or to receive them. Travel at home or abroad is blessed by good fortune as is business, and shopkeepers or anyone else working in trade can expect a profitable day. If you have time and energy it would be well spent on general maintenance inside and outside the house.

WHAT TO AVOID TODAY

If you're thinking of having your hair cut, postpone it until another day to avoid disappointment. On a more serious note, this is not the right time to begin a period of mourning or to attend a funeral: try to focus your attention on the positive things in your life.

Personal problems may come to the fore now if you were born in the following years of the Ram: 1931, 1943, 1955, 1967, 1979.

29TH DAY OF THE 11TH MONTH – FRIDAY, 3 JANUARY

THE HOURS OF FORTUNE

23–01	M	07–09	G	15–17	B
01–03	B	09–11	G	17–19	M
03–05	B	11–13	B	19–21	M
05–07	G	13–15	G	21–23	M

ADVICE FOR THE DAY

Lucky stars are still shining on anyone who is travelling, going to parties or meeting friends, and you shouldn't miss this opportunity to resolve romantic difficulties. Be prepared to take financial risks now; anyone who is starting up a business can look forward to a profitable future. This is also an appropriate time to retrieve outstanding debts. You can also feel secure that you're doing the right thing if you're signing a contract. This is a l day to put your creative talents to use, particularly if you're making or designing clothes. This is a suitable time to choose wine or to brew your own. Finally, if someone close to you has died recently, this is an appropriate day to arrange or to attend a funeral.

WHAT TO AVOID TODAY

Try to keep your mind on practical not spiritual matters; tomorrow is a more auspicious day for prayer or quiet reflection. You're also advised not to agree to the sale of property — there could be hidden problems in store.

This is an unlucky day for anyone born in the following years of the Monkey: 1920, 1932, 1944, 1956, 1968.

30TH DAY OF THE 11TH MONTH – SATURDAY, 4 JANUARY

THE HOURS OF FORTUNE

23–01	G	07–09	M	15–17	M
01–03	B	09–11	M	17–19	B
03–05	G	11–13	B	19–21	M
05–07	G	13–15	G	21–23	B

ADVICE FOR THE DAY

If you have time and energy on your hands it would be well spent on general maintenance in your house or garden.

WHAT TO AVOID TODAY

There's misfortune associated with water today so be careful if you're doing anything from swimming to unblocking drains.

Be prepared for quarrels throughout the day if you were born in the following Years of the Cock: 1921, 1933, 1945, 1957, 1969.

TWELFTH MONTH

Chinese families smear the lips of the Kitchen god with honey to ensure that he bears a good report of them to the Jade Emperor in Heaven.

1ST DAY OF THE 12TH MONTH –
SUNDAY, 5 JANUARY

Hsiao Han, which begins at 10.12 this morning, is a traditional reminder that the coldest weather of winter is approaching.

THE HOURS OF FORTUNE

23–01	B	07–09	G	15–17	M
01–03	B	09–11	G	17–19	M
03–05	G	11–13	B	19–21	B
05–07	M	13–15	G	21–23	G

ADVICE FOR THE DAY

You should start the month off by ironing out personal problems and working out plans for the months ahead. It's a good day for prayer or religious ceremonies and you should put some time aside for quiet thought. If you are planning to meet friends or are beginning a romance make the most of the opportunities that come you way and you could be in for an unexpected surprise. If you're owed money by friends or business associates you shouldn't have any problems retrieving it now. This is a pleasurable day if you enjoy shopping and you can expect to find some bargains; but don't get too carried away and make sure you stock up on essential supplies.

WHAT TO AVOID TODAY

This is a bad day for gardeners and anyone else working on the land and you're advised to steer clear of sowing seeds and planting trees or crops. You should also be extra careful if you're mending clothes or home furnishings.

This is a day of disagreements and personal problems for

anyone born in the following years of the Dog: 1922, 1934, 1946, 1958, 1970.

2ND DAY OF THE 12TH MONTH – MONDAY, 6 JANUARY

THE HOURS OF FORTUNE

23–01	M	07–09	M	15–17	M
01–03	B	09–11	G	17–19	B
03–05	G	11–13	G	19–21	G
05–07	M	13–15	B	21–23	B

ADVICE FOR THE DAY

Instead of complaining about your luck you should count your blessings today and try to get the most out of the places that you go to or the people that you meet. Don't turn down opportunities because this could be the day when your prayers are unexpectedly answered. It's an auspicious time to announce an engagement and it's generally a lucky time to give or receive presents. Good fortune is on the side of anyone who is on the move to a new house or emigrating, but its not going to be an easy day for anyone setting off on a business trip or a holiday. It's generally a positive time for practical work around the house, so, if you've been postponing necessary DIY for a long time, start work on it now and you'll be pleasantly surprised with your efforts.

WHAT TO AVOID TODAY

If you've recently been through a personal loss you should try to forget about the past and make plans for the future. There's the possibility of an an accident in the kitchen and cooks are advised to take extra care if they're making soups or sauces.

Be prepared for difficulties at home and work if you were born in the following years of the Pig: 1923, 1935, 1947, 1959, 1971.

3RD DAY OF THE 12TH MONTH – TUESDAY, 7 JANUARY

THE HOURS OF FORTUNE

23–01	B	07–09	M	15–17	B
01–03	B	09–11	G	17–19	M
03–05	G	11–13	M	19–21	M
05–07	G	13–15	B	21–23	G

ADVICE FOR THE DAY

Don't be afraid to ask for help now and you could find that your prayers are unexpectedly answered. If you delayed travel plans yesterday you can set off on a journey with confidence. If you're at home today turn your attention to work that may need doing in your bedroom or in the garden. This is also the time to set traps or lay poison if you've been having problems with mice or other vermin.

WHAT TO AVOID TODAY

Don't attempt to repair gutters or drains unless it's absolutely necessary and make sure that your footing is secure if you're climbing ladders.

This is a day of upheavals for anyone born in the following years of the Rat: 1924, 1936, 1948, 1960, 1972.

4TH DAY OF THE 12TH MONTH –
WEDNESDAY, 8 JANUARY

THE HOURS OF FORTUNE

23–01	G	07–09	M	15–17	M
01–03	B	09–11	G	17–19	M
03–05	G	11–13	G	19–21	G
05–07	G	13–15	B	21–23	M

ADVICE FOR THE DAY

Don't put new projects into action because this is a broken day within the month. There's very little good fortune around now, but it is a good time to clear away rubbish or to knock down old sheds or walls.

WHAT TO AVOID TODAY

Stay well away from lawsuits and contracts today but if you are involved in any sort of legal action don't set your expectations too high. On a more practical note, there's a good word of advice for gardeners: handle shovels, trowels and other digging equipment very carefully.

This is a day of setbacks for anyone born in the following years of the Ox: 1925, 1937, 1949, 1961, 1973.

5TH DAY OF THE 12TH MONTH –
THURSDAY, 9 JANUARY

THE HOURS OF FORTUNE

23–01	G	07–09	G	15–17	G
01–03	B	09–11	G	17–19	G
03–05	B	11–13	B	19–21	M
05–07	M	13–15	B	21–23	M

ADVICE FOR THE DAY

This is an ideal day for prayer or quiet reflection and a few moments spent in relaxation could put you in a much stronger frame of mind to cope with the day's problems. The future looks bright for anyone who is expecting exam results or beginning a new educational course. Travel at home or abroad is blessed by good fortune and you should feel confident about the future if you're emigrating or moving to a new house. The financial prospects are excellent if you're setting up in business or finalizing a business deal. The forecast ends on an encouraging note for gardeners and anyone working with electrical kitchen appliances or building house extensions.

WHAT TO AVOID TODAY

Think twice before you lend money, even to friends — it may not be returned as promised. Don't be tempted to use up drink or food supplies that you've been saving for a celebration — be strict with yourself today. Finally, there's the possibility of an accident in your bedroom, so don't try to tidy up or to move furniture.

Be prepared for disagreements throughout the day if you were born in the following years of the Tiger: 1926, 1938, 1950, 1962, 1974.

6TH DAY OF THE 12TH MONTH – FRIDAY, 10 JANUARY

THE HOURS OF FORTUNE

23–01	G	07–09	G	15–17	G
01–03	B	09–11	B	17–19	G
03–05	G	11–13	M	19–21	M
05–07	B	13–15	B	21–23	M

ADVICE FOR THE DAY

Don't be frightened of asking others for help or advice now: you could find that your request is answered sooner than you think. It's an ideal time to start a new college or evening course; if you make a commitment to your studies now the rewards will be greater than you imagined. If you're marrying today you can look forward to happiness and financial security in the years ahead, and the forecast is also promising if you're making a business commitment. There's a word of support for anyone working on home maintenance, particularly on home extensions. Finally, this is an appropriate time to arrange or attend a funeral and you will find that the support that you receive from family and friends will carry you through.

WHAT TO AVOID TODAY

There are mixed blessings for farmers or gardeners today. While the forecast for digging or ploughing is excellent, you're advised not to plant seeds, shrubs or trees. This is also a bad time to buy, cut or arrange flowers.

Don't take unnecessary risks now if you were born in the following years of the Rabbit: 1927, 1939, 1951, 1963, 1975.

7TH DAY OF THE 12TH MONTH – SATURDAY, 11 JANUARY

THE HOURS OF FORTUNE

23–01	G	07–09	B	15–17	G
01–03	B	09–11	G	17–19	G
03–05	G	11–13	M	19–21	G
05–07	G	13–15	B	21–23	G

ADVICE FOR THE DAY

This is a good day for worship or quiet reflection and you could find that your prayers are unexpectedly answered. If you're setting off on a hunting or fishing trip you can expect a good catch but, on a more practical note, you should also take this opportunity to get rid of vermin or insects that may have infested your home or garden. You can look forward to a successful day's work if you're an enthusiastic dressmaker or knitter, but the news is also good for anyone who feels it's time to mend torn clothes or damaged furnishings that they have been ignoring for a long time.

WHAT TO AVOID TODAY

There's an air of misfortune in the kitchen today so don't spend more time there than you have to. Make sure that you handle hot plates or dishes with care and don't attempt re-decoration work there.

This is an unlucky day for anyone born in the following years of the Dragon: 1928, 1940, 1952, 1964, 1976.

8TH DAY OF THE 12TH MONTH –
SUNDAY, 21 JANUARY

Today commemorates the occasion when Sakyamuni, the historical Buddha, attained enlightenment.

THE HOURS OF FORTUNE

23–01	M	07–09	M	15–17	M
01–03	B	09–11	B	17–19	G
03–05	G	11–13	G	19–21	G
05–07	B	13–15	B	21–23	G

ADVICE FOR THE DAY

This is generally a positive day for prayer, worship and religious ceremony. Don't turn down opportunities to meet or make new friends and you could be in store for a pleasant romantic surprise. This is an excellent time to finalize business or holiday travel arrangements and travel at home or abroad is blessed by good fortune. Finally, if you've been feeling ill recently this is an appropriate day to begin a period of convalescence or to ease yourself back into the demands of everyday life.

WHAT TO AVOID TODAY

Unless you have the strength to face arguments and domestic upheavals in the coming months don't get married today. On a less serious note, don't get your hair cut – you'll only be disappointed with the results.

Personal problems may come to the fore now if you were born in the following years of the Snake: 1929, 1941, 1953, 1965, 1977.

9TH DAY OF THE 12TH MONTH – MONDAY, 13 JANUARY

THE HOURS OF FORTUNE

23–01	M	07–09	G	15–17	G
01–03	B	09–11	G	17–19	G
03–05	B	11–13	B	19–21	M
05–07	G	13–15	B	21–23	M

ADVICE FOR THE DAY

This is a good day for religious ceremony or for quiet prayer. On a more active note, this is a lucky day to travel, and if you've been having difficulty finalizing travel plans everything should fall into place now. Anyone who works in a creative field or whose hobby is painting, sewing, carving or writing can look forward to a successful day. You shouldn't feel guilty about putting time aside for yourself now and if you're in need of a haircut or other beauty treatment this is a good a time as any to relax and enjoy yourself.

WHAT TO AVOID TODAY

If you've been through a period of personal difficulties or upheavals this could be a particularly painful day for you. Don't try to push the past behind you but come to terms with what has happened. You're also advised not to arrange or attend a funeral today.

This is a day of delays and disagreements if you were born in the following years of the Horse: 1918, 1930, 1942, 1954, 1966, 1978.

10TH DAY OF THE 12TH MONTH –
TUESDAY, 14 JANUARY

THE HOURS OF FORTUNE

23–01	G	07–09	M	15–17	G
01–03	B	09–11	G	17–19	G
03–05	G	11–13	M	19–21	M
05–07	G	13–15	B	21–23	B

ADVICE FOR THE DAY

Since this is a broken day within the year you should turn your attention to cleaning your house thoroughly. The Almanac also suggests that you put some time aside for quiet reflection.

WHAT TO AVOID TODAY

This is an unlucky day for anything connected with funerals or mourning. If you are recovering from the loss of a relative or friend it may be a long time before you return to your normal routine.

This is a day of disappointments for anyone born in the following years of the Ram: 1931, 1943, 1955, 1967, 1979.

11TH DAY OF THE 12TH MONTH –
WEDNESDAY, 15 JANUARY

THE HOURS OF FORTUNE

23–01	B	07–09	G	15–17	B
01–03	B	09–11	M	17–19	M
03–05	G	11–13	G	19–21	B
05–07	G	13–15	B	21–23	M

ADVICE FOR THE DAY

This is a perfect day to put plans into effect and put your energies to good use. Feel free to travel as far afield as you like since it's likely to be a day free of delays and accidents. Don't turn down social invitations because you could be in for an unexpected surprise when you least expect it. It's also the right time to sort out romantic problems or to begin a new romance. It's a particularly lucky day to marry since the gods of fortune will be watching over you now and, on a more immediate level, it's a perfect day to give or to receive presents.

If you're moving house within your own country or abroad you can look forward to stability or prosperity in your new home. There's also a special word of support in today's forecast for anyone working with animals or thinking of buying a new pet. If, however, you're spending the day at home and you have time on your hands, turn your attention to cleaning, gardening or general house maintenance.

WHAT TO AVOID TODAY

Try to keep yourself busy and keep your mind on practical matters. Try to postpone religious ceremonies until another time and don't allow yourself to mull over worries. Although today's forecast advises you to concentrate on work around the home, handle electrical goods carefully and be careful when you're using the cooker.

Don't take unnecessary risks now if you were born in the following years of the Monkey: 1920, 1932, 1944, 1956, 1968, 1980.

12TH DAY OF THE 12TH MONTH – THURSDAY, 16 JANUARY

THE HOURS OF FORTUNE

23–01	M	07–09	M	15–17	M
01–03	B	09–11	G	17–19	B
03–05	G	11–13	G	19–21	G
05–07	G	13–15	B	21–23	M

ADVICE FOR THE DAY

The fortunes have changed since yesterday and it's now the right time to turn your attention to spiritual matters, at least for part of the day. There should be good news on the way if you're waiting for exam results or if you're hoping to start a full- or part-time college course. It's no longer a lucky time to marry, but it is an ideal day to get engaged and to give or receive presents. Travel, romance and friendships are still well-starred and you're advised to make the most of your opportunities. You can look forward to a flourishing career if you're opening a business or finalizing a business deal. Meanwhile, on the home front, concentrate on cooking and DIY, particularly in your kitchen.

WHAT TO AVOID TODAY

Since there's good luck associated with cooking, feel free to attempt even the most difficult recipes, but be extra cautious when you're making sauces or handling alcohol. You should also watch out for an accident involving water, particularly if you're gardening.

This is an unlucky day for anyone born in the following years of the Cock: 1921, 1933, 1945, 1957, 1969.

13TH DAY OF THE 12TH MONTH – FRIDAY, 17 JANUARY

THE HOURS OF FORTUNE

23–01	M	07–09	M	15–17	B
01–03	B	09–11	G	17–19	G
03–05	G	11–13	M	19–21	B
05–07	G	13–15	B	21–23	G

ADVICE FOR THE DAY

The Almanac carries very little advice today. It's a suitable time to deal with pest control so whether it's mice or ants that have infested your house or garden, now is the time to get rid of them. This is also an appropriate day to attend a funeral or to make funeral arrangements.

WHAT TO AVOID TODAY

Beware of an accident if you're handling water. Take extra care if you're mending gutters, repairing drains, watering the garden or even washing your hair.

This is a day of delays and disagreements for anyone born in the following years of the Dog: 1922, 1934, 1946, 1958, 1970.

14TH DAY OF THE 12TH MONTH – SATURDAY, 18 JANUARY

THE HOURS OF FORTUNE

23–01	G	07–09	G	15–17	G
01–03	B	09–11	G	17–19	M
03–05	M	11–13	M	19–21	G
05–07	G	13–15	B	21–23	B

ADVICE FOR THE DAY

Make an extra effort to meet friends and to attend parties or dinners, you could be in for an unexpected surprise. This is also an ideal day to begin a romance or to resolve romantic differences. The news is good for anyone getting engaged and you can expect to receive some welcome gifts. Good fortune is also on your side if you're moving house or emigrating. This should prove to be a successful day in the garden, so if you've been thinking of planting, weeding or pruning, this is the time to do it. The day's forecast ends with a word of support for farmers, builders and home-brew enthusiasts.

WHAT TO AVOID TODAY

If you're thinking of going sailing or rowing you're in for a day of trouble and you'd be wise to postpone it until tomorrow. You're also warned not to commit yourself to legal contracts or to initiate legal action.

Domestic problems may come to the fore now if you were born in the following years of the Pig: 1923, 1935, 1947, 1959, 1971.

15TH DAY OF THE 12TH MONTH – SUNDAY, 19 JANUARY

THE HOURS OF FORTUNE

23–01	B	07–09	M	15–17	M
01–03	B	09–11	M	17–19	G
03–05	G	11–13	B	19–21	M
05–07	M	13–15	B	21–23	M

ADVICE FOR THE DAY

This is an excellent time for prayer, worship and quiet reflection. You can look forward to a day free from delays and accidents if you're travelling by land, sea or air. If you put some time aside today for cleaning your house or gardening you should be more than pleased with your efforts by the end of the day. If you've just heard news of a death in the family or have been through a personal upheaval, give yourself time to recover and don't expect too much of yourself.

WHAT TO AVOID TODAY

Don't over-indulge in food or drink and don't be tempted to break into food or drink that you may have been saving for a special occasion. You should also wear as little jewellery as possible and, if you're thinking of investing in expensive jewellery, get a second opinion before you buy. You're generally advised to handle money carefully today because what may look like a good investment may turn out to be a financial disaster.

Be prepared for problems in your domestic life if you were born in the following years of the Rat: 1924, 1936, 1948, 1960, 1972.

16TH DAY OF THE 12TH MONTH – MONDAY, 20 JANUARY

This is the festival of the sage and teacher, Lao Tzu, who is reputed to have lived c.550 BC (see 1st day of the 7th month).

THE HOURS OF FORTUNE

23–01	G	07–09	M	15–17	G
01–03	B	09–11	B	17–19	M
03–05	G	11–13	M	19–21	G
05–07	G	13–15	B	21–23	G

ADVICE FOR THE DAY

Don't over-exert yourself today and don't take unnecessary risks. There's very little luck around since this is a broken day within the month but you are advised to take this opportunity to clear away rubbish or to demolish old sheds or walls.

WHAT TO AVOID TODAY

Beware of accidents in the garden and steer clear of planting or cutting flowers.

This is a day of upheavals for anyone born in the following years of the Ox: 1925, 1937, 1949, 1961, 1973.

17TH DAY OF THE 12TH MONTH – TUESDAY, 21 JANUARY

Ta Han, which begins at 3.30 this morning, is a traditional reminder that the coldest time of the year has begun.

THE HOURS OF FORTUNE

23–01	G	07–09	B	15–17	G
01–03	B	09–11	G	17–19	G
03–05	B	11–13	M	19–21	G
05–07	M	13–15	B	21–23	G

ADVICE FOR THE DAY

Others are willing to listen to you now or to act on your behalf so don't be afraid of asking them for advice. Journeys by land, sea or air are blessed by good fortune and travel difficulties that you may have had in the past few weeks should be ironed out now. Financial and career prospects are excellent if you're opening a business or negotiating a business deal. There's also a positive forecast for farmers, agricultural workers and enthusiastic gardeners. The rest of today's advice is given over to DIY enthusiasts who can look forward to a fruitful day.

WHAT TO AVOID TODAY

There's bad fortune lurking in the kitchen throughout the day and you're advised not to repair faulty electrical goods and to handle hot pans or dishes with care. Besides the kitchen there's also misfortune connected with work in the bedroom so don't attempt to move furniture or clear out cupboards there.

Be prepared for unwelcome news now if you were born in the following years of the Tiger: 1926, 1938, 1950, 1962, 1974.

18TH DAY OF THE 12TH MONTH –
WEDNESDAY, 22 JANUARY

THE HOURS OF FORTUNE

23–01	M		07–09	M		15–17	M
01–03	B		09–11	M		17–19	G
03–05	M		11–13	G		19–21	M
05–07	B		13–15	B		21–23	G

ADVICE FOR THE DAY

For the second day running you shouldn't be afraid to ask others for advice, but this is also an ideal time to reflect on personal concerns. There's still good fortune associated with travelling and you can look forward to a day free of delays whether you're making your usual trip to work or emigrating to a new country. Financial matters are well-starred so you can afford to take a risk. There's the prospect of many stable and prosperous years ahead of you if you're getting married today and, on a more immediate note, it's the perfect time to give or receive presents, whatever the celebration. Finally, the Almanac says it's a suitable time to arrange or to attend a funeral but, if you've recently been through any kind of loss, give yourself time to mourn and to recover.

WHAT TO AVOID TODAY

Steer clear of legal matters and don't agree to a verbal or written contract — you could be letting yourself in for more trouble than you bargained for. This is not a day to pamper yourself, no matter how much you think you deserve it, so concentrate on practical or spiritual matters instead.

This is an unlucky day for anyone born in the following years of the Rabbit: 1927, 1939, 1951, 1963, 1975.

19TH DAY OF THE 12TH MONTH –
THURSDAY, 23 JANUARY

THE HOURS OF FORTUNE

23–01	M	07–09	B	15–17	G
01–03	B	09–11	M	17–19	M
03–05	B	11–13	G	19–21	M
05–07	G	13–15	B	21–23	M

ADVICE FOR THE DAY

Don't be afraid to ask for help – this could be the day
when your prayers are unexpectedly answered. You can
look forward to a fruitful day if you're working in the
garden or greenhouse, particularly if you're planting
seeds, trees or shrubs. The forecast is good for sports
enthusiasts and there's a special mention for anyone going
fishing or hunting. On the domestic front you're advised
to lay traps or insect repellent if you've been troubled by
insects, mice or other vermin.

WHAT TO AVOID TODAY

If you've been hoping to buy property, don't make a hasty
decision today. Give yourself at least another day before
you make a financial commitment. If you've been through
a period of depression or upheaval recently this is not the
appropriate time to mull over your worries; keep yourself
busy instead.

This could be an unhappy day for you if you were born in
the following years of the Dragon: 1928, 1940, 1952,
1964, 1976.

20TH DAY OF THE 12TH MONTH – FRIDAY, 24 JANUARY

This is the festival of Lu Pan, the god of carpenters, whose statue can usually be found in woodwork shops.

THE HOURS OF FORTUNE

23–01	G	07–09	M	15–17	G
01–03	B	09–11	B	17–19	M
03–05	G	11–13	G	19–21	M
05–07	G	13–15	B	21–23	B

ADVICE FOR THE DAY

This is a positive day for prayer, worship or quiet reflection. Don't miss the opportunity to meet friends or accept social invitations: you could be in for an unexpected surprise. There's likely to be good news in store if you're waiting for exam results, and if you're making plans to enrol on a full- or part-time college course you can expect to reap rewards in the future. If you're feeling under the weather you should try to consult a doctor now; if you're starting a course of health treatments it should prove to be very effective. If you're working at home, turn your attention to general maintenance work in your bedroom or bathroom.

WHAT TO AVOID TODAY

This is an unlucky day to arrange or to attend a funeral. There's also a dismal forecast for anyone getting married now, so, unless you're prepared for arguments in the coming months, postpone the celebration until another day.

This is a day of setbacks for anyone born in the following years of the Snake: 1929, 1941, 1953, 1965, 1977.

21ST DAY OF THE 12TH MONTH – SATURDAY, 25 JANUARY

THE HOURS OF FORTUNE

23–01	B	07–09	M	15–17	G
01–03	B	09–11	M	17–19	G
03–05	M	11–13	B	19–21	B
05–07	M	13–15	B	21–23	M

ADVICE FOR THE DAY

This is a well-starred day to sign a contract or negotiate business deals. If you work with your hands, whether as a dressmaker, carpenter or artist, you can look forward to a very successful day. On the domestic front, it's an ideal time for structural alterations in the house or for making home-brewed beer and wine. Finally, it's an appropriate day to deal with funeral arrangements or come to terms with a personal loss.

WHAT TO AVOID TODAY

Anyone working on the land should avoid digging or ploughing.

Be prepared for disappointments throughout the day if you were born in the following years of the Horse: 1918, 1930, 1942, 1954, 1966, 1978.

22ND DAY OF THE 12TH MONTH – SUNDAY, 26 JANUARY

THE HOURS OF FORTUNE

23–01	M	07–09	M	15–17	G
01–03	B	09–11	G	17–19	B
03–05	G	11–13	G	19–21	M
05–07	G	13–15	B	21–23	G

ADVICE FOR THE DAY

Since this is a broken day within the year you should focus your attention on domestic matters. Now is the time to sort through cupboards, or sheds, to clear away rubbish and to give the house a thorough clean.

WHAT TO AVOID TODAY

You could be risking your health if you spend too long in the kitchen and the Almanac specifically advises you not to make sauces and soups, or brew wine. If you've recently been through an emotional upheaval this could prove to be a particularly painful time for you, so try to keep your mind occupied with practical matters.

Personal problems may come to the fore now if you were born in the following years of the Ram: 1919, 1931, 1943, 1955, 1967, 1979.

23RD DAY OF THE 12TH MONTH – MONDAY, 27 JANUARY

THE HOURS OF FORTUNE

23–01	M	07–09	M	15–17	B
01–03	B	09–11	M	17–19	M
03–05	G	11–13	M	19–21	G
05–07	G	13–15	B	21–23	M

ADVICE FOR THE DAY

If you didn't have the time or energy to clean your house yesterday there's still time to do it today. It might not prove to be as difficult or as boring as you imagine. Feel free to make travel plans and don't worry about delays or accidents if you're setting off on journeys by land, sea or air. In fact, it's a well-starred time for anyone who is on the move, whether it's for a fortnight's holiday or to settle in a new country. Don't be afraid to take financial risks – they're likely to prove profitable. Finally, it's an excellent day for DIY enthusiasts to approach difficult jobs around the house that they may have been postponing.

WHAT TO AVOID TODAY

Although it's an auspicious day for house maintenance, you shouldn't attempt plumbing work yourself: call in an expert instead. You should also be extra cautious if you're going sailing or swimming.

This is a day of arguments for anyone born in the following years of the Monkey: 1920, 1932, 1944, 1956, 1968, 1980.

24TH DAY OF THE 12TH MONTH – TUESDAY, 28 JANUARY

At midnight tonight the Kitchen god makes his ascent to Heaven. Throughout the year he has carefully watched human behaviour and now he is going to make a character report to the Jade Emperor. Before his effigy is taken down from the kitchen and burnt – so that his spirit can rise to Heaven – his lips are smeared with honey to ensure that he will say only sweet things.

THE HOURS OF FORTUNE

23–01	G	07–09	M	15–17	M
01–03	B	09–11	M	17–19	B
03–05	G	11–13	M	19–21	G
05–07	G	13–15	B	21–23	M

ADVICE FOR THE DAY

There is still good fortune associated with travel and financial negotiations. The gods are on your side if you're making wedding plans, and if you're getting married you can look forward to a stable family life.

Finally, if you have time on your hands, turn your attention to painting and decorating or electrical repair work in your kitchen. On a more sombre note, it's a suitable time to make funeral arrangements or to allow yourself time to recover from a period of loss or upheaval.

WHAT TO AVOID TODAY

Beware of an accident if you're going swimming or taking a bath today. You should also avoid initiating legal action or giving evidence in court.

Your plans may not work out as you expected now if you

were born in the following years of the Cock: 1921, 1933, 1945, 1957, 1969.

25TH DAY OF THE 12TH MONTH – WEDNESDAY, 29 JANUARY

THE HOURS OF FORTUNE

23–01	G	07–09	G	15–17	M
01–03	B	09–11	M	17–19	G
03–05	M	11–13	B	19–21	B
05–07	M	13–15	B	21–23	G

ADVICE FOR THE DAY

You should set to work today on painting and decorating around the house or on general maintenance in the garden. There's also a good forecast for anyone doing manual work, particularly weaving or darning. If you're interested in sport you should have a satisfying and safe day.

WHAT TO AVOID TODAY

Don't be tempted to use food or drink supplies that you've been storing – there could be unexpected guests on the way. Don't take financial risks now and avoid lending money, even to close friends, as they may not keep their repayment promises. Check that your jewellery is in a safe place, and if you're wearing expensive jewellery make sure you fasten it carefully.

This is an unlucky day for anyone born in the following years of the Dog: 1922, 1934, 1946, 1958, 1970.

26TH DAY OF THE 12TH MONTH – THURSDAY, 30 JANUARY

THE HOURS OF FORTUNE

23–01	G		07–09	M		15–17	G
01–03	B		09–11	B		17–19	G
03–05	M		11–13	M		19–21	G
05–07	M		13–15	B		21–23	B

ADVICE FOR THE DAY

Since a new moon appears today you should put some time aside for quiet reflection, but it's also a time to catch up on your social life. Take this opportunity to meet or make friends and to solve romantic differences.

WHAT TO AVOID TODAY

There's likely to be travel delays throughout the day and you're also advised to take necessary safety precautions before you begin a journey. You're also advised to have a rest from gardening because there could be an unexpected accident. Finally, if you've been through a period of loss, try to stay as close as possible to your normal routine, and if someone close to you has died don't make funeral arrangements now, wait until tomorrow.

Don't take unnecessary risks now if you were born in the following years of the Pig: 1923, 1935, 1947, 1959, 1971.

27TH DAY OF THE 12TH MONTH – FRIDAY, 31 JANUARY

THE HOURS OF FORTUNE

23–01	B	07–09	B	15–17	G
01–03	B	09–11	G	17–19	G
03–05	M	11–13	G	19–21	G
05–07	M	13–15	B	21–23	G

ADVICE FOR THE DAY

It's a good day for general cleaning and if you've been troubled by insects or vermin in your house or garden you should take the necessary steps to get rid of them. Work should go well for carpenters or anyone working with or handling wood. On a more personal note, if you've been thinking of having your hair cut this is an excellent time to visit the hairdresser.

WHAT TO AVOID TODAY

This is a day of accidents in the kitchen so be careful when handling hot liquids and don't attempt to repair crockery or electrical goods.

This is a day of delays and disagreements for anyone born in the following years of the Rat: 1924, 1936, 1948, 1960, 1972.

28TH DAY OF THE 12TH MONTH – SATURDAY, 1 FEBRUARY

THE HOURS OF FORTUNE

23–01	M	07–09	M	15–17	M
01–03	B	09–11	G	17–19	G
03–05	M	11–13	G	19–21	M
05–07	B	13–15	B	21–23	G

ADVICE FOR THE DAY

Since this is a broken day within the month don't make plans or take risks. The day is only suited to minor demolition work around the house or garden.

WHAT TO AVOID TODAY

Think twice before you make career decisions and be prepared for financial setbacks in the months ahead if you're opening a business now.

Be prepared for unexpected or unpleasant news now if you were born in the following years of the Ox: 1925, 1937, 1949, 1961, 1973.

29TH DAY OF THE 12TH MONTH – SUNDAY, 2 FEBRUARY

This is the day when the Northern Dipper, a star in the Tzu Wei (Purple or Pole Star) group, descends to earth. If he is honoured now he will grant long life in return.

THE HOURS OF FORTUNE

23–01	M	07–09	G	15–17	G
01–03	B	09–11	G	17–19	M
03–05	B	11–13	M	19–21	M
05–07	M	13–15	B	21–23	M

ADVICE FOR THE DAY

This is an appropriate day to think through problems or to ask others for help or support. It's generally an excellent day for financial dealing, so if you're thinking of investing money, lending or borrowing money or opening a business you can look forward to good returns. Don't neglect your personal appearance: now is the ideal time to treat yourself to a haircut.

WHAT TO AVOID TODAY

There's the possibility of an accident in your bedroom and you're advised not to move your bed or even change your bed linen. Looking to the future, it's an unlucky time to buy property, so don't rush into the purchase of a house until you are sure that you've been given sufficient background information.

This is an unlucky day for anyone born in the following years of the Tiger: 1926, 1938, 1950, 1962, 1974.

30TH DAY OF THE 12TH MONTH – MONDAY, 3 FEBRUARY

THE HOURS OF FORTUNE

23–01	G	07–09	G	15–17	G
01–03	B	09–11	G	17–19	M
03–05	M	11–13	G	19–21	M
05–07	B	13–15	B	21–23	B

ADVICE FOR THE DAY

This is New Year's Eve, one of the busiest days in the Chinese year. Debts should be settled by now, the house cleaned and food prepared. It's an excellent time to think through new educational projects, to set off on a journey, to move to a new house or to emigrate. If you're getting married you'll be blessed by good fortune in the coming years, and if you're expecting to receive presents you'll be more than pleased with the quality and quantity of the gifts that you receive. Even though tomorrow is a holiday this is a lucky day to finalize business plans or to open a business. If you've been feeling ill don't be afraid to consult a doctor — it's unlikely to be serious. If you've been thinking of going on a shopping trip you should find bargains today, and try to put some time aside to treat yourself to a haircut. Finally, if there are repairs that need doing around the house, try to complete them today, so you are free to enjoy yourself tomorrow.

WHAT TO AVOID TODAY

Don't get involved in legal negotiations and avoid initiating legal action even if you think you have a watertight case. This is also an unlucky day to mull over problems, to begin a period of mourning, or to arrange a funeral.

This is a day of upheavals for anyone born in the following years of the Rabbit: 1927, 1939, 1951, 1963, 1975.

11 90
FEML
$ 95.00